# THE HOUSE ON THE HILL

## THE SAMFORD HOUSE OF INDUSTRY

## 1764-1930

*Ill fares the land, to hastening ills a prey,*
*Where wealth accumulates, and men decay:*
*Princes and lords may flourish, or may fade;*
*A breath can make them, as a breath has made:*
*But a bold peasantry, their country's pride,*
*When once destroy'd, can never be supplied.*
                                        *Goldsmith.*

**SHEILA HARDY**

*For Jasmine and Mina*

**Acknowledgement**

As always, I am indebted to Suffolk County Council for providing us with a superb Record Office that contains the archival material that forms the basis of this book. My thanks too, to the staff of the SRO who are unfailingly helpful and understanding, especially when they find time to let me share 'a great discovery' with them.

My thanks to Maurice Dowe who knew, and was able to draw, exactly what I wanted.

To Sue Kerswell who allows me to stretch friendship to its limits when I ask her to read and comment on my work. Her judgement is highly valued, as is her unstinting support. Thank you seems inadequate.

And finally, I could achieve nothing without the love of my husband. His fortitude and patience in putting up with my absorption in whatever is the current subject is boundless. Not only does he encourage, he is always ready to offer calm and practical assistance, especially when my computer appears to be developing a mind of its own!

# CONTENTS

I      Who looks after the poor?

II      The increase in poverty in the eighteenth century; the amalgamation of parishes to form Houses of Industry; the first fifty years of the Samford Union House.

III      The New Poor Law; the growth of bureaucracy; 'the deserving and undeserving' poor.

IV      A personal history – Anne Candler's story.

V      Medical matters.

VI      What happened to the children?

VII      Law and order within the House.

VIII      Visitors to the House

IX      Vagrants and bona fide travellers.

X      Humanity to the inmates.

XI      In time of war.

XII      After death; the burial ground.

XIII      Masters and Matrons; Labour masters and Laundresses; Porters and Chaplains.

XIV      The building; schedule; changes through the years.

Author's Note

In most cases, when I have quoted, I have retained the spelling and grammar of the original text. In the eighteenth century and the first half of the nineteenth, spelling was not fixed and in many cases was dependent on the pronunciation of the writer. Hence we have such gems of Suffolk appearing in phrases like, 'relief was paid to John Smith, he having brook his leg.'

# I

'The greatest of evils and the worst of crimes is poverty.'
**George Bernard Shaw.**

What to do about rising unemployment and homelessness and where to find the money to meet the demands of benefit payments were some of the problems that occupied the government as recently as the last decade of the twentieth century. How are jobs to be created when traditional markets are declining? If people are retrained to work in new trades, what guarantee is there that there will be enough work for them in those particular areas? And if the unemployed go off to new localities in search of work, where are they to live? What too, is to be done about the growing number of one-parent families; how are errant fathers, who fall behind with or have never contributed to paternity payments, to be traced and made to pay? Who is to provide specialised or long-term medical care for the sick and what is to be done with the increasing numbers of the old and infirm when they are no longer able to care for themselves?

However contemporary these problems may seem, they are certainly not new! Indeed, they have been with us in some form or another since man began living in groups bigger than the immediate family. But it is only within the last hundred years or so that the State has taken responsibility for dealing with them.

I will try to keep my 'history lesson' as brief as possible but it is a necessary one if we are to understand how and why Houses of Industry, Union Houses or Workhouses came into being. In the Middle Ages when the population was much smaller than it is today and people lived in compact groups based on a village or small market town, responsibility for the poor – that is, those without work or on such a meagre wage they could not support themselves and their families – often fell to the religious orders. Monasteries provided food and lodging for the needy, hospital care for the sick and aged and education for orphans. In feudal villages the local landowner, in conjunction with the parish priest, would have assumed responsibility for the care of his workers, while the religiously based Mediaeval Craft Guilds made financial provision for their own needy members.

By Elizabethan times, with the monastic orders dispersed, the Parish became the focal point for assistance. Churchwardens held great power locally and it was they and the members of the Church Council or Vestry Committee who annually elected from their number the Overseers of the Poor to dispense the aid that was required.

But before they could pay **out**, they needed to collect the funds **in.** We know that wealthy merchants and landowners regarded it as their religious duty to provide for others. It is often said, rather cynically, that they tried to buy their way into heaven by subscribing to the building of a church or the provision of almshouses. Even if this was so, those left behind had cause to be thankful that benefactors did leave sufficient funds to endow orphanages, schools, hospitals and housing. Many of those large scale endowments are still with us serving a useful purpose, while the smaller ones like the rent from a field to provide red flannel petticoats for widows; winter coals for the aged or a Christmas Dinner for apprentices may have dwindled in both income and those requiring the assistance.

Although very welcome, these endowments did not deal with everyday running costs, so to meet these a Poor Rate was imposed on everyone within a Parish who lived in a property over a certain value.

In addition, most Parishes had premises at their disposal, usually known as the 'Towne' House or more properly defining its usage, the 'Poores House'. Here a homeless family could be temporarily housed or the very elderly brought to end their days.

"Relief of the aged and sick, apprenticeships for the young and the provision of work for the able-bodied" were three parts of the Elizabethan Code for dealing with the poor. And the system worked well while times were good but fluctuations in trade and agriculture imposed impossible burdens on both sides. The falling off in a trade or depression in agriculture meant a laying-off of workers who would then need help in supporting their families. This led to an increase in the Poor Rate to meet that demand while in turn, the people who had to pay the rate were also finding it hard to make ends meet. In addition they were expected to meet all the other taxes imposed by the government. In the eighteenth century for example, those taxes were needed to pay for the expense of being almost continually at war with other countries throughout the century.

The seventeen hundreds saw great change; this is the period often referred to in our older school books as the Agrarian and Industrial Revolutions; a period of upheaval, in so far as the traditional way of doing things came to an end. For generations manufacturing had been based on the home. Wool, the staple of this country, went through its various early processes in the cottage homes of the workers; the spun yarn being taken off to weavers in larger houses who sent the resultant cloth to be disposed of by merchants in towns and cities like Ipswich and Norwich. Most agricultural workers, with the help of their wives and children supplemented their incomes with this cottage industry.

The growth of industry and the development of factories following mechanisation led to a shift in population. Many young people left the precarious life of farming in the hope of a regular income in a factory. Those who remained in rural areas found that there was no longer a demand for their spinning or knitting skills and in some cases there was also little farm work available as landowners rushed to turn their arable land over to pasture for sheep to satisfy the demands of the new factories. So, in the countryside there was widespread unemployment and when agricultural jobs had gone, so too had the cottage that went with the job, resulting in homelessness. This in turn encouraged a drift to town in search of work putting even more strain on the limited housing resources there. Existing houses were split either into tenements – separate units – or let out on a single room basis, whole families crowding into the limited space. It is hardly surprising that men went off seeking work, hoping to be able to send for their families but often being forced to abandon them. Sometimes both parents went, leaving the children who, they knew, would be looked after by the Parish.

Whenever there was a lull in fighting, and often this meant during the winter months, the ordinary soldiers and sailors were dismissed to return to their homes. Unless they had managed to save some of their pay, they were dependent on either casual employment or their Parish to support them. Many preferred to stay in towns rather than return to the countryside so they swelled the urban population and often were behind some of the more violent crimes. The romantic figure of the mounted highwayman was in reality as nasty a piece of work as his footpad counterpart who preyed on members of the public going about their business in town. The disbanded soldiery was often responsible too, for the spread of venereal and other diseases and their winter liaisons frequently left behind late summer babies. Abandoned without means, mothers and children were forced to throw themselves upon the mercy of the Parish Overseers for subsistence. Pursuit of the putative father was often a futile business, especially in towns.

The story I hope to unfold to you is based on one particular area, and that a rural one, and in its telling I hope to avoid some of the generalisations which are sometimes encountered in history text books. However, there are certain principles that applied throughout the country when Parish help, or relief as it was known, was dispensed. Considered by some to have been the biggest drawback to freedom of movement of labour and by others a sensible deployment of funds was the Settlement Order. This was a hangover from days long gone when to qualify for assistance one needed to have been born and bred in the Parish. Settlement could also be acquired if one was apprenticed there, had worked there for at least a year or rented a property worth £10 a year, in other words one would have made some contribution to the Poor Rates. It was this Settlement Act which was responsible for the heartrending stories of individuals, usually mothers about to give birth, being harried from the parish in which they happened to be, to be sent back to their home parish. A payment was usually given by the expelling Overseers to assist the traveller to return. Heartless as this might sound, the Parish Poor Rate was not limitless and the Overseers' first duty was to their own parishioners.

As the century progressed the problem of caring for those in need increased as the gap widened between the very wealthy and the very poor. The causes for this were many. Ironically, it was the increased prosperity of the country with its major export of the intensively produced cereal crops that was responsible for much of the hardship. Since high prices could be gained from foreign buyers, merchants and traders expected the same on the home market. The price of bread rose rapidly. In the past the cost of a loaf had acted as a marker for wages, but these no longer kept pace with the rises. As bread was the staple food of most poor families, many faced starvation, as they were unable to find the money to purchase this basic necessity. So, more and more applications were made to the Parish Overseers for assistance. In many cases the response was to lay down a code of practice – so much cash allowed according to the current price of a loaf, the payments adjusted to so much per adult with a sliding scale of payments for the number of children and their ages. In other cases a deal was struck with a local baker to provide the quartern (four pound) loaves that were then handed out to those who had the requisite authority from the Overseers. But as the situation worsened it was necessary to take more drastic measures to alleviate the situation.

There was still an underlying suspicion on the part of many that poverty was self-induced. If one worked hard, then one should be able to maintain oneself and one's family. It was allowed that being widowed and orphaned, falling sick or ageing was beyond one's control and therefore demanding of help and compassion but for the rest, unemployment was frequently equated with laziness. To discourage the loafers and idlers who took advantage of the hand-outs, requests for relief were to be severely tested and ultimately, particularly in towns, relief was refused unless the applicant entered a Workhouse. An Act passed in 1723 allowed for the setting up of such establishments; their purpose to provide paid work and somewhere to live. The fact that many of these were badly run led to the fearful reputation they acquired that is still within folk memory to this day.

Rural Suffolk took advantage of another option, that of combining with other parishes to share the burden of provision for the poor. The county was divided into administrative areas based on the old Hundreds and it was these that provided the basis for the Union Houses.

Before we begin the story of the Samford Hundred House, I must ask the reader to try not to judge the past by the standards of the present day. Although human nature changes very little, our expectations of life do. So, the things we take for granted as being necessary for our day-to-day living would have been unknown to our predecessors of two hundred and fifty or so years ago. To understand the story of the House of Industry you need to remember that in the countryside there were no roads as such, merely cart tracks which were kept in reasonable state by the filling in of potholes with stones lifted from the fields by women and young children and then put in place by agricultural labourers. Children were regarded as part of the work force from quite a young age. Housing was sparse and overcrowded. There had been a prolonged period of neglect of rural housing. Large estates that had been given over to pasturage often had an absentee landlord who was either unaware or careless of the need to keep his housing stock in good repair. So roofing thatch decayed and walls of lath and plaster crumbled. The tenant who was already paying a high proportion of his yearly income on rent could ill afford to undertake the repairs that rightly belonged to his landlord. In some cases, greedy landlords divided a reasonable sized house into a terrace of three or four units causing further overcrowding that led to excessive demands upon the wells supplying water as well as acute problems over the disposal of human waste products. House division also cut down the garden available to individual tenants. Land that had previously supplied one family with sufficient vegetables for their needs as well as supporting a pig and hens now had to be shared out amongst several.

Inside the house beds, that is simple straw mattresses laid on the floor or on rough frames with simple wool coverlets, were shared by parents and children, often in one room. If the children occupied a separate room, it was unlikely that the shared beds contained only those of the same sex. In many families, bedding consisted of whatever old bundles of rags were available. Only those items with a strict utilitarian purpose would find their way into these homes. Basic needs were met but there was little room for trifles or ornaments that were purely decorative.

An example of how few possessions made up a home in those days may be seen in the case of Robert Shapard, who being unable to pay his yearly rent, had his household goods seized in lieu.

| | |
|---|---|
| 1 bed as it stands | £ 1.1.0. |
| 1 table | 2.6. |
| 3 chairs | 1.0. |
| 1 joint stool | 1.0. |
| 1 oval table | 2.6. |
| 1 pair of tongs & andirons | 2.6. |
| bellows & saltbox | 2.0. |
| 1 tub with bands | 5.0. |
| 1 iron pot | 4.0. |
| 2 skillets & chafing dish | 2.0. |
| warming pan | 1.6. |
| frying pan & spoon | 2.6. |
| 2 Sore & Bulton hutch* | 1.6. |
| apples | 4.0. |
| 1 box iron | 2.6. |

As we can see, his bed was the most valuable item he possessed (which is why beds feature so widely in Wills of the time) and 'as it stands' refers to the bedding that went with it. I have no idea what trade Shapard followed but the high valuation placed upon the apples suggests that there was a large quantity of them so either he had an orchard and was an apple seller or possibly he was a cider maker. *A hutch could be an oaken chest with a lid used for storage of corn or bread. Sometimes the term applied to a dresser with a storage cupboard in the centre. As for 'Sore and Bulton', I can only offer the mundane explanation that these were either the makers' names or the dialect for 'saw and built on'.

As a comparison with Shapard's these are the contents of the home of an Ipswich butcher. Offered for sale after his death were a table, 2 cupboards, a couch, six chairs, a screen and four pictures, the contents of his parlour. In the kitchen there was a spinning wheel and an iron hanging pot and a jack bellows, two chests, a cupboard, five chairs, a joined/joint stool and earthenware vessels. In the parlour chamber, a bed and two cribs (small beds) and a cradle. He also had ten further chairs, some old beds and a chest and another cupboard. The cellar of his house was used as a store. The advertisement taken from the **Ipswich Journal** gives us a wealth of detail. We can deduce that the butcher had been reasonably affluent since he had a comfortable parlour in which he and his wife and family might sit apart from the servant(s). We learn too that he and his family had slept in beds in the parlour chamber that might adjoin the parlour or be situated above it. The other beds and furniture may have been used by the servants who would have slept in the attics or in the kitchen. Most interesting perhaps is the reference to the spinning wheel. The butcher's wife probably spun the yarn that provided the cloth to make clothes for her family.

Clothes were frequently handed down throughout a family and between employers and their servants. Foreign travellers to England were amazed to discover that an elegantly dressed young man or woman could well be a man/maid servant, off duty in his/her employer's cast off clothes. In the case of Lord Chedworth, of whom we will hear later, he actually got his valet to 'wear-in' his boots for him. Male clothing for the most part consisted of coarse linen shirts, a waistcoat, leather breeches and a topcoat. Both men and women wore knitted woollen stockings. Smock frocks were the usual working garb for men, while for working women aprons covered the simple skirts and blouses worn over petticoats. Shawls provided warmth outside, topcoats for women being usual only for the wealthy. Hats for the men and simple bonnets or caps for women completed the ensemble.

Other aspects of the way in which life then was different will emerge as we unfold this story. But we should remember that the threat of sudden destitution was one that hung over the heads of all – even the very rich with misguided investments or reckless gambling could find themselves in dire straits. One problem that has not changed down the years is the need to make provision for one's old age as the following newspaper item shows.

"Mr William Manley formerly an attorney of great practice died recently. The mutability of human affairs was strongly exemplified in the fate of the deceased. His practice for several years as a solicitor was extensive, lucrative and honourable; and he was esteemed, visited and employed by many of the first families in the neighbourhood; but he departed this life in the Parish Workhouse."

**The Ipswich Journal 1804.**

## II

"Some days since, the Workhouse in the Parish of St James Westminster, which was almost finished, was blown down by a sudden gust of wind, which caused much Joy among the Poor, who made Bonfires and Illuminations on that Occasion." Aug.1726.

In the **Ipswich Journal** for the week ending the 9 June 1764, among the advertisements for houses to let; positions vacant and those wanted; the one hundred stacks of shrub wood fit for brick-kiln burning or common kitchen-firing available at Great Wenham and the advance notice of the Cock-fights to be held at the King's Head during the three days of the Ipswich Race Meeting, was a rather larger and much more formal advertisement which must have caused any local gentlemen – and the odd lady too, to sit up and read more attentively.

Similar notices had appeared over the past year or so but this one had particular relevance to the inhabitants of that part of Suffolk known as the Samford Hundred. Couched in the legalistic jargon of the period it read:

*"Whereas by an Act passed in the last Session of this present Parliament, entitled, 'An Act for the better Relief and Employment of the Poor in the Hundred of Samford in the County of Suffolk,' it is enacted that from and after the $24^{th}$ Day of this present Month of June, every Person who shall be seised (in possession of the freehold*

*of) in his or her own Right of Lands or tenements rated to the Poor's Rate within the said Hundred at the value of £30 per Annum, also all the Rectors and Vicars of the several Rectories and Vicarages within the said Hundred, and also every Person who then shall be rated to the Poor's Rate in one or more Parish or parishes within the said Hundred for Lands, Tenements or Heridaments or Tythes occupied or enjoyed by him or her at the value of £60 per Annum, shall be and are incorporated Guardians of the Poor within the said Hundred.*

*"And it is further enacted, that the said Guardians shall meet at the White Elm Inn at Copdock on Tuesday, 26 June to put the said Act in Execution, particularly to choose (by way of Ballot) out of the Guardians, 24 Directors of the Poor within the said Hundred; also a Treasurer and a Clerk.*

*"Churchwardens and Overseers, being given due notice, to attend the first meeting with their Books – the Accounts for the seven years from Easter 1756- 65 – such books to be left in custody of the President who shall be chosen at such meeting."*

Here was change indeed! Not only was the individual Parish losing its right to administer Poor Relief as and when it saw fit but the major contributors to the Poor Rate were being compelled to carry out the Government's policy, becoming in fact, unpaid civil servants. Imagine how it would be if you, as a Community taxpayer in one of the higher bands, suddenly found yourself with your fellow taxpayers expected to carry out the government's policies for the administration of local services. To a degree, this has already happened. Over the last few years, those who took on the voluntary role of school governors have been given more and more responsibility for the running of each individual school, administering its budget and hiring, and possibly firing, the staff.

We are not told exactly how many gentlemen turned up for the 10 o'clock meeting at the White Elm. What is certain is that it was only gentlemen, for although there were some lady land owners who qualified in their own right, they were not, of course, actually to participate in the business meeting. They were allowed a voice in the proceedings by appointing a male proxy to act for them. The only proviso was that the person chosen should himself be of Guardian status.

The White Elm at Copdock was chosen because it was centrally placed within the Samford Hundred and was situated on the main London road. A busy coaching inn, it was well used to catering for large numbers of travellers and their horses.

The local Overseers, often small tenant farmers or tradesmen who had been elected to their office at the annual Parish Meeting, armed with their precious account books came from Shotley, Erwarton, Chelmondiston, Harkstead, Holbrook, Woolverstone, Freston, Wherstead, Tattingstone, Stutton, Brantham, East Bergholt, Bentley, Sproughton, Burstall, Hintlesham, Chattisham, Shelley, Washbrook, Copdock, Belstead, Capel St Mary, Great Wenham, Little Wenham, Holton St Mary, Higham, Stratford St Mary and Raydon. Presumably they deposited their books and took their leave. However, although they were resigning some of their power, they were not redundant, indeed they would still be needed to help the new Guardians carry out their work at local level.

The list of assembled knights, squires and clergy (and some of the clergy were also knights or squires) reads like pages from the 1760s version of *Who's Who*. Strict decorum was required in recording the status of those present so we start with the baronet Sir John Barker. Then follow those who were regarded as 'gentlemen' and therefore accorded the abbreviated 'Esq' after their names; Thomas Staunton, Thomas White, Robert Harland, William Berners and James Sewell. Next came the clerical gentlemen; the Reverends Richard Canning, Tobias Rustat, Martin Nunn, Titus Stebbing, William Garrod, Thomas Warren and Stephen White. Last in this particular social pecking order came the wealthy farmers simply known as Mister: Mr. William Vesey, Lark (yes, really!) Tarver, Henry Bacon, John Lewis, Nathaniel Whimper, John Hall, Thomas Woodward, William Brooks, Thomas Alderton and Lott Knights. From these, twenty-four were chosen to be Directors. It would appear that they were elected for their suitability and popularity rather than where they lived, for among those elected were Thomas White, Esq.

and the Revd. Titus Stebbing both of whom lived in Tattingstone. (The Revd. Stebbing may not have been pleased to have his time taken up just then with such matters, for it was only ten days before his marriage to Miss Dale of Clare was due to take place.) The estate owner, Mr William Berners of Woolverstone and wealthy farmers Thomas Alderton of Shotley and Thomas Woodward of Sproughton were also chosen. Sir Richard Savage Lloyd, MP whose home was Hintlesham Hall was elected Chairman. The two salaried posts of Treasurer and Clerk went to Ipswich bookseller John Shave and the attorney John Juby. Their salaries were fixed at five guineas (£5.5.0.) for the Treasurer and £4.0.0. for the Clerk.

They were legally bound to form themselves into a new Corporation. That having been done they then settled upon a design for the common seal that would be used on all official documents. The chosen device of a spinning wheel cut in steel with the words Samford Hundred Suffolk around it, proclaimed the industry that would be carried on within the proposed workhouse. Having got that far, the meeting was adjourned for three days until 29 June.

It was then, in the White Horse in Ipswich, that the new Directors got down to the serious business of where they should build this new House and perhaps, more important, how they were to finance the project.

In that edition of the **Ipswich Journal**, mentioned earlier, there had been an advertisement placed by the Guardians of Mutford and Lothingland Hundred who were seeking a parcel of land of around 50 acres. This seems to have been considered a sufficient size on which to build a Workhouse and provide some agricultural land to help support the inmates. Edmund Jennings of Tattingstone had just such a parcel of land that might suit the Samford Directors. Situated close to the parish church, it was a freehold estate of approximately 52 acres on which stood a barn and other outbuildings. It was currently being farmed by Joseph Mason. After much discussion, the Directors adjourned the meeting until 5 pm and empowered Lott Knight and Thomas Alderton to negotiate with Jennings. They had been given the brief to purchase land for not more than £600. They and the rest of the Directors must have been overjoyed when they reported that for £298 they had secured a 999 years lease on the land known as Fryers Pightle, Broom Hill, Topyard Field, Backhouse Field, Church Field, Further Fenn, Oak Field, First Fenn and Sink Meadow.

A week later the question of compensation for the tenant, Mason was raised. There were still four years to run on his lease but he was prepared to give immediate possession of Backhouse Field and the orchard in return for £18.0.0. It was here that the building would be situated. The rest of the land, including the barn, Mason would give up on the 10 October 1766. That meant there were still two years of his tenancy left but for that he would accept £40.0.0. in compensation. The Directors also agreed to indemnify him for any damage done to his crops during the building process or by the paupers after the building was erected. But they also granted themselves the liberty of entering upon twenty acres during the ensuing spring and having it sown with hayseeds, clover or rye grass. In addition they laid claim to the straw and chaff from Mason's final year's corn crop.

The site turned out to be conveniently placed on several scores; it was almost at the centre of the Hundred, being not more than nine miles to the farthest village in most directions; it was at the top of a hill which meant that fresh air could blow through the building and it had a fast running stream close by. However, hardly had the ink dried on the land deal before negotiations were afoot to sell some of this parcel of land to Thomas White who already owned much of the land in the village. He paid the Directors £205 for three pieces, amounting to just over 15 acres and gave them a three acre piece he already owned known either as Pond Grove or Holly Hill.

The next step was to decide what form the building should take; who should be responsible for erecting it and how to raise the money to pay for it. The Directors did not have any corporate money to play with, so initially each Director or Guardian pledged a £100 a piece. At the meeting on the 30 June, the Revd.Rustat from Stutton pledged a loan of a thousand pounds at 4½ % interest. Other loans were raised from a variety of sources; one, that of £500, came from the Grey Coat Boys and Blue Coat Girls Charity School in Ipswich. The Trustees however, drove a hard bargain, adding an extra ½ % to the interest rate on their loan. Another method of raising immediate funds was to mortgage the money expected from the Poor Rate. For example, Edmund Jennings, gave £500 plus 4 ½ % interest on a mortgage on $1/20^{th}$ of the Poor Rate. The following year the Revd. Canning pledged £600 against $1/16^{th}$ of the Rate, while an Ipswich master mariner gave £150 for $1/66^{th}$ and a gentleman from the town pledged £300 for $1/33^{rd}$ of the Rate.

Just how much money would be needed to set up the whole operation became clearer when tenders for the building were received. Having viewed the architects' plans for a House of Industry, the Directors ordered that they should be placed on public view in Mr Shave's office in Ipswich for the attention of local building contractors – or bricklayers, as they were then known.

At their next meeting, again at the White Horse in Ipswich, they received five sealed bids for the contract. The highest from Nuthall was for £4,650. Aldis came close behind at £4,620, Hayward and Robinson managed to lop off £500 with their bids of £4,164 and £4,159 respectively. Undercutting them all was Andrew Chandler of Nacton with his offer of £4,029.9s.0d.

It would be cynical to suggest that his price was the only reason Chandler got the contract. It no doubt contributed but I suggest that he was chosen because his work was known to most, if not all, the Directors. Chandler had built the Carlford and Colneis Hundred House (now Amberfield School) at Nacton some ten years earlier. The Nacton House was vigorously supported by Sir Philip Broke who no doubt showed it off to his fellow landowning neighbours. In fact, it was Chandler who had delivered the original plans and elevations to the Directors with proposals for the building. But before he got the final contract, Captain Robert Harland, another sea-farer like Broke, was deputed to look over the plans thoroughly and find an independent and 'skilful workman' to examine the scantlings (specimens) of the timber and other materials to be used.

Contracts were drawn up and exchanged at Michaelmas 1764. Among the specifications Chandler agreed to "Dig all the Foundations and Cellars to a proper depth, as showed by the Drawings, and to remove Earth to some proper place, so as to leave the Ground level, the Bottom of the Privies to be two feet below the Surface of the Earth. All Foundations below Ground of outside wall to be two bricks and a half, footings one brick".

Work was to start in 1765 and be completed by Lady Day (25 March) 1766. The Directors and Assistant Guardians might well be pleased with the progress they had made but there were others with very different ideas. At the meeting on 15 December 1764 it was revealed that a letter making threats upon the lives of some of the Directors had been discovered in Raydon. So seriously was the letter taken that a general meeting of all the Guardians was called at the White Elm on the 18$^{th}$ so that all might be acquainted with the contents of the letter and discuss what action should be taken. The letter, reproduced as it was written, is a prime example of eighteenth century writing, using capital letters for most nouns, commas but rarely full stops and a spelling based very largely on the speech of the writer. It reads:

*"Gentlemen this to aquaint you all Consorning the Bilding of this Workhous think to starve the poore they are Stephen Wite Stratford, Lows of Barssild (Burstall) Wite of Tatason Loyd Hintlesham but Let them tak Care of them Selves for the farst that is to hap on shall theare Brans be Blown out and that soon as sure as death and faile not and the hous shall not be bilt a toyle for theare shall be 3000 men planted soon and wil di att it and pull Wites hous downe."*

Even if one did not take seriously the threat to blow out the brains of the gentlemen mentioned, what was a matter of concern was the possibility a very large number of disaffected men who could gather and wreak havoc upon the new building. The decision of the meeting was that a reward of £100 should be given to those who helped to bring about the conviction of the writer/s of the letter. Thus an advertisement appeared in the **Ipswich Journal** a week later that gave the letter in full with the additional detail that it had been found between 5 and 6 in the morning of Wednesday 12 December lying in the King's Highway in Raydon between the houses of Mr Pilborough and Mr Cook. The Guardians promised that they would endeavour to procure His Majesty's most gracious pardon for anyone concerned in writing or dropping the letter, other than the person who actually wrote the original. This advertisement continued to appear throughout January.

Nothing more was reported on the subject and the building work went ahead at the planned date. Chandler was to receive four staged payments of £500 with the final half of the initial sum paid when the Guardians were satisfied that everything was in order. Thomas White was put in charge of these payments. Being on the spot, living as he did at The Place in Tattingstone, he was able to keep a keen eye on the progress of the building. And progress speedily it did. By the 29 September 1765 White was certifying that the first floor had been laid while the roof tiling was finished by December.

Perhaps the threat to the security of the House had not gone away entirely. On 21 December a policy for £3000 was taken out with the Sun Fire Insurance Office for accidental damage by fire. The premium was £7.18s.6d.

Once building was underway, there were other important concerns to be dealt with. Having decided that the inmates would best be employed spinning wool into yarn, negotiations had to take place with the local growers who would provide the raw material. Then there was the very important question of who should be responsible for the day-to-day running of the place. Obviously, given the fact that this was to be a House of Industry, the man chosen must have a good working knowledge of the wool trade; preferably a master craftsman who had experience of dealing with a work force as well as merchants and traders. Two other requirements had to be met; the man should be married with his wife prepared to work with the female inmates and both should, if possible, have had smallpox. Captain Harland was deputed to find a suitable person to superintend the House while the Revd. Mr Rustat was given the task of fitting up two of the rooms within the House for 'habitation' by whoever was selected. He was also directed to buy such furniture as he thought fit up to a limit of £15.

Advertisements for the post were placed in national as well as local newspapers and from the applications received Edward Pearson and his wife Mary were duly appointed on 24 June 1766. Pearson, who came from Norwich, was a specialist woolcomber, that is one who understood the business of selecting the right lengths of wool ready for spinning. His salary as 'Governour' was fixed at £40 per annum, while Mrs Pearson, now to be known as 'Governess' received £15. In addition they received free board and lodging on the premises.

On the day that the Directors interviewed and appointed the Pearsons, they had another piece of business to attend to, namely the widening of the road leading to the entrance to the House. What we now know as School Road leading into Lemons Hill was originally nothing more than a sandy lane, (which is what the locals called it). It was not wide enough to take all the traffic that would be using it in future, so the order went out to 'rebuild' it. What is not clear from the Account Book and Directors' Minute Book of this period is just how much pauper labour was involved in the building projects. It would have made sense to employ where possible those currently in receipt of Poor Relief.

It has been said that the Samford House was built to take five hundred inmates. That seems an exaggerated figure and certainly, initially, in 1766, the Directors were not expecting to house even as many as two hundred, that is assuming that every bed that was ordered was to sleep two. We may find that difficult to comprehend but in those days entire families might share the same bed. It was also quite common for a female servant to share a bed with her mistress and even in wealthy families, unmarried offspring were unlikely to have a bed to themselves. And a traveller would take it for granted that he would be unlikely to have single occupancy of a bed in an inn. So it is quite likely that the younger inmates at least shared one of the hundred bedsteads, (made to the same specifications as those in use in the Nacton House,) which were on the Directors' initial shopping list.

And what a shopping list it was! To help pay for it all more loans had to be raised. Lott Knight lent £800 and the Revd. Rustat, another £600. Messrs Sewell, Brook, Canning and Knight formed the committee that was to consider materials and clothing. In April 1765 they placed advertisements three times in the **London Daily Advertiser** and the **General Evening Post** requesting sealed bids and samples of goods offered. Where possible supplies were purchased in Ipswich or the surrounding area but some suppliers came from London. To start with the aforementioned beds had to be fitted out. First came an order for mattress and bolster cases made from strong, West Country striped ticking. An extra-sturdy woollen cloth sheeting, often used at sea and so known as 'Fearnought', was used for coverlets. Sheeting of various thicknesses was ordered and woollen material for blankets. Chicken feathers to fill the bolsters were ordered by the pound.

Next came equipment for the kitchens and dining hall; coppers, iron cooking pots, copper irons, coal grates, fenders, boilers, pewter chamber pots, wooden bowls, spoons and ladles. Already we can see the pictures conjured up, if not in Dickens's **Oliver Twist,** certainly by those stage and cinematic presentations of **Oliver!** Coppers and wooden bowls really do evoke the waif asking for more gruel. Yet common sense tells us that for mass catering in a period when cooking was done over an open fire, large pans would be needed. Similarly, at that time most ordinary people used wooden plates or trenchers and spoons in their own homes.

Since beer was regarded as a standard part of the English diet, it was natural that the House should brew its own. The original specifications for the Brew house were found to be too small so before the requisite equipment was purchased, the building was extended.

It is very hard for us to imagine how limited possessions were at that period. I dislike generalisations but on the whole, most working men and women would have possessed a very small wardrobe. In many cases it would have amounted to the clothes they wore every day, covered perhaps by a smock frock or apron, with slightly newer or better ones for Sunday. Clothes were still, on the whole made either by a member of the family or a local seamstress or itinerant tailor. There was always a good market for second-hand garments so 'best clothes' were often the first things sold in order to buy food or pay the rent. For those entering the House of Industry, the chances were that the clothes they stood up in had become threadbare and verminous. So, it was essential, for hygienic reasons as much as any other, that all inmates should be issued with a fresh set of clothing on their entry.

The shopping lists for clothing tells us not only what was the standard apparel of the period but also something of the materials used, names of cloth now totally unfamiliar. All men were issued with hardwearing leather breeches. Their shirts were made of 'Broad Hamburgh stuff', presumably a coarse woollen material popular with the German market; Kersey, a coarse ribbed narrow cloth was used for waistcoats and a Yorkshire plain cloth for topcoats. (The terms broad and narrow here refer to the width of the cloth.) To complete the ensemble, they were issued with a felt hat, knitted stockings and handkerchiefs made from checked Scotch linen. Children wore scaled down versions of adult clothing, so boys wore much the same as the men except their shirt material was of narrow Dowlas (Calico) the same as the girls had for their shifts. The women had thick Dowlas for their shifts – a garment that acted as an undergarment by day and nightdress for bed. The women wore gowns made of Padua serge (a ribbed material) and coats (that is a short jacket) of half Kersey. Both women and girls wore aprons made from a check material and they and the children had knitted stockings. Everyone was also given a pair of shoes. The actual numbers ordered in 1766 were:

| Men | 60 pairs | Girls | 70 pairs |
| Boys | 70 pairs | Children | 40 pairs |
| Women | 60 pairs | | |

As time went on, replacements would be provided from within the House. Shoes would be made and repaired upon the premises and the children would be employed in knitting the long woollen stockings.

But for the moment all these items had to be made. A Mrs Cuff was employed to cut out all the shirts and shifts. This lady was probably a mistress of her trade for she also undertook to provide the staff to make up the garments. For cutting out the shirts and shifts she charged 3d. per dozen and her tariff for sewing up garments was:

| | |
|---|---|
| Men's shirts | 5/- per dozen |
| Women's shifts | 4/- per dozen |
| Boys' shirts | 4/- per dozen |
| Girls' shifts | 3/- per dozen |
| Children's shifts | 2/6 per dozen |
| Women's caps | 1/6 per dozen |
| Girls' caps | 1/3 per dozen |
| Children's caps | 1/3 per dozen |
| Sheets | 4/- per dozen pairs. |

If one looks at portraits from the eighteenth century one sees that it was customary for all women and children to wear a simple, usually white, close fitting cap. Readers of **Cranford** will recall the consternation several of the ladies in the novel felt if they were caught by an unexpected caller still wearing their domestic or morning cap. So the wearing of caps in the House was simply part of a general trend not a symbol of being a pauper.

While Mrs Cuff was busy in her workroom in Ipswich, Andrew Chandler was now supervising the interior of the House, beginning with the Dining room.

The new Governor, Edward Pearson was given the go-ahead to have the appropriate number of spinning wheels made and so that work could begin immediately the House opened he was empowered to buy-in a sufficient quantity of wool. The Directors had questioned what they should do about maintaining Pearson and his family until such time as there was actual work for him to do so it was important to give him some form of employment. Another important purchase was a cart and a horse to pull it. This would have been used for a variety of purposes, the most important being that of bringing in the families to the House, conveying goods to and from the House and on occasions acting as an ambulance for the sick or a hearse for the dead.

The staff were also catered for. Three bedsteads with sacking bases overlaid with goose feather mattresses and pillows were made especially by a Mr Iron, upholsterer for the use of the Governor and his family and for the occasional use of the duty surgeon. They had the added refinement of china furniture in their bedrooms. Not for them pewter chamber pots and washbasins. An eight-day clock was also ordered so that good time keeping could be ensured.

The building was finished and the grounds were laid out. The importance of fresh air for good health was well understood in the eighteenth century and the authorities were eager to make sure that as little illness as possible should sweep through the building. For that reason, not only were windows or ventilators placed opposite each other on either side of the building allowing air to blow through the sleeping, living and working areas but 'airing grounds' were included in the plans, so that the inmates could take exercise as well as breathe fresh air. The 'airing grounds' were placed at the rear of the building where, unfortunately it was felt by some, they could be seen by those using the lane in front of the church (the present Church Road). The rector complained and at one of their regular meetings during 1766, the Directors decreed that 'all the paling next to the road opposite Tattingstone Church be forthwith done.' The wooden fences would in due time be replaced by high brick walls topped with broken glass but that repressive period was still a long way off.

Smallpox was the scourge of the eighteenth century. Many of those who received Poor Rate assistance from their parish had suffered from the disease that required long and careful nursing. The high mortality rate left families severely depleted, often deprived of one or other parent. Although inoculation was being encouraged, it would be sometime before it was accepted as matter of course. It was bad enough trying to contain an outbreak in an individual cottage in a village, how much more of a problem it would be to prevent an epidemic within the House. The answer was to have an isolation area to which all sufferers could be consigned. So the Directors asked Thomas White and the Revd. Stebbing to look for and have staked out a suitable area for a Smallpox House.

By the 28 June 1766, the Directors had almost completed their arrangements. At the meeting on that day they put in an order for the coal required for general heating, cooking and laundry purposes. They also made several important appointments. William Finch from Woodbridge was appointed as House baker, a post for which he was paid 6/- a week with board and lodging provided for him, his wife and child. A Mrs Dalton was taken on as nurse on a short-term contract until the following Easter at a salary of two shillings and ten pence (2/10d.) per week. The other appointment was for a qualified physician who, in return for an annual salary of £60.0.0. was expected to attend the House twice a week on specified days to deal with all routine medical matters. The doctor was further expected to be qualified in "all branches of Physick" as well as surgery and midwifery. In addition, he could be called out at any time for an emergency and he was expected to provide the medicine that he prescribed for his patients. There was no shortage of applicants. The Parish Poor Rate had always reimbursed local doctors who treated those in need and the additional income that generated was often very important to a struggling practitioner. Dr. John Clubbe of Ipswich who was put on a three-year contract was a young man of twenty-five, probably newly qualified and thus overjoyed to find himself with a regular salary.

With medical matters in mind, the Directors also turned their attention to the disposal of the dead. A contract was placed with Mr Betts of Holbrook to provide coffins and to make a bier on which the coffin was carried prior to interment. Where possible bodies were to be returned to the parish from which the deceased had come with the relations or parish paying for the burial. However this was not always feasible, especially in the case of itinerants and those who had died from an infectious disease, so the answer was for the House to have its own burial ground.

The Directors left the decision on this matter to the members of the Weekly Committee. Once the House was up and running, this committee was formed from those Guardians who were not necessarily Directors. They became responsible for superintending the day-to-day business of the House but were also there to watch the interests of the inmates and investigate any complaints they might have. So it was the Weekly Committee that decided that a 'burying ground' should be set out at the upper end of Back Lane Field and that a hedge of fast growing quickthorn should screen it.

In early September advertisements were placed for the supply of food and essential basic household items like candles and soap. Again, most of the suppliers were local and were expected to supply samples of their wares to be inspected by the Board. The contract for beef and mutton went to Barzillai Hare of Woolverstone. I mention him in particular only because of his unusual forename. I need hardly point out just what these contracts must have meant to local tradesmen, especially as they knew that they would be on-going.

There were still one or two last minute things to be done. The post of chaplain had not yet been dealt with, so the Revd. Stebbing agreed to act as such until an appointment was made. Mr Lark Tarver undertook to supply some necessary 'tools of the trade' for the chaplain, namely a surplice and a burying cloth. Then someone must have suddenly realised – perhaps it was Mrs Pearson – that no provision had been made for an area where linen lines might be set up. So the Weekly Committee promptly carried out a survey and located a suitable site and at the same time ordered that a garden should be laid out too.

Finally came the big day. On Wednesday, 1$^{st}$ October 1766, the doors of the new House of Industry for Samford Hundred opened to receive the first intake of paupers. As with the rest of the operation from the inception of the Corporation in 1764, through the erection of the massive building, the fund raising and all the other very necessary parts of the scheme, that first week's intake had been planned with great precision. The parishes within the Hundred were divided into four areas for administrative purposes, so on that opening Wednesday, it was the poor of Sproughton, Higham, Chattisham, Little Wenham, Capel St Mary, Belstead and Brantham who were the first to enjoy whatever delights the place had to offer. And if one was sick or starving, homeless or used to massive overcrowding, then without doubt, the sparkling new building with its fresh clean white-washed walls and new furnishings, the rows of clean beds with proper bedding in place of rags and the prospect of three meals a day must have seemed blissful, even if one had to surrender personal liberty for a time.

Thursday saw the admission of candidates from Hintlesham, Raydon, Copdock, Washbrook, Freston, Holbrook and Great Wenham. Tattingstone people came in on Friday along with those from Stutton, Stratford St Mary, Bentley, Harkstead, Burstall and Shelley. The final intake on Saturday was from East Bergholt, Shotley, Erwarton, Chelmondiston, Woolverstone, Wherstead and Holton St Mary.

It would be a mistake to think that there was a steady stream waiting to cross the threshold. Indeed there was probably only a handful on each day. Many of those admitted initially would have been those too sick to be cared for at home, orphaned children and pregnant women as well as the able-bodied who were destitute.

During the first few months of that autumn and winter, both the Directors and the Governor and his staff would have been finding out what worked and what still needed to be done to make for the smooth running of the House. A routine had to be established; so it was decided that in summer the inmates would rise at five, take breakfast between six and seven, work until the dinner hour at noon; work again until supper at five until six with two hours leisure until bedtime at eight. Getting up time was a couple of hours later in the winter. Again we need to remember that these hours were probably kept by those outside the House too. 'Early to bed early to rise' was not just a virtue; it was a necessity in the days when the only form of artificial lighting was by candles, which were expensive, or very weak rush lights.

Another of the things looked at was the diet of the inmates. It was essential that this should be as nourishing as possible. The last thing the authorities needed was an ailing population. The whole purpose of the place was to produce an end product, in this case spun yarn, which would produce an income both to support the worker and provide them with some savings to use when they left the House. And as far as the sick were concerned, the sooner they could be cured and sent back home, the better. It was also essential that the children in their care were well nourished for as soon as they were old enough, an apprenticeship or employment of some kind would be found for them. Unhealthy, weakly children could become a charge on the Poor Rate perhaps for a life time, so it was essential to make sure that there were as few of these as possible.

So yet another task for the Directors was to agree a Bill of Fare for the House. No doubt in this they were guided by the experience gained from other Houses in Suffolk. Three meals were served and when one examines the menu, one sees careful planning was used.

Sunday:
Bread & cheese.   Beef & dumplings/pudding.      Bread & cheese.
Monday:
Beef broth.       Baked suet pudding.            Bread & cheese.
Tuesday:
Bread & cheese.   Boiled pork.                   Bread & cheese.
Wednesday:
Pease broth.      Mutton & dumplings/pudding.    Bread & cheese.
Thursday:
Mutton broth.     Bread & cheese.                Bread & cheese.
Friday:
Bread & cheese.   Beef & dumplings.              Bread & cheese.
Saturday:
Bread & cheese.   Beef broth.                    Bread & butter.

By our standards this seems very boring yet there was a healthy emphasis on protein by providing cheese every day. Most poor people would have been unlikely to have meat at home very often, let alone four times a week as here. There was, of course a strong carbohydrate intake as well as fat in the suet puddings and dumplings. Wednesday's 'pease broth' would have been quite a tasty 'pea and ham' soup using the liquid in which the pork had been boiled on the previous day. The peas of that period were probably closer to the dried peas that older readers may remember from school dinners. Again, the peas were high in protein and when cooked and mashed formed the cake-like pudding of the nursery rhyme, which, you will recall, could be stretched out to last nine days!

The bread too, would have been more like our present day wholemeal. Refined white bread was popular with the wealthy in towns except among those who had read the treatise written in 1757 **"Poison Detected or Frightful Truths and Alarming to the British Metropolis."** This revealed that there was a widespread use of alum to whiten flour and that often this was mixed with human urine, lime and chalk and on occasions, ground human bones taken from graveyards. It was found that alum was likely to cause constipation so to counteract this, purgatives were added to the flour. While a healthy person might be able to withstand the ill effects of the 'refined' bread, the very young and infirm could not. Part of the high infant mortality rate of the time was caused by infants being weaned on this bread mixed with milk. Similarly, this was a dish considered suitable for invalids. And the milk used in towns was often far less good than that in the country, coming as it did from cows that were kept in urban sheds, fed on discarded vegetable peelings and old, fusty hay.

The fact that vegetables do not appear on the House's Bill of Fare does not mean that they were not part of the diet. Certainly some would have been included daily, mainly those in season which could be grown in the fields surrounding the house. Potatoes were still not as widely used, as there were to become in the next century, which is why there is so much emphasis on bread. Beer was also issued as part of the diet. It offered a certain amount of nourishment as well as helping to giving a feeling of a full stomach. Children under the age of seven, invalids and nursing mothers would receive a daily ration of milk.

The Dietary, as it was known, having been set, it continued without deviation until the summer when the pork dinner was dropped for the season. This was a sensible hygienic move rather than a cost cutting exercise. In the days before refrigeration, pork was notoriously difficult to keep fresh. The records do not state what was substituted but one can't help thinking that it was probably more bread and cheese.

The physical needs of the inmates having been addressed, the Directors now turned their thoughts to the spiritual. John Betts, the carpenter from Holbrook who already held the contract for the supply of coffins, was charged with the task of fitting out a Chapel in a room next to the one in which the Committee met. He was to make a prayer desk some 3ft x 4ft and set it on a platform raised 18 inches off the floor. This was to be placed against a wall that would be wainscoted (panelled with wood) up to the ceiling. He was also to provide seats for the Governor and his family and six benches, each 14 feet long with side rails for the use of the inmates. The benches cost 6/6d each while a bill for £1.15.0. was submitted for the Governor's seating. A large Bible and the Book of Common Prayer and a small book of Burial Prayers completed the requirements of the chapel. Later a salaried chaplain would be appointed.

On a more mundane but very necessary level was the appointment of Thomas Abbott to "shave the Poor every Saturday". For this he received a quarterly payment of £1.1.0. but he was expected to provide his own soap. Again we must remember that the working man was unlikely to own a razor and that the village barber made his living from weekly shaves, hair cutting – and a bit of home spun dentistry! What is not clear from the records at that time is if Abbott was himself an inmate but it is likely, as the Directors tried to utilise any specific trade that came into the House. A case in point being John Arnold, a leather worker who came into the House just after it opened. Within a few weeks the Directors had bought in leather and set him up in business.

Within a couple of weeks of opening, the first of the farm livestock was purchased; a cow and her calf. Work was put in hand to build 'a Hog Court' for the accommodation of the boar that was the beginning of the piggery. And so that the arable land might be cultivated a plough was also ordered.

Although the Directors and Guardians had much of their time taken up with the House and all that entailed, they still had to consider the needs of the poor who would not automatically be taken into the House. Each week several of the Directors would meet to hear the cases presented to them by the Overseers of the individual parishes. They would then decide on the monetary relief that should be given to those who needed temporary help. And it was not always just money that was available. Take the case of John Willes of Stutton. We are not told what his problem was but he was granted 5/- a week for his general maintenance (rent and food). And since he was "allowed a straw bed and other necessarys", it is safe to assume that he was bed-ridden, perhaps with some form of spinal injury. Another sick man was James Twaits of Burstall who was allowed 6/- a week to support himself and his child until he was well again. Perhaps the wife of William Coal of Higham had died or maybe she was seriously ill. Either way the Board took responsibility for housing four of his children within the House. But we do know that William must have been in work as he was charged three shillings a week towards their maintenance. Those who were seriously sick and too ill to be removed to the sick wards were allowed payments towards their nursing care and extra food as well as rent. Sometimes these payments went on much longer than was anticipated. The widow Twitchett, who may have been related to the later Master of the House, was taken ill in 1771. Each week the carefully written note appears in the Weekly Committee book that she has been granted three shillings. This went on for many weeks until the note reads, "the widow Twitchett to be relieved with three shillings for the week past and nine shillings for three weeks to come *if she so long live.*"

(My italics.) Not only did she survive the next three weeks, she went on for at least another two months.

In April 1769, the Weekly Committee had to consider the case of Robert Fallows who came originally from Hintlesham. Robert had received a job offer and so asked to be discharged from the House. The Committee agreed that he should go and that he could leave his family behind on condition that he paid three shillings every week until Michaelmas to the Governor of the House for the maintenance of his family.

The mid eighteenth century had a more pragmatic approach to children born out of wedlock than the later Victorians were to have. Where possible, the father was identified and made to take financial responsibility for the offspring, hence the hundred blank 'Bonds for Bastardy' that were printed at this time along with the blank warrants and certificates ready for the Parish Overseers to fill out when necessary. Often, quite large sums were put down by the father for the child's maintenance. In cases where the mother was unable to claim against the father, an allowance could be made to her from the Board. Thus we read of Ann Deal who was allowed sixpence a week to maintain her 'base-born' child up to the sum of £4.14.0. This means that she had some help for almost three years.

Another eye-opener for these days when we take certain things for granted, is the fact that the Samford Union of parishes was responsible for payments for those of their residents who ended up behind bars. Isaac Squirrell of Harkstead found himself in Ipswich Bridewell (House of Correction or gaol situated behind Westgate Street.) At that time there was neither provision for a salary for gaolers or money made available for the maintenance of prisoners. They had to rely on their friends or charity for food. For example, the Assize judges always sent a donation to the gaol to provide bread and beer for the prisoners.) So the Directors found themselves liable to pay 5/- a week to the Keeper of the Bridewell for Isaac's maintenance. Similarly, payments had to be made to other Union Houses if a Samford resident should be taken in to them. And later, when the Woodbridge Union at Melton turned into the County

Asylum, patients transferred there had to be paid for by their own Union.

In February of 1767, Edward Pearson, the Governor, went to Norwich to sell the yarn produced within the House. The income from this was needed to help offset the rising numbers that were coming into the House. In March another twenty-six bedsteads were ordered plus six armed chairs and one dozen ordinary or common chairs. In that month too, more sows and pigs were bought in to increase the House's herd. And we are informed that Isaac Hutchinson had now taken over the Saturday shaving at 7/6d. a week, and spent the rest of his time employed in mending shoes for 2/6d. Since Hutchinson certainly was an inmate we can deduce that Abbott was too and that he had gained his discharge from the House. We are also pleased to learn that John Willes of Stutton has recovered from his illness and has been allowed two pairs of breeches and a pair of shoes, presumably so that he may once again take up employment. On a sad note we are told that Simon Fenn is to get 2/- a week to help him with his wife who is 'disordered in her mind'. In April the Governor was charged with the purchase of more chamber pots. And bricks were ordered to lay down a "proper drain", so presumably the numbers using the privies had increased.

An interesting appointment took place at this time. Although the idea of universal education was still a very long way off, the authorities were well aware that employment opportunities were greater for those who were literate and numerate. The man working on the land would expect his sons to follow him and his daughters to go into local service, but the Directors of the House who had to find employment for the orphaned or abandoned children in their care knew that they stood a better chance of securing good offers if the candidate had received a basic education. So, in 1767, Abraham Whiney, an inmate with some education himself, was employed on a three-month contract to teach the children to read. This was by no means a full-time education. Whiney had the children on Mondays, Wednesdays and Fridays. In return for his teaching, Whiney received about £3.5.0. a quarter. From this salary he would be expected to contribute to his keep but he would be able to save too, towards the day when he could leave the House.

A reminder that the House was operating as a House of Industry, comes in April 1767, when we read that the best spinners were to be paid 5d a day with the rest being paid in proportion to their ability. As a comparison of prices, that same month, it was decreed that Parish Officers, namely the Overseers who were responsible for bringing their needy parishioners to the House, were to receive travelling expenses of 6d a mile for those using a cart and 3d a mile for those on horseback. What is not clear is if this payment was for the round trip or merely one way. On the back cover of one of the Account Books there is a list of all the parishes in the Samford Hundred with their distance from the House so that the Treasurer was in no doubt as to how much he should pay out to a claimant.

1767 was a bad year for smallpox and at the end of it the Directors voted that Dr Clubbe be given an additional remuneration for all his hard work. William Talmarsh, Tattingstone's sexton was also given 10/6 that Christmas as an acknowledgement of the increased work he had had in digging graves and tolling the bell for burials. The following year, the Directors were pressing hard for universal inoculation. Obviously it was more economic to pay doctors to inoculate those who could not afford the treatment, rather than the Poor Rate bearing the expense of nursing cases through the sickness either at home or in the House. In 1771, the Board decreed, "if any of the Poore in the House choose to be inoculated, Mr Brooke or his son shall be employed in doing so providing it be at 5/3d. a head." In a further attempt to curtail the spread of the disease it was decreed that anyone falling ill with smallpox should be removed as soon as possible to the Sick House and the rest of the family be inoculated immediately. Anyone knowingly harbouring an undeclared case of the disease was liable to prosecution. On the other hand, anyone willing to undertake the nursing of smallpox cases was paid around 15/- a week. We hear of a Mrs Norman in the parish of St.Clement's in Ipswich who was paid a regular £2.10.0. a week for nursing Anne Gilders and her daughter from Shotley. These payments went on for some time. In the House itself, Ann Askew, an inmate who had helped out with nursing and general care of the sick between Christmas and Easter was rewarded with 10/6d. On the other hand, Richard Peck, whose wife had died in the epidemic, and his two sons William and Joseph who survived, were now actively seeking employment so were granted 25/- each to buy a new wardrobe.

We shall discover as we review the two hundred years of the House's existence that the building and the site did not remain static. On a very practical level in 1768 "the Brickwork for the Necessary to be built up higher and done immediately." The earth closets and urinals – the privies or 'necessary houses' as they were also known were to be a constant source of anxiety for the Directors. In that same years more building took place, the first being the erection of a Porter's Lodge. The Minute for this particular item states that it was "for preventing the poor going out or people coming into the House." It had become necessary to impose more discipline upon the inmates. Once a person had entered, he/she was not expected to wander in and out at will, particularly if he/she was wearing clothes belonging to the House. There was a danger that these might get 'mislaid' – stolen or sold – perhaps for drink. Then the wanderer might return not only without the clothes but inebriated. Drink was a problem of the period and one that had to be controlled in a large community. One volatile member could very easily upset the smooth running of the place.

Then there was a need to keep others out. Visiting was allowed at permitted times but there were unscrupulous folk who would try to gatecrash to see what they could get in the way of free food or other goods. Much later than this there is a reference to the son of the House nurse being found to have about his person a quantity of tea that belonged to the House.

By 1769, the Directors had children in the House who were old enough to be found employment. The Overseers of individual parishes had always been responsible for negotiating apprenticeships for their orphan or needy young people but now this fell to the Directors or Assistant Guardians. Where possible, children were found positions in their native parishes. This meant that they could return to live near to members of their extended family or family friends. We are given details of two arrangements that were made at that time. Thomas Dardy was taken into service by Mr Howard of Brantham from November 1769 until 'old Michaelmas' 1772. [In 1752 the Julian calendar was replaced in order to bring England in line with most European countries that followed the Gregorian style. To correct a discrepancy of some eleven days, the $2^{nd}$ September 1752 was followed by the $14^{th}$. Michaelmas (29 Sept.) had always been an important date for such things as tenancies and hiring agreements and for some time people still calculated Michaelmas by the old calendar.] The Board provided him with a coat, waistcoat, breeches, three shirts, three pairs of stockings, and two pairs of shoes. At the same time, Ann Woods was taken into service for one year by Mrs Lewis, also of Brantham. Her wardrobe consisted of a gown, two shifts and two pairs of stockings, a pair of shoes, one pair of stays, two caps, two handkerchiefs, a mantle and an apron. Mrs Lewis agreed that she would pay Ann a guinea for the year's service. So that was two less mouths to feed and backs to clothe. We shall hear more of the Board's treatment of children later.

But for the next few years the important thing was for the House to run as smoothly as possible; the labour within it to produce as much yarn as could be sold for the best returns and to keep the Poor Rates within reasonable bounds for those who had to pay them. Over the years the rates rose steadily. The Board had to cope with rising prices on the one hand and falling employment on the other, which in turn increased the demands on the Poor Rate. Added to this, many of the original short-term loans on the building were coming to maturity and money had to be found to repay them. In some cases the lender could be persuaded to re-invest his capital but at the price of a higher interest rate. However well the Treasurer might balance the books, an unforeseen event could alter everything. This might be a virulent outbreak of smallpox, or the spread of a farm disease such as foot and mouth or swine fever that could lead to acute food shortages and high prices, as well as a sudden decline in agricultural employment. Severe weather would have wide repercussions too; from the long term, shortages and high prices of any crop that managed to survive prolonged frost and snow, flooding or lack of summer sunshine, for example through to the more immediate problem of the sick and elderly needing extra food and warmth to prevent their dying from hypothermia.

An additional burden arose when the Government went to war against the colonists in America and then found themselves fighting the French, Spanish and Dutch. Then, the Militia, which normally did training service for a few weeks each year, was called up for active service to join the ranks of the enlisted men. Since the government made no financial provision for the dependents of service personnel, it was not long before the families were applying to the Board for out-relief and in the case of very large families it was often cheaper to take the children into the care of the House. Should the serviceman die in action then it was more than likely that the whole family would be forced into the House until such time as the widow and the older children could earn sufficient for the support of the family in lodgings outside.

In 1786, Edward Pearson, the Governor of the House, died. For twenty years he had carried out his duties to the complete satisfaction of the Board and he had become an established figure among the local population. For his widow, his death meant the loss not only of his income but her home and income too. Unless she had managed to save enough to support her, she would be faced with either finding another post or – perhaps unthinkable – ending up as an inmate. The problem was solved in an unusual way. When the post was advertised, her son Robert, who like his father had practised as a woolcomber, presented himself as a candidate. Instead of his wife being considered as Matron, his mother was put forward. Since Mrs Pearson was known to the Board, the pair were appointed – at a salary which had not increased for the Governor since 1766 and Mary Pearson's salary was actually reduced from £15 to £10. In all probability because of her age she was to do less and the £5.0.0 went towards the salary of the Nurse who acted as her deputy. For his salary, Robert found that he was to take on some of the duties of the Clerk to the Board.

One of the first jobs he had to undertake in this capacity was to placate Mr Flory, a farmer in the village of Tattingstone who sought compensation for the damage done to one of his fields of wheat. Apparently some of the Workhouse cows had managed to get into it and enjoyed a feast on the fresh young shoots. Understandably, Mr Flory was furious and the Board was forced to pay out £2.0.0. to cover his loss.

In the following year it became obvious that the numbers of people applying for assistance was growing and that many of them were those who could not claim to be legitimate residents of Samford Hundred. So great had the problem become that it was necessary for the Board to purchase a cart for the specific purpose of removing paupers to the place of their legal settlement. Better to pay a one off removal fee than to have to undertake to feed and lodge 'outsiders' in the hope of claiming off another area. The horse and cart was expected to travel up to thirty miles in summer months and twenty in winter. A subsistence allowance was paid for both the accompanying officers and the paupers, for if the destination was above the daily mileage, then accommodation would have to be sought at an Inn along the road.

Pearson left in 1797 and was replaced by a Mr. Twitchett. From the handwriting in the Minute Books it is clear that he was not as literate as Pearson had been. It is also possible that he and Mrs Twitchett were neither as trustworthy nor as good at maintaining discipline as their predecessors. The Board found it necessary to lay down that "the Governor and Matron shall not in future buy or sell any goods belonging to and for the use of the Corporation without order." One wonders quite what they had been up to. Had they been engaged in transactions that gave them backhanders? Whatever they had done, had been discovered. Perhaps it was pure coincidence that it was about this time it was decided that a Constable should be appointed to the House. And the second directive shows that there has been some slipping in standards. "The Governor and Matron to both attend the Poor at all their meals to keep good order, help them to their Provisions and see there is no waste – **and no want** – and that proper persons shall go round both at Dinner and Supper and deliver Beer to each person by a horn and that what may be left by one shall be filled up and given to the next. That children may have as much as may be thought necessary." The need to keep good order is further stressed when in October 1795 a set of stocks was introduced into the Dining Room in which the disorderly were to be placed. And had there been problems of males trying to get into the female airing-ground? This seems to be the obvious reason why the order was given to add another two feet of brickwork to the dividing wall in the courtyard. The actual Minute on this says that the blacksmith from Bentley is to "do the ironwork". This could, of course refer to adjustments to any gate there might have been but it is more likely that iron spikes were embedded into the top of the brickwork.

An indication that the Board was going through hard times financially was the decision to let off part of the arable land it owned to the Revd. Andrew Grant, rector of Tattingstone. It is likely that this land was part of what is now known as Glebe Farm. The remaining twenty-two acres, apart from a small portion, were laid down with hayseeds and Dutch clover for the grazing and pasturing of their cows and horses, although two of the horses were sold off at that time. The area that had been retained was to be "dug and cultivated by the Poor for growing potatoes, carrots, cabbages, beans and peas and other vegetables thought to be beneficial to the Poor." The increased use of vegetables suggests that meat and cheese costs were rising and meals needed padding out.

That was only a very small measure. More money was required in 1795. The Trustees of Holton School lent against their Parish Poor Rate with the expectation of 4½ % interest but a Mr Jarrold wanted 5% on his loan of £200 as did Mr Thompson of Sproughton on his £400. The increased demands for assistance were so great that in most parishes the Poor Rate for the year was doubled! It was expected to raise £2828.13.3 ½d. This was to meet the out-relief that was now being paid at the weekly rate of 6d per head for a man and wife and two children. The third child received 8d, the fourth and ensuing children 9d. allowable on all children up to the age of twelve when they might reasonably be expected to work. This allowance could mount up to a sizeable sum in some cases and the more indolent found it easier to seek parish aid than to go and seek work.

How to balance the books must have been a constant nightmare for the Treasurer who that year had his accounts audited by Golding Constable of East Bergholt. (This affluent miller, who took his duties as a Guardian very seriously, is of course now better known to us as the father of the artist John Constable.) It was decided that one way of cutting costs was to opt for cheaper materials to be used in making clothes for those within the House, so a striped cloth made of hemp was substituted for wool. It is somewhat ironic that a House of Industry producing woollen yarn could no longer afford to buy in woollen cloth. And an attempt to keep people out of the House, by paying an extra threepence a pound to those who did spinning in their own homes had the effect of pushing up the quantity of yarn produced to the detriment of that produced in the House. So the bonus was stopped after a few months.

More and more we see desperate measures being taken. One was the pursuit of Bastardy Orders. No longer was the laissez faire approach adopted; a Sheriff's officer was appointed to actually track down the errant fathers. The public was actively encouraged to inform on each other; a reward of £1.11.6. being paid for every successful Order served. If a 'base-born 'child could be removed from the House and the responsibility of the Guardians as a result of information received then another guinea was added to that figure.

As the eighteenth century drew to a close, the nation was facing numerous problems, not least the threat of the country as a whole becoming bankrupt by the prolonged war with France. Taxation in various forms was crippling and the Poor Rates were becoming an ever-increasing burden, especially upon those in the countryside. Something had to be done to relieve the situation nationwide. There was a widespread belief amongst the government and those who held power that the present system of helping the poor was in fact producing a labouring class that was no longer interested in labouring; the system which rewarded a man for having a large number of children which he could rely on the parish to keep was encouraging early marriage and a lack of prudence. So the Act of 1764 was repealed and in its place in 1799 came **An Act for the Better and More effectual Relief and Employment of the Poor in the Hundred of Samford.** This stated that "whereas the House and other buildings were erected and fitted up …and a great number have been received and maintained and employed; and a considerable sum of money hath been borrowed and is now due and owing on the Credit of the Assessments…and the numbers of the Poor have greatly increased and the produce of the (Poor Rate) Assessment is not sufficient to maintain and pay off the money borrowed… All JPs residing within the Hundred or five miles thereof; All rectors and vicars and all who hereafter occupy property rated at the Poor Rate value of £60.0.0. are to become Guardians of the Poor." In other words, we are almost back to where we started.

# III

'People would be required to stand on their own feet instead of relying solely on the state when they lost their job, fell sick or retired... "We want to encourage adults to save for themselves to help ride out difficult times:..(the welfare state) becomes about government helping people to help themselves, rather than doing everything for people or simply handing out benefits to the people." ' **The Prime Minister, the Rt.Hon. Tony Blair**
**The Daily Telegraph, 27.4. 2001.**

Thirty-five years had passed since the first Directors had drawn up their plans for the Samford Union House. Suffolk had been in the forefront of adopting this method of housing and occupying its poor. The differing sizes of the villages meant that it was the most economical way but now throughout the country many other areas were examining the system and realising the advantages of housing all their paupers under one roof rather than each village or small town maintaining its own establishment.

In Samford several of those who had been involved with the House since its inception were still Directors but among the new ones appear some now familiar names. Capt., later Admiral, Harland, has been succeeded by his son Sir Robert, as the leading figure. Richard Savage Lloyd, Thomas Shave, Nathaniel Whimper, Golding Constable, and Thomas Woodward all provide continuity while new to us, though they may have been serving for several years already, are Charles Berners, jun. Robert Bradstreet, Charles Collinson, the

Revds. Joseph Tweed and Henry Denny Berners. Thomas White of Tattingstone has retired to be succeeded by his heir, Lord Chedworth. The father and son John and Thomas Gosnall from Bentley, John Stubbin, William Deane, Robert Baker, Hayward Rush, Thomas Jarmain, John Cooke, Isaac Everett, James Smith, John Josselyn jun., James Fisher and Cooper William Brooke were all elected. Twenty-four other suitable 'persons' were elected as Acting Guardians at the first of the re-organised meetings that was held, as future ones were to be, at the White Horse, not in Ipswich but in Capel St Mary. Meetings were to be quarterly, on the Tuesday after 25 March, 24 June, 29 September and 25 December. It was agreed that the main purpose of these meetings was to audit the Accounts.

Each quarter twelve of the forty-eight Guardians, six of whom must be Directors, were on duty to be responsible for the "inspection, direction, management and provision of the Poor". At first sight it appears that the new Board was getting off lightly compared with the previous one that had been meeting monthly. However, under the new system, three of them, one a Director, had to meet between 10 am and noon every Wednesday at the House. In the event of some crisis this might be more often. In fact things were very much as they had been. But perhaps there had been a slackening in standards and it was necessary to remind those involved that the responsibility was to be taken seriously. Any Director or Assistant Guardian who failed to attend a meeting without a really good excuse, having been duly reminded of the date via a notice in the **Ipswich Journal**, was liable to a fine, 20/- for a Director, 11/- for one of the Acting Guardians.

One of the first things to be agreed was that the Board should have the power to purchase up to forty acres of extra land. Did this indicate that the Directors were anticipating the need to extend the building and with it the various outbuildings and exercise grounds?

All the records of this first meeting show a hardening of attitude towards the Poor compared with that shown in 1766. They started with the basic requirements of re-appointing all the staff, the Governor and Matron, the surgeons and apothecary and the Anglican

Chaplain and outlining their actual positions. A resident schoolmaster and mistress were also employed to teach the children to read and hear them recite the Catechism once a week. And a new appointment, that of Constable, was made. Finally they re-stated that it was the duty of the Board to provide a proper stock of hemp, wool and other materials as well as the proper tools with which to carry out the work that was produced within the House.

However, there was not always sufficient employment being offered to the House from the Norwich weavers. So for the first time the House entered into arrangements with outside employers. Those men who could not be employed in spinning or some other trade within the House, could be hired out to local farmers, especially at harvest time. However, the hirer had to undertake to feed and lodge the workers for the period of their employment. On the face of it this seems a sensible measure but in many cases, it gave farmers the opportunity to get rid of permanent employees in the knowledge that they could get them back on a temporary basis. Payment for the labour of inmates was paid directly to the House. "Such profit from Work or Labour of the Poor shall be paid to the Treasurer. Provided nevertheless that such Rewards shall, out of the said Profits, be distributed to such of the said Poor Persons as shall be industrious and skilful, in proportion to the quantity and quality of their work... but no part of such rewards shall be expended by Poor Persons in the purchase of Spirituous Liquor the drinking of which by any of the said Poor Persons, the Governor and Matron are hereby strictly enjoined to prohibit and prevent."

This was not just a repressive measure or the adoption of a high moral tone, but a simple expedient necessary for the smooth running of the House. The eighteenth and early nineteenth centuries were notorious for the amount of alcohol consumed by all classes of society. The wealthy drank quantities of imported wines and spirits. The literature of the period is full of examples, including all those references to smuggled liquor. Drunkenness amongst young men was rife and many are the stories of the middle-aged, both men and women, forced to take the waters at Bath to relieve gout, thought to be brought on by excessive amounts of drink, port in particular. However, the medical profession put a great deal of faith in the efficacy of wine and spirits as we can see in this extract from the **Diary of Parson Woodforde**. 'Mr Thorne (the doctor) came to see Nancy this Morning. He strongly recommends Port Wine and to drink more than less. She drank today between a Pint and a Quart without having the lest (least) effect upon the Brain. She has not drank less than a pint for many days.'

    The effects of the sale of cheap spirits, particularly gin, upon the poor are best seen in Hogarth's painting **Gin Lane**. Horrifying stories of the deaths of children caused by inebriate mothers and nurses fill the newspapers of the time. Children, cruelly abused by drunken fathers, in time also turned to drink. Those too poor to buy the means to make a proper meal for themselves and their families could buy a pennyworth of gin, more than enough to quench the immediate desire for food. And the cheap gin was readily available from outlets other than inns or taverns. There had been a time when it had even been on sale in the House. That practice had been abolished but there was a danger that when men were out working they would have access to alcohol and bring it back in with them. The problems that could arise in the House through drunkenness were many. Apart from fights, which could blow up over the smallest thing, there was also the question of damage to property and possible injury to innocent parties caught up in a fracas. Drink was also known to inflame tempers and at a period when the authorities were in constant fear of the people rising up in rebellion as they had done in France, it was essential that no opportunity be given for a 'revolutionary' to foment unrest. So, no spirits, but the beer ration continued.

    The hardening of attitude is shown further by the reminder to all the poor, both inmates and those in the parishes, that under an Act passed in the 17$^{th}$ year of the reign of George II, "All persons who are idle and disorderly and who are able, but neglect or refuse to work or maintain themselves and their Families, may be prosecuted for such Offences…and upon conviction shall be punished in such Manner as idleness and disorderly persons are." In other words, the truly needy will be helped but those who make no effort will not. We are working towards the time when there was an actual division into 'the deserving poor' and those who were classed as making no effort to help themselves. And the Board also drew up a "code of Punishment for those Poor who were found guilty of profane cursing and swearing, lewd, indecent or disorderly conduct, the neglect of or refusal to perform work or service, such work or service being suitable to their age, strength and ability." This applied to both sexes. Those under the age of twelve were to receive "moderate correction", most likely the use of a cane, or "abatement in diet" - the loss of a meal. Sometimes they might be marked out by having to wear different clothing as well as having their rations cut. All offenders over twelve could be sent into solitary confinement, be denied food or be placed in the stocks. However, none of these punishments was to last longer than twelve hours. The most punitive measure was reserved for those who stole from the House itself. The first offence alone carried a sentence of twenty-one days in the House of Correction or prison in Ipswich. The phrase "stealing from the House" usually applied to the clothing the inmate wore. In order to be accused of stealing it, it was necessary to have left the House without permission. It was sometimes the case that an inmate would abscond, sell his or her clothing, get brought back to the House to be re-clothed and then sent to serve the time in prison. All of this cost the Directors – and the Poor Rate payers – unnecessary and additional strain on a budget that was already stretched to the limits.

Cost cutting exercises were undertaken where children were concerned. For example, pressure was put on relations to care for orphaned or abandoned children. Even more pressure was put on employers. Churchwardens and Overseers had a duty to 'encourage' locals to take the young people from their own parish rather than choosing from across the Hundred. If he were known, responsibility for the support of an illegitimate child fell to the father's parish. Further attempts to cut costs led to all the women's clothing for use within the House being made by the female inmates. This was a sensible measure but it meant that those who had previously undertaken the work lost out. It is possible that if all the local Houses adopted this policy, the seamstresses of Ipswich and Stowmarket could in turn find themselves forced into the Workhouse.

Some clues as to the actual workings of the House appear in the printed regulations governing conduct found in the records for 1801.

1. All single women coming to the House pregnant and lying-in there to be confined six months after being put to bed.
2. All Persons upon admission be confined to the House for six weeks.
3. All women after being put to bed, to attend Chapel and return thanks.
4. Paupers to go out once a month and no oftener.
5. Persons may visit the House once a week on Saturdays between one o'clock and four.
6. All persons coming to the House and residing there as Paupers to wear the dress of the Hundred.
7. Hours for coming home, 8pm in summer and 6pm in winter.

The expression 'being put to bed' refers of course to the birth of a child. The unmarried mother was denied her freedom for six months in order to ensure that she fed her child. Nowadays we would talk about her bonding with it and therefore being less likely to abscond leaving the child behind. All women who gave birth in the House, like similar women everywhere, were expected to attend the service of Thanksgiving after Child-Birth, referred to in the Book of Common Prayer as the Churching of Women. The prayers said emphasised the great dangers involved in childbirth "the snares of death compassed me round about: and the pains of hell gat hold of me." The 1980 Alternative Service Book included a thanksgiving for birth, much more joyous and involving both parents.

We may think that being admitted to the Union was tantamount to entering prison but the inmates were allowed out occasionally. Once a month may seem niggardly but it was the same as that allowed outside for living-in servants, for example.

Furthermore it was sensible; more often could lead to all sorts of temptations. Similarly one should look at the limited visiting time remembering that Saturday afternoon might well be the only time working people had free. (It was not that many years ago that hospital visiting in this country was limited to two hours on a Sunday afternoon.) As for the 'curfew' time, that too was commonsense for a time when life was governed by the hours of daylight rather than a clock. And while we are comparing the everyday life of those within the House with those working people outside, we should note that those inside were able (and expected) to attend Divine Service on Sundays and Festivals and also Daily prayers before breakfast and supper. Christmas Day, the two days following it, Good Friday, Easter Monday and Whitsun Monday were all taken as holidays from work just as they would be for those living in the community. However, it is worth noting that should the 26 December happen to fall on a Tuesday the Board would be expected to meet.

Again the wearing of the House 'dress' was sensible. Every inmate had a set of clean clothes issued to them and their own, often filthy rags were taken away to be cleaned and stored until the owner left the House. One can argue that the 'uniform' was demeaning and marked out the pauper from others outside. On the other hand, within the House, all were equal and in many cases their clothing was better than they would have had outside.

As the Industrial Revolution took a firmer hold on the country as a whole, the Board had to face the hard fact that the piecemeal efforts of spinning yarn to be sent elsewhere for weaving was no longer an economic option. Work was needed for more than the few spinners resident in the House, so in 1802, the Governor was instructed to write and invite George Christian of Norwich to set up a manufactory within the House. Machinery to weave the yarn into cloth was purchased and Christian, at a salary of 5/- a week, plus board and lodging, soon had the House living up to its original title of House of Industry.

There is no proof for how well this did at the beginning but in 1807 there was an attempt at diversification. Getting right away from wool, the Board set up a straw hat manufactory. It is not clear if the straw was locally grown or imported but although straw hats were in fashion, the Union House venture did not last long.

Apart from the regular income that the weaving produced, there are few references to the work until 1823 when a Mr Noble took over the running of the manufactory. At that time sixty inmates were employed in various capacities, combing the wool, spinning, doubling and twisting the yarn and finally making it up into worsted. The business must have been doing reasonably well as in 1829 the Board sanctioned the erection of a building where the preparatory stages of washing, dyeing and scouring of the wool and worsted might take place. Another indication of profitability is that in 1826 the Board had felt sufficiently secure to vote that they put aside £100 per quarter into a Sinking Fund with the idea of liquidating the debt of £3,700 they had on the building. However, in 1830 it became necessary to reduce the payments to the fund to £50 a quarter. And in May 1835 Mr Noble was given notice and the manufactory came to an end. This was not necessarily because there was a decline in the trade, rather that there were new moves afoot. A cryptic remark in the Minutes that in future those boys who would have been taught the weaving business were to be sent out to become farm labourers gives us a clue as to what was happening.

1834 was an important milestone in the history of the Poor Law, in so far as that was when the **Poor Law Amendment Act** came into force. The main purpose of this Act was to abolish as far as possible, out-door relief to all except the very old and the infirm. In future everyone else seeking help would have to enter the House. It was anticipated that by making the regime within as harsh as possible under the new system, this would act as a deterrent to those, men in particular, who were able-bodied and could work – they just needed to try harder to find it. Thus it was that the idea of a House of Industry producing a worthwhile product and providing training for the young now disappeared. However, some form of work had to be found to occupy those who were able-bodied and it was at this time that the picking of oakum was introduced. A note in the Minutes for

30 November 1842 reads, "Mr Catchpole reported having purchased at Harwich 8 cwts (1 hundredweight = 112lbs.) of old rope for the purpose of the employment of the able-bodied in the House in picking the same into oakum." As we shall see in a later chapter, inmates were usually given bundles to work on weighing about 1½ lbs. The individual fibres of the rope were pulled out ready to be re-used for other purposes, mainly for caulking ships and sometimes houses made from timber planking. It is interesting that Catchpole went to Harwich for his old ropes rather than Ipswich. Perhaps this is an indication of the increasing number of ships using the former port. That eight hundredweights of oakum must have lasted almost twelve months. The following year the Master bought another load; this time it was 6 cwts. and we are told that it cost £8.2.0. Unfortunately, there is no indication of how much the picked oakum fetched, but one must assume that it was a sum worth having.

Parliament's attempt to achieve a uniform system throughout the whole country meant that 15,000 or so small parochial Workhouses were abolished to be replaced by some 600 Unions, such as Suffolk had had for half a century or more. Supreme control was centralised in the three Commissioners appointed by the Crown. From these gentlemen, sometimes referred to as 'the three tyrants of Somerset House', came in 1834 the first of many questionnaires to be filled in. Question five asked for the numbers within the workhouse and the greatest number it was capable of holding. The Board's reply was that they could accept four hundred and thirty three, but at that time they had four hundred and fifteen inmates. The average was three hundred and thirty. The steep rise in occupants at that period highlights how widespread was the unemployment of the period. Question eight asked "What is the gross cost per head weekly, including clothes, food and medication and what is the total amount of monies expended for the relief of your Indoor paupers for the year ended Lady Day 1834?" From the reply we learn that the weekly costs per inmate ranged between 2s.3d to 3s.4d. The total running costs for the House including salaries, books, stationery, repairs and the interest of the original debt came to £2725.14s.0d.

In 1836 following a proposal made by Dr Kay, one of the Assistant Poor Law Commissioners that the inmates should be classified into four classes, sorting out the able-bodied from the rest, it was necessary to erect new walls dividing the original exercise yards crossways.

The impact of control by the Commissioners did not happen overnight of course, and for several years the Guardians of the Samford Union were able to maintain much of their independence while acting within the guidelines laid down by the New Poor Law. But there was increasing, and for us a familiar, bureaucracy. For example, in 1841 the Board received a letter from Sir John Walsham, an Assistant Commissioner, detailing the method of taking the new averages required by the Commission and requesting the return of 'Quarterly Abstract Form 66' and the 'Quarterly Statements A.4 Form 12'.

The following year they required more statistics, this time relating to the numbers of married persons in the House within the year ending 30 March. Of that number, the Board was required to specify how many had been in the house more than five years and how many less than five. Of the latter how many had been admitted more than once and how often. While of those who had been in for five or more years, how many of them were over fifty years in age. Finally, what was the number of married persons who had died since the passing of the Poor Law Amendment Act? One can imagine that the poor Clerk to the Board spent many hours trawling through the various record books in order to gather the information required, no doubt often asking himself what the Commissioners would do with it all when they had it.

By 1847 the Poor Law Board (PLB) was able to take firm control of the system only to be replaced in turn in 1871 by the Local Government Board (LGB). The Minutes for the 21$^{st}$ March 1849 record the last meeting of the fifteen Directors and twelve Acting Guardians under the old regime. A week later the announcement comes that, "In compliance with a letter from the Poor Law Board to the Clerk of the Samford Incorporation, dated 28 February 1849, the following met at the Samford Union House." They were Thomas Burch Western, lord of the Manor of Tattingstone, John Berners of Woolverstone, the Hon. Revd. Frederick de Grey of Copdock, the Revd. Thomas Mills and Charles Lillingstone. All these wealthy and noble gentlemen were to be ex officio Guardians of the reconstructed Samford Board. They did little at this first meeting beyond confirming that all the present holders of office within the House should remain in place. It would appear that the five ex officio members were little more than figure heads, the main work of the committees being carried on as before by the old Directors and Guardians. The only significant change seems to have been the provision of a water closet for the new Board.

Thus the Guardians were now unable to use their discretion about how they should act in certain cases. It is from this time, I believe, that the image of the harsh, repressive Board of Guardians is drawn. Time and again in the Minutes the phrase, "the Board has no power to do this..." recurs in respect of requests to help; a family to migrate to Canada, someone to receive some form of specialised hospital care or a child to travel to join a relation in another part of the country. Every major decision that the Board now makes has to be communicated to and receive authorisation from the PLB or LGB.

Most of the old Minute Books are covered in soft kid leather that has not only preserved them but has made them a delight for the modern researcher to handle. The handwriting within them is usually a pleasure to read though this depends very much on who was doing the actual Minute taking. Up until 1837, the books have been simple plain ruled books, purchased no doubt from the local stationery supplier in Ipswich but the one that starts in that year is very much a standard official document. It opens with printed details of the New Act and then goes on to give specimen Minutes for various meetings so that the Guardians, although lay people, should be in no doubt as to how they should conduct themselves.

Appended to the inside cover of the Minute book for 1839 are the printed leaflets describing work opportunities in Australia. These sheets offer a fascinating insight into such things as the number of ships leaving for the other side of the world, the length of the journey and the arrangements prospective passengers were expected to make. The fare for those travelling 'cabin class' was forty guineas while those who went out 'steerage' paid only twenty but had to provide all their own equipment including bedding, cutlery and crockery. While it now sounds ludicrous to us, it did of course mean that the immigrants had the basic essentials of life when they arrived in the new country. Free passages were offered to young married agricultural labourers, shepherds, carpenters, smiths, wheelwrights, bricklayers and masons if accompanied by their wives. This was similar to the assisted passages or ten pound ticket offered to British migrants after the Second World War. Any unmarried female with £5.0.0. and a spirit of adventure could also find a new life in Australia. It was the duty of the Guardians to encourage those who were able-bodied and unemployed to apply for a passage to either Australia or Canada.

Some found themselves in Canada whether they wanted to be or not. Such was the case of a Chattisham man named House who having joined the 43$^{rd}$ Regiment was sent off to Canada leaving his wife and two children chargeable to the Parish. They were all taken into the House but the wife, Catherine, an Irishwoman asked the Board to send her back to her native land. The Guardians must have decided that it was worth spending up to £3.10.0d. for their journey and maintenance en route rather than maintaining them indefinitely within the House.

During this period of the 1840s out-relief was given only for those suffering from illness or infirmity. The list of ailments is not dissimilar to the present day – asthma, rheumatism, lumbago, cough, measles, fever, and general debility. Frequently a woman's condition was described as rendering her "unable to do for her family". Although that phrase meant general household care, many women found themselves having to become the breadwinner of the family as well as the carer. When Lucy Double managed to secure a position that would support her and her two illegitimate children she asked permission to leave the older child, a boy of eight who was ill at the time, temporarily in the House. Permission was granted. But Lucy was somewhat tardy in reclaiming her son and some time later we learn that the Master was instructed to take the boy, now restored to health, to Colchester where his mother was then living. It was also leaned that Lucy had recently married. The dismissal of the child to its lawful parents, underlined the point emphasised under the new laws that stepfathers were expected to take financial responsibility for their wife's children.

Phrases like "ordered to come to the House" seem to us with the distance of years, harsh indeed. Yet when David Dickerson and his family from Washbrook were so ordered, it was because David had met with an accident and was thus unable to work. Similarly, when William Parker of Little Wenham, with his wife and seven children was turned out of his cottage – the reason unspecified but probably because he had been made redundant by his farmer employer – they all found refuge in the House. Had the Union House not been there, where else would they have gone?

The Board was under constant pressure from the Poor Law Commissioners to cut costs wherever possible and at the same time had to contend with recalcitrant parishes that refused to either pay the rate demanded of them or deliberately held back their payments until the last possible moment. With the Board having to account to the Commissioners and the Master having to account to the Board, it is hardly surprising that life for the inmates became much harsher at least for those who were designated as 'able-bodied'. These were denied the little luxuries that fell to the aged and infirm. The tobacco and snuff rations are mentioned elsewhere. But the food rations for the 'able-bodied' were also carefully monitored. Strangely, it was two women who drew attention to the restriction of food. Maria Lewis was brought before the Board by the Master for her refusal to work. She complained that what she was required to do was too strenuous on the meagre diet provided in the House. Spurred on by her example, Martha Welham who was in the same room as Maria also complained about the quality of the meat and the tea with which they were provided.

It is likely that originally, most of the staff had received the same food as the inmates but over the years, the officers expected, and demanded, more and better meals. On one occasion, questions were asked about the milk supplied to the House and it was revealed that only the staff and the children under seven received "new" milk, that is the full cream variety. The inmates were served skimmed milk in their tea and later, coffee. A pint of coffee with milk and sugar was first introduced in 1895 at dinner-time on Sundays and Thursdays. It would be interesting to know how widespread was the consumption of coffee outside the House at that period.

# IV

## 'A multiplicity of great misfortune'

"To Anne Candler for teaching the children to read....10s.0d."
**Minutes of the Samford House 1794**

The weekly **Ipswich Journal** which had provided Suffolk with a record of events at national and local level since 1720 was, like every newspaper since that time, often reliant on certain items to act as space fillers. In the eighteenth century these often took the form of verses; compositions by the famous, for example the poet laureate, Thomas Wharton's **Ode to New Year's Day, 1788,** to those of the lesser known or even anonymous local poet.

From the 1780s, at regular intervals, poems would appear within its pages bearing the address 'Tattingstone', 'Tattingstone Poor-House' and 'Tattingstone House of Industry'. The earlier poems bear the accompanying insignia of 'A.C.'

In a letter addressed to, "The Printers of the Ipswich Journal", the poet asked that "by inserting these lines (the poem **On the Death of a Most Benevolent Gentleman, Metcalfe Russell, esq.**) I believe you will oblige some of the readers of your Journal. It is not the first favour that you have been pleased to indulge the author with... but a multiplicity of great misfortune has compelled me to take refuge in the House of Industry for some time... Your most humble and obedient servant, Anne Candler."

I have told Anne's story in a fictionalised form elsewhere, but her history does provide us with a unique record of how one twist of fate could change a life, or lives, so that within a matter of weeks one could go from independence to total dependence on others.

Anne was born in November 1740, the youngest of the three surviving children of William and Anne Moore. William was a master glover in Yoxford, Suffolk. His wife was one several daughters who had enjoyed a comfortable upbringing in the home of a successful civil servant. A slump in native glove-making, the result of the market being flooded with cheap foreign imports, led to the Moores leaving Yoxford and settling in the busy and overcrowded parish of St Margaret's in Ipswich. Of Anne's early life, there is little record; we can assume that she received a basic education from her mother before Mrs Moore's death left the girl to become her father's companion. We also know that she somehow gained the friendship of Mary Firmin, the daughter of a wealthy Ipswich businessman.

On the 28 February 1763, at the age of 21, Anne married William Candler, a year or so her junior and like her, at the time of the wedding a resident in the parish of St Margaret's. Unlike many who married at that period, both Anne and William were able to sign their names in the marriage register. Both have a good strong hand with each letter carefully formed – and whatever later editors may have written, Anne herself spelt her name with an 'e'! William's writing borders on the flamboyant with the 'd' in Candler arching in a perfect curve to form almost an eyebrow' to the lower part of the letter. This suggests that he was confident in the use of a pen, so not an illiterate field worker or manual labourer. My gut feeling is that William, and perhaps Anne too, was in good service, possibly at Christchurch mansion. Although the Fonnereau family had bought the house well before the birth of either of them, it had for the previous hundred years been in the hands of the Devereux family. Quite what their influence was upon the young Candlers I cannot prove but it is significant that they named one of their sons Devereux which must have somewhat startled the rural vicar who was accustomed to the Thomas, Samuel, William and the occasional Robert who were brought for baptism. Another son bore the name of Peregrine, which I take to reflect Anne's literary interest, the novel, **Peregrine Pickle** by Smollett having been published in 1751. Similarly, after she had named her daughters after various relations, she again indulged her fancies by naming the youngest, Clarissa, probably influenced by Samuel Richardson's **Clarissa Harlowe**, which had been published in 1747-48.

The newlyweds set up home in Sproughton where William's family lived. There is no actual evidence of how William earned his living but I suspect that he may have been employed in some capacity by Mr.Collinson, the owner of the Chantry estate. Whatever he did, it was not long before William had become weighed down by the pressures of family life. He spent much of his free time with like-minded fellows at Wildman's Alehouse in the village. Once, while on a drinking spree at the Black Horse in Ipswich, he succumbed to the alluring promises of a recruiting sergeant, accepted the 'King's Shilling' and woke up to find he had enlisted in the Army. Anne, through the good offices of friends, managed to extricate him in return for his joining the local Militia which, at that time, was only required to go into camp for two weeks in the year.

The family grew and so did William's desire for freedom. Matters came to a head in the year 1777 following a visit from his younger brother, on leave from the Guards in which he had enlisted four years earlier. William invited his brother to Sunday dinner and afterwards the two went for a walk. The brothers must have drunk late into the night and Anne did not see William until Monday evening when he returned home "thoughtful and gloomy". He left for work on Tuesday morning but failed to return home that night. Nothing was heard of him until on the Friday someone brought Anne the news that her husband had enlisted with the Guards in Colchester.

This was devastating for Anne. She was left without any means of support with six children, the eldest of whom was fourteen, the youngest barely eighteen months. Although friends might help her in the short term, it was almost inevitable that she would have to apply for assistance from the Poor Rates. One of the first Anne had to call on after William's defection was Mr Woodward, from the Hall. This prosperous farmer was Sproughton's representative on the Board of Guardians and as such, he would be able to support her claim for assistance. He bluntly told her to forget about her husband, a worthless rascal in his opinion. Consultations took place and Anne was advised that although her friends Miss Firmin and Mr Collinson would pay her rent, it would be better for all concerned if four of the six children were sent to the Tattingstone House that had been open then for some ten years. Ann, the eldest and Clara the baby stayed with their mother. Anne herself was very ill for the first three months following William's departure so her elder daughter was required to take on the nursing of her mother as well as the care of her small sister. During this time, Anne received outdoor relief in the form of bread and money to pay for additional nursing care. This was not the first time that the Candlers had sought Parish Relief. In 1763, the physician for the area, Dr.Rodbard had been paid for the treatment he had given, probably to Anne in childbirth. Again, the following year, the Overseers' Accounts note "To surgeon Rodbard £2.2.0. for W.Candler's wife in bed and medicine. 3/- by order to William Candler." Whilst between Easter and October 1765 - "To William Candler at sundry times 9/-"

During the next two years Anne managed "by industry and the frequent donations of kind friends to live protected from want." It is possible that her 'industry' took the form of knitting or spinning but in my fictional account of her life, I had her open a 'Dame School'. At that time, literate women often undertook to look after others' children by the day and teach them the rudiments of the three Rs in return for a small fee.

Anne's eldest daughter was found a position in domestic service so Catherine, the elder of the four children in the House was brought home to live with her mother until such time as she too could be found employment. Unfortunately, just when it looked as if things were getting better for the family, Candler returned to Sproughton on leave. Officially still attached to the Army, he was presently 'stood down'. This meant that he was able to take employment but, should the necessity arise, he could be recalled immediately to military service. William had done well for himself and he cajoled Anne to join him in London where he had found work. He promised they would make a new life for themselves and the children. Painting a rosy picture of the opportunities that lay in store for them, especially for the children, Anne agreed to join him in early April 1780.

At a purely practical level, once it had become known to the Poor Law Guardians that Candler was in regular employment he would have been required to pay full maintenance for the children in the House or remove them altogether. So, Anne gave up her home in Sproughton, put a few of her belongings into store but sent the best furniture by boat from Ipswich up to the new lodgings in London. Within two hours of her arrival all her friends' misgivings were proved right. Failing to meet her at the appointed time, when William did turn up he had been drinking heavily and demanded what little money she had. Her initial disappointment turned to horror when she saw the lodgings he had found for them. They were worse than anything she could have imagined. Within two months of her arrival the Gordon Riots occurred and William was recalled to his regiment to help quell the rioters. Anne and the child were left for several weeks, almost penniless, to fend for themselves in an alien environment. When Candler returned, Anne realised that he was not interested in family life and when a sea-faring relative of Candler offered her a return voyage to Ipswich she took it gladly.

They came ashore at Stoke from where she and little Clara walked to Sproughton. She had to return there for that was the only place where she could claim Poor Law assistance and she speedily visited the Overseer who gave her the necessary admission papers to enter the House at Tattingstone. She had lost her home; her furniture had been left in London and the few belongings she had left in store were sold to pay towards her keep in the House. Anne was now a pauper.

From the bare outline of her history that Anne was later to write, we learn several details about life in the House and the workings of the Poor Law. Contrary to the belief that once one entered the House one was totally isolated from the outside world, visitors were allowed and inmates were able to maintain contact through letters. During her time in London, Anne had written regularly to Miss Firmin and about a month after her entry into the House, she wrote to tell her of her new address. "To my infinite surprise, in two or three days (I) had the delight of seeing her! She requested of the Governess that I might be permitted to walk with her in the garden; and soon perceiving my situation lamented this additional misfortune; and gave me the kindest assurances of the continuation of her friendship. Not many days after she sent her servant with a letter, and a guinea enclosed from my kind friend and benefactor J.Collinson, Esq. This was sometime in October."

The situation that Miss Firmin had perceived was that Anne was pregnant. In March 1781 at the age of forty, she was delivered of twin sons. It was a difficult confinement; with a space of three hours between each child and for several days her life was in danger. At a time when death in childbirth was very high, it is perhaps a tribute to the nursing care that she received in the maternity ward within the House that Anne survived. She was, however, more fortunate than most in that her friends sent supplies to speed her recovery. From the Guardians' point of view, they now had even more Candler children to feed, clothe, educate and ultimately find employment for. The situation was alleviated somewhat when the twins died, one at fourteen weeks the other a month later.

Three years passed. William had been discharged from the Army and he came to visit Anne in the House. He proposed that they should again live together in Sproughton. In her written account, Anne says she refused to consider the proposal until such time as he had found employment, somewhere to live and sufficient means to furnish one room at least. She was at pains to explain to the ladies to whom her 'history' was addressed that she was being sensible in thinking carefully before joining Candler. In actual fact, she probably had little option. Once Candler was in employment and had some form of lodging, then the Guardians would demand that he shoulder the responsibility for his family. Had this been fifty years later he might have found he had to pay the arrears for his family's maintenance.

It must have felt exceedingly strange to Anne to find herself back in lodgings in Sproughton after three years of communal living among a very mixed society of women. Any happiness she might have felt was short lived for the very day she joined Candler he "was seized with a shivering fit, which was followed by a fever of the most alarming kind." She nursed him for the next seven weeks, "during which time the Revd. Mr.G... procured us an allowance from the House." But Candler did not get any better and as what money she had was running out, she was again advised that they and Clarissa should all go into the House. "This was in fact the only step I could take, and here all my prospects of comfort ended."

It was a good six months before William was fit enough to be discharged from the House to seek work. He returned to Sproughton, met up with his old drinking companions and "became so utterly degraded in appearance, manner and morals as determined me to renounce the idea of ever living with him again." As far as she knew, he rejoined the Army and disappeared from her life forever.

Anne remained in the House for twenty years. In that time her children were found employment and all but two of them moved away from the area and more or less lost contact with their mother. Clarissa and Lucy married and raised families in Copdock and Holton St Mary.

So what did Anne do all day? Like all other able-bodied inmates she would have been expected to work for her keep and for the little pocket money that might provide additional comforts or savings against the time of her discharge if that ever came about. We know that Anne must have spent some of her money on paper, pens and ink for the poems she wrote. She must also have had access to the **Ipswich Journal** for not only did she send her poems to the editor; some of those poems were prompted by news items that she had read. She may also have bought her own stock of candles to supplement the standard House issue. She says "I have been obliged to write the greater part (of the letter to the ladies) by candlelight as I have very little leisure by day."

You may remember that I said earlier that in my fictional account I had Anne teaching in her own little school. For the purposes of this present volume, I started to read through all the Minute books and Account books of the Samford House of Industry. Imagine my amazement when I discovered that in the Accounts for 1794 the quarterly sum of 10s.0d had been paid to Anne Candler for "teaching the children to read"!

In 1801, Mrs Elizabeth Cobbold, wife of John Cobbold, the brewer of Ipswich, herself a poet of no mean repute, became Anne's patron. She gathered together the poems that had appeared in the **Ipswich Journal** as well as many others and seeking subscribers from among the wealthy, the intelligentsia and the philanthropic members of local society, she was responsible for the publication of **POETICAL ATTEMPTS by Anne Candler, A Suffolk Cottager.**

One of the subscribers to the volume was John Howe, Lord Chedworth. He was the nephew and heir to Thomas White, the Tattingstone landowner who was one of the original Directors of the House of Industry. Chedworth too, became a Guardian during the time that Anne was an inmate. A highly intelligent man, he was a lawyer by profession and in this capacity he gave free legal advice to many in the Ipswich area. He was also extremely well read, spending many hours preparing an academic study of Shakespeare's plays. He had a great love of the theatre generally and often enlivened his correspondence with his friends with detailed analysis of the plays he had seen. He was also a Greek and Latin scholar – he liberally sprinkles his letters with classical quotations. He had strong views too, on religious matters and as a peer he took seriously his duty to attend the House of Lords. Yet for all that, he remained a man of the people, happy to mix with all and sundry. A man of inherited wealth, much of which was swindled out of him by an unscrupulous land agent, money meant little to him beyond what it could do for the comfort of others. Thus he was more than happy to purchase several copies of the limited edition of Anne's poetical works.

The sale of the book raised sufficient funds for Anne finally to leave the House and go to live in a little furnished cottage in Holton St Mary, close to her daughter and grandchildren. She was then sixty-three years of age.

Two poems marked her leaving. The first, subtitled, **'Written in Tattingstone House of Industry, February, 1802'** gives some insight into the life she had endured for the past twenty years. Here were all the thoughts she had harboured but dared not express until she was sure that she really was going. On the other hand, I cannot help feeling that perhaps some of the sentiments she expresses are those that she thought her readers would want to hear, painting as she does, the picture of herself as a reclusive sensitive creature surrounded by 'disgusting objects'. The poem was intended as a tribute to Elizabeth Cobbold, the friend she has found beyond the melancholy walls. In addition both poems show the strong religious views of the period.

### Reflections On My Own Situation

How many years are past and gone
How altered I appear.
How many strange events have known
Since first I entered here?

Within these dreary walls confined,
    A lone recluse, I live,
And with the dregs of human kind,
    A niggard alms receive.

Uncultivated, void of sense,
    Unsocial, insincere,
Their rude behaviour gives offence,
    Their language wounds the ear.

Disgusting objects swarm around,
    Throughout confusions reign;
Where feuds and discontent abound,
    Remonstrance proves in vain.

No sympathising friend I find,
    Unknown is friendship here;
Not one to soothe, or calm the mind,
    When overwhelmed with care.

Peace, peace, my heart, thy duty calls,
    With cautious steps proceed:
Beyond these melancholy walls,
    I've found a friend indeed!

I gaze on numbers in distress,
    Compare their state with mine:
Can I reflect, and not confess
    A Providence divine?

And I might bend beneath the rod,
    And equal want deplore,
But that a good and gracious God
    Is pleased to give me more....

The poem continues for thirteen more stanzas in which Anne debates the battle of good and evil that she has had to face equating them to the battles and sufferings endured in fairy stories: she ponders the question of fate and remarks that somehow she has been marked out for special attention, finally she prays,

> Look down, O God! In me behold
> How helpless mortals are,
> Nor leave me friendless, poor and old,
> But guide me with thy care.

Three months later she wrote **On Perusing the History of Jacob** – with its subtitle of **After I had left Tattingstone House of Industry - 24 May 1802.**

'Am I the very same, who used to be
Still sighing for her long-lost liberty?
For twenty years and more I mourned the loss;
The laws were rigorous, every task seemed cross,
The bondage irksome, and the treatment hard,
From social converse and from friends debarred;
Excess of grief the gathering ills portend,
But Jacob's God has raised me up a friend,
Blest is that gift the Almighty deigns to send.

Like me, for twenty years, did Jacob find
Men were unfeeling, selfish and unkind…

[There follows a long description of Jacob's trials]

'So may my eve of life be more serene,
More tranquil than the former part has been;
This cheering ray no threatening clouds overcast,
That may too much resemble what is past.
O! let me spend the short remains of life
In peace and quiet, far from noise and strife,

My conduct such as best becomes my age
And something useful still my time engage:
Like Mary let me choose the needful part,
But not with pious fraud or specious art,
At gloomy eve, when Sol withdraws his light,
I'll beg of God to keep me through the night,
I'll bless his goodness each returning day,
And those who gave the bed whereon I lay.'

As far as is known, Anne did spend her last years in peace and quiet. Her death at the age of seventy-four was reported in the Ipswich Journal of the 17th September 1814.

# V

'For my own part, I like a medical man on a footing with the servants; they are often all the cleverer...
'The standard of the (medical) profession is low, my dear sir. I mean in knowledge and skill; not in social status, for our medical men are most of them connected with respectable townspeople here.' **George Eliot, Middlemarch**


Of all those involved with the care of the poor, doctors seemed to occupy the most difficult position. They were professional men but at the same time they were paid employees of the Directors and Board and therefore finally answerable to them. In 1766 when the House appointed young Mr Clubbe as their first physician, the medical profession as we know it was still in its infancy. Between medieval times and the eighteenth century the separate spheres of apothecary, unlicensed practitioner, physician and surgeon had gradually been coming together. The improvement in training and major scientific discoveries had all contributed to a greatly improved service that was able to remove itself from the barber/surgeon image. However, the newly qualified physician had to establish himself before he was able to command the fees that would ensure him and his family a comfortable living. Thus the salaried position offered by a Workhouse was one to be sought after.

John Clubbe was recruited at an annual salary of £60 to devote two days a week to any patients within the House who might need his services. He was expected to treat all ailments and prescribe such medicines and ointments, as he deemed necessary. As he was also expected to cover the costs of these from his salary, one might anticipate that he would have been somewhat sparing in their use. It was his duty to attend in the case of a difficult confinement and to perform minor operations such as the removal of external tumours. A bed was provided for his use when called upon for night duty. In 1769, when he took on the role of providing out-care in one of the Districts too, his salary was doubled. The Medical Officer could also act as an adviser to the Board, as perhaps Clubbe did in 1768. We read, "ordered that a beathing tubb be made for the use of the House. Mr Clubbe to procure the same." He did. And the following year it was noted as having cost three guineas.

The medical work within the parishes grew greatly over the next few years and it was not long before groups of neighbouring parishes within the Hundred were formed into districts for the provision of medical care. The 'Division' or district surgeon was often in a difficult position over where his duty lay. As a doctor he was approached to treat an ailing patient – and often his conscience told him this was an urgent case – but as the Board's physician he could not treat a pauper unless that person had been issued with a medical certificate by the local Overseer. Sometimes it was almost too late by the time the requisite form had been issued but should the doctor act off his own initiative and treat the patient, then he could not be sure that he would receive his remuneration.

In the early years, most of the doctor's work revolved round the treating of the numerous outbreaks of smallpox. To combat the disease, periodic purges were held to vaccinate as many of the local population as possible. This was a costly business for the Board but a useful addition to the doctor's income. In 1795, for example, forty-four parishioners in

Sproughton were vaccinated at a cost of 5/3d. each. In 1823, Dr Spurgeon vaccinated 286 and received £28.12s. but Dr Martin who was by then both surgeon to the House as well as the Holbrook district netted £50.16s. for his 508 vaccinations. Most of these mass vaccinations took place in private houses within the various villages, the householder being paid for the use of a room; in 1825, 7/6d. was the going rate for the rental. A note in the Minutes of 1861 informs the Board that Widow Clarke of East Bergholt was unwilling to loan her premises any more having not received payment for the previous occasion. In addition to the rental cost there was another for the beer supplied to the recipients of the vaccination.

The doctors were expected to keep meticulous records of all their dealings so that their bills might be checked. Woe betide the man who failed to fill in his returns correctly or was late with them. In 1824, Mr Brooke, another of the district doctors, submitted his bill for the vaccinations he had carried out that year but it took five years before the Board finally settled his account in 1829 because he had "not been able to furnish the amount of numbers." Dr Spurgeon was one who was often in trouble. The Clerk recorded in 1832 that he "have three months notice to quit the care of the sick poor of his division unless he chooses to attend the next quarterly meeting of the Board to apologise for his letter of 31 January and also for having refused Medicine to two families in East Bergholt." He was called before the Board again in 1838 for failing to keep his records correctly. He countered the Board's reprimand with the argument that his salary was altogether inadequate for the labour and inconvenience involved. However, he was reminded that it was a legal requirement of the Poor Law Commissioners that demanded the keeping of the Weekly Medical Returns Book of Sickness and Mortality. Having been warned he would be dismissed if he did not comply, Spurgeon reluctantly agreed to abide by the rules. But he was not to be browbeaten and several weeks later he complained bitterly to the Board that the postal charges he had to pay were not covered by his 'inadequate' salary. The cry that the doctors were not paid enough was a constant one, yet most of them stayed in the Poor Law service for many years. Dr Martin, for instance, retired in 1860 having been in the service of the Guardians for the House and the Holbrook district for thirty-seven years. His house in Holbrook painted by the artist John Preston Neale shows that his life style was very much that of a country gentleman. Further, he cannot have thought there was much to complain about in the position for on his retirement, he recommended his partner and son-in-law, Dr Albert Fleming as his replacement.

Fleming was duly appointed Medical Officer for the Holbrook District at a salary of £61.17.8 with another £35.0.0. for his work in the House. His duties there were to include attendance every Monday, Thursday and Saturday at hours to suit his convenience and on such other occasions as the Governor thought his attendance necessary. It was also made clear to him that he was only to give medical treatment, relief or medicine to those who had the proper documents issued by the person "lawfully qualified to give such an order", that is the Relieving Officer or one of the Parish Overseers. Within six months, Fleming had been reprimanded for treating John Paine of Holbrook who, although suffering from fever, did not have the requisite documentation.

Much of the doctors' work was dealing with routine problems, one of which was to help ease those men who were unable to work because of a severe hernia. In 1825 the Board took out an annual subscription of 5 guineas to the Rupture Society. The purpose of this, it was noted in the Minutes, was so that they could be supplied with fifteen trusses for use within the House and the Hundred. John Bloomfield of Brantham was one of those given an order for a truss in 1851. Women's needs were not neglected either; in 1852 an abdominal support was ordered for Martha Cox of Capel.

Another of the doctors' duties was to decide if a patient needed to be brought into the House for medical and nursing care that could not be given at home. Similarly, those who became too old or infirm to care for themselves and had no one to help them were recommended to the House. Thus it was that over the years the House began to develop the move towards its final stage of being a geriatric hospital. Not everyone who came into the House was a pauper in the sense that they had little or no means of support. As early as 1831 we read of Sarah Day who had become incapable of taking care of herself. She had property to the value of £160 so three shillings and threepence was deducted weekly from that for her maintenance with an additional two shillings and sixpence for 'extra diet'. In other words she was in a position to have extra milk and butter and possibly additional meat purchased for her.

The medical profession at that time, perhaps rightly, put great faith in the curative powers of good mutton broth and either porter (stout) or brandy. In 1851 Drs. Grosse and Spurgeon had their orders for meat and porter queried. It seems that they ordered far more than the other doctors. The order for a piece of mutton with which to make the broth was frequently given both for those within the House and those who were in receipt of Out-relief. And it was the failure of a proper order for the purchase of a piece of mutton that was to cause an outcry in the county and focus attention on the Board of Guardians of the Samford Union. Above the pseudonym of 'Observer' the following letter appeared in the **Ipswich Journal** of 27 April 1861.

"Sir,

In one of the parishes of the Tattingstone Union the following instructive cases have just occurred. Two deaths among the labouring poor have taken place – the one a fine young man of twenty-five, the other an aged one past work – under circumstances now to be related. The young man a few days since was compelled to leave his work in the fields through an attack of pneumonia, and returned to the cottage, where for five years past he has been the support and solace of a mother, a widow. For some time past he has been supporting by his weekly wages, a sister, whom his poor mother needed at home as her nurse. A medical man (not the parish doctor, or the club one, for the young man was considered to have no claim on either,) was sent for to preserve, if possible, this valuable life. Well, a little mutton broth is ordered by this gentleman to be given to the patient. On finding however, that the poor widow has not a shilling to buy the mutton with, he gives her a written recommendation to the overseer of the parish for this bit of mutton. The note is taken by mistake to one of the Guardians, then to the overseer, but 'no effects'; afterwards to an ex-overseer, with the same result. In the fourth place it is handed to the second overseer, who recommends the mutton to be procured at the butcher's, with the promise of the poor woman to pay for it herself if the parish refuses to so. The result thus far of all these applications is stated to the medical man, who indignantly, but humanely, puts his hands into his own pocket for the required shilling. The mutton is now bought, and the broth made; but the patient is dying and cannot take it. In an hour after he is in that state where 'they hunger no more' and where 'there is no more death', leaving his widowed mother and sister to the tender mercies of Guardians and Overseers.

"The case of the poor old man past labour is this. As the club (of which he had been a member) had recently failed, the Union allowed him two loaves of bread and 15 pence weekly. Of this money an allowance of 1/- was paid weekly for a lodging. Hence three pence a week was all that this poor man had wherewith to procure everything needful except bread. This continued for eight months, until, in short, according to the parish doctor's certificate, bronchitis and typhoid lent their united aid to relieve this honest hard-working, godly man, of his sufferings and the parish of its burden. Is it that there is no charity in the land? Far from it. But the moment a poor man seeks parish relief everybody's heart towards him – but especially those of Guardians, Overseers, relieving Officers, et id genus omne – is turned from flesh to stone."

One can imagine the storm this caused in the tea and coffee cups of the gentlemen of the Board and others as they read their copies of the **Journal**. One of the first to respond was Mr Fisher Alderton of Shotley who made the following statement to the Board:

"I am Overseer for this parish. I knew James Whiting who died on Monday 22 April. He was one of the persons alluded to in a letter...He had been in the employ of Mr C.A.Screiber who holds a farm in this parish, for two or three years past as a common labourer and at wages for the past twelve months of 12/- per week besides making Hay and Wheat Harvest. He was a single man about 25 and hiring a cottage and large yard at a rent of £4.4.0. per annum. His mother a woman about 60 years of age resided with him and kept his house. Whiting appeared to be a healthy man. On Thursday 18 April in the afternoon Whiting's mother came to my house and applied to me as Overseer to grant an order for the supply of 2lbs. of mutton which had been recommended by the certificate of Mr Keane, surgeon of Holbrook who attended her son and stated her son was very ill. Whiting had worked up to the previous Monday three days before and received his wages as usual. I told her I knew he had been earning 12/- a week constantly and had only been out three days. I therefore thought if he needed mutton he could provide it for himself. I also told her that as the certificate was not from the Union surgeon I did not think meat would be allowed. I refused the application. Whiting died on the Monday following and I have heard from inflammation on the chest. I knew also Susan Whiting, the sister of the aforesaid James. She is about 23 and was in my service as Cook at wages of £8.0.0. per annum, service which she quitted in April 1860 and went to reside with her brother. At the time of her quitting my service she urged as a reason for so doing that her mother who was unwell needed her attendance. My wife told her that she did not need to resign her service for that as all the attendance her mother needed could be rendered by neighbours. She also offered and arranged to pay for the attendance of a neighbour upon the mother but the daughter persisted in quitting her place. I have considered her maintenance for the past year an unnecessary burthen upon her brother, the deceased.

"I also knew Joseph Dunnett. He was aged labourer residing in Shotley and who died a few days previous to Whiting. He had been in receipt of out-relief – viz.1s.3d and 2 quartern loaves per week. About three days prior to his death one of his neighbours came to me and brought a certificate signed by Mr Fleming the Union Medical Officer recommending half a pint of brandy. I directed the party to procure the brandy and gave order to that effect. I had no further application made to me. Two or three days before his death another of his neighbours called at my house and said Dunnett thought he would like an egg and asked if I would send a few. My wife sent 10 new laid eggs, some of which were in the house at the time of his decease. Beyond these applications none other were made to me as Overseer or otherwise by Dunnett or by any party on his behalf. Had such application been made to me in such case I should at once have attended to it."

There was much speculation as to the identity of 'Observer'; the general opinion being that it was the locum vicar of Shotley. As such, he had only been in the village a short time and, according to Mr Alderton was not in a position to know all the background details to either case. Several important historical facts emerge here, not least the reference to 'the club'. Many working men, particularly those with families, had joined one of the many Friendly Societies that had proliferated during the century, set up to assist their members when in need. Often supported by a Temperance group, men met together at the end of the working week for a short time of social relaxation – hence the use of the term 'club'. At the weekly meeting they made a small payment that was meant to guarantee that in time of sickness, they would receive either financial assistance or the doctor's bill would be met. Such insurance was supposed to take away the need for calling upon the Poor Law. The larger societies did indeed offer adequate cover, but there were many cases of smaller, particularly local societies being under-funded and therefore unable to cope with the demands made upon them. However, in Whiting's case, being young, unmarried and normally in good health it appeared that he had not bothered to take out any form of medical insurance.

Alderton gives some very useful contemporary detail as to wages paid and the cost of rent. He also gives background information about both the Whiting household and attitudes of the period. For example, although Widow Whiting was in need of some assistance, Alderton could not see why a neighbour should not have been hired to give this. In fact Mrs Alderton had offered to foot the bill for it in order to keep Susan Whiting as her cook. Quite apart from how good Susan might be as a cook and therefore a loss to the Alderton household, the Overseer's attitude was that he failed to understand her giving up a paid position where she lived-in to return home to become an added expense for her brother. As far as the refusal to give the order for the mutton was concerned, Alderton was simply carrying out the official policy. Whiting had not been declared a pauper since he was in paid work. As he had only been off sick for three days, it was hard to understand why there was not a shilling available in the house to cover the cost of the mutton. In the case of Joseph Dunnett, Alderton felt even more aggrieved that he was being cast as the villain of the piece. He had, when asked, signed an order for brandy for Dunnett but had received no other official request for assistance. And, when he had been approached by Dunnett's neighbours who told him that the old chap fancied an egg, rather than bothering the Board to pay for this, Mrs Alderton had promptly sent him ten new-laid ones from her own hens.

Next to add to this saga was Benjamin Sparling, a Shotley farmer who was also Churchwarden and a Guardian. He said that on the 19th Susan Whiting had come to his house with a certificate signed by Mr Keane and told him that Mr Alderton had refused the application. "I told her to go to the butcher's and get the mutton and by no means to let her brother want for it. She then left me under the impression that she would go at once and get the mutton. I also said I was sure it would be allowed by the Relieving Officer and that if not, they could but pay for it. On the following Monday, the day of Whiting's death and the day for the Relieving Officer to attend in the Parish, I sent for the Relieving Officer to call on me that I might speak on the case, and discovered that Whiting's sister had not applied for or obtained the mutton." (And now comes another piece of valuable information.) "Whiting had been a member of the Hundred Benefit Club until a few months of his decease when he withdrew and on last Easter Monday (he) joined another Benefit Club at an entrance fee of 5/-, a book of Rules 6d., dinner 3/- and he treated the company to beer – total 9s.2d." (This was obviously not a temperance society! However, the lavish treating of the company amounted to 8d worth of beer.)

"The Sunday after Mr Hibbs alluded to these cases in his sermon, the labourers in my employ expressed themselves indignant at the discourse and stated that if Dunnett wanted, it was because he did not make his wants known, and as to Whiting, if he wanted, he did not ought." Again we have the man with the inside knowledge talking. One can almost hear the labouring men among the congregation having their say. The novelist Thomas Hardy would have loved this episode! Perhaps there may be a case of consciences pricking but the congregation did not feel that the Revd. Mr Hibbs as a temporary vicar had the right to stir up all this trouble.

Mr Sparling was questioned by the rest of the Board about Dunnett's having only 1s.3d. a week to live on. In reply to the question what happened about his rent, they were told that he lived with his nephew and contributed a penny a week towards the rent but he actually owed for the previous nine weeks. The odd bit of occasional paid labour helped the old man out but his neighbours were adamant that he never complained he was in need.

The Guardians decided to write to the Revd. Hibbs to ask for an explanation of his letter. Unfortunately, they did not get much in the way of a reply beyond the enigmatic remark that "Observer must remain an observer." However, for the Guardians matters had been taken up elsewhere and they now had to submit their evidence to Sir John Walsham of the Poor Law Board for his thorough investigation.

This was not the last of the Whiting affair. In July Dr Fleming reported that on a visit to the Widow Whiting he found her "dining off a slop basin" – in other words she had nothing to eat beyond bread soaked either in a little milk or more likely, tea. When he had remarked that surely she had been allowed extra relief since the death of her son, she replied that it had been cut off and an order given for her to go into the House. This she adamantly refused to do, saying that she would rather lie there and die first. Remembering the furore over the Dunnett case as well as her son's death, Fleming thought that if she did indeed die, then the blame would be put on him. So he gave her 2s.6d. from his own pocket and recommended both mutton and porter.

Hearing this, the Board felt that she really should come into the House where proper nursing could be provided and her every want taken care of. However, she continued to refuse this option. The Guardians consulted the Poor Law Board who, no doubt also recalling the past publicity, wrote at the end of August to say that the Guardians had no power to compel any destitute person who applied for relief to come into the House if he or she refused. They then gave the Guardians a loophole that if she refused, the Guardians would probably think it right to instruct their Relieving Officer to watch her case, and afford such temporary relief in kind as either the medical Officer, if he was in attendance, or the Relieving Officer himself might deem to be absolutely requisite during the intervals of the meetings of the Guardians, in the event of the case becoming one of greater necessity. The story teller in me would have liked more details, as for example, where was daughter Susan while her mother lay so ill? Had she found employment – if not, why not? But this case was not a piece of fiction but a real one taken from the pages of a Minute Book and as such provided only the details that were relevant on that specific occasion.

It is probable that the district Medical Officers had most insight into the needs of the poor. Often they were called upon to visit homes that even the most sympathetic parson or Christian lady would baulk at. By the 1860s it was reports from doctors that were having some influence on the authorities of their duty to examine carefully the housing needs of the poor. Mr Edwards, a district Medical Officer, attended the inquest at Washbrook on Charles, the infant son of George Adams. Apparently, the damp and unsanitary condition of the house had caused the child's death. Both the coroner and the jury directed Mr Edwards to bring to the attention of the Board the fact that the house was unfit for human habitation. It would appear from the fact that the Board then wrote to the Washbrook Parish Surveyor who had powers to act under the Nuisances Removal Act, that a great part of the problem was the disposal of human waste products. It was likely that these were simply emptied straight into the stream in front of the houses. The practice was responsible for frequent outbreaks of typhus and typhoid fever. Ten years earlier, in 1851 there had been complaints about the cesspools in a property in Sproughton owned by Mr Condor of Ipswich. Washbrook had also had complaints at the same time about 'the nuisance' in some cottages owned by Mr Harwood.

The Guardians felt so strongly about the appalling conditions that many of the villagers lived in that they petitioned the government to help facilitate those who might alleviate the situation. They wrote of the insufficiency and inadequacy of tenements of the labouring classes in rural districts asking that the government should pass "some remedial law for the better regulation and supervision of such tenements…The condition of the dwellings of the Poor is such as to be injurious to health and dangerous to the morals and well being of the inhabitants. That the dwellings are often occupied by large families having only one sleeping room wherein all the members of the family are promiscuously crowded without respect to numbers, sex or age." Their recommendation to Her Majesty's Government was that "we would humbly suggest that facilities be given to Societies having for their principal object the improvement of the dwellings of the poor." This was a reference to what we would now term Housing Association groups but it was to be another fifty years or more before subsidised Local Authority Housing was available for those unable to meet the rents of private landlords. In the meantime the petition was sent with the backing of the East Suffolk Member of Parliament, Sir Fitzroy Kelly. Attorney-General in 1858-9, he felt so strongly in favour of the motion that he was willing to bring it in as a Private Member's Bill if necessary.

In 1869 there was another sad case. The Stannard family of Bentley all went down with Diphtheria; two of the children dying as a consequence. The authorities agreed that their deaths had been preventable; caused by the poor construction and bad state of repair of the cottage in which the family lived. The roof let in so much rain that a mouldy dampness was ever present in the sleeping apartment and the 'nuisance' was compounded by an open cesspool behind the house which received all kinds of refuse and the drainage from adjacent buildings.

Problems within the House itself surfaced in 1867 when in October there were so many cases of ophthalmia (a highly infectious inflammation of the eyes) that it became necessary to provide a quarantine ward for them, well removed from every one else. A room at the extreme south-east corner on the men's side was chosen. It was apparently "a light and cheerful room" and it required only to be fitted with an open fireplace. Medical knowledge had advanced sufficiently to recognise that the eye infection was spread through the use of communal washing facilities, so every bed was supplied with an individual washbasin and towel rack. Tables and chairs were brought in for meals and 'a night stool', a form of commode provided, so that the patients were truly isolated from any external contact.

How to maintain good standards of hygiene and sanitation were ever pressing concerns. In June 1862 the Poor Law Commissioner's Report recommended that better ventilation was needed in the Old Men's Day Room. It was suggested that this would be materially assisted if a partition was taken down and better still that the lavatory should be situated elsewhere. Bearing in mind that we are still at the stage of earth closets, the sense of this is immediately apparent to the more sensitive noses of today! The Inspector also recommended that the lavatory (using the term in its original meaning of a place to wash) adjoining the Girls' Schoolroom should be equipped with zinc or galvanised iron washbasins. The drain in the Boys' lavatory was to be trapped and the Inspector drew attention to a leaking pipe and recommended the installation of washbasins for this area too.

When the House had first opened, nursing often fell to those competent women who had had the misfortune to become inmates. In 1769, Elizabeth Hasleton and Mary Fenn who were employed in the "Sick House" were given extra payments for their work with smallpox patients. As time went on, so the post of nurse and Matron's assistant became fully paid posts advertised as other posts were. As with teaching, nursing was for many a self-taught art, the regulation and the proper training came much later. Dickens's Sarah Gamp is probably not too wide of the mark. The middle class young ladies who joined the Anglican Sisterhoods and those like Florence Nightingale who had received specialised training from the German Lutheran Deaconesses of Kaiserwerth, were to become the backbone of hospital nursing. They often relate in their diaries that night duty, in particular, was undertaken by women of the lower classes. These, besides being lacking in anything other than the most rudimentary medical knowledge, were often inebriated when they came on duty.

The longest serving of the nurses was Hannah Baskett. It would appear that she was originally appointed in 1837 as a schoolmistress. Quite when she changed roles is not recorded but she continued to act as a Nurse until 1874 by which time she was in her late seventies. Two interesting cases cropped up in the House in October 1868 and February 1869. Nurse Goldsmith had been appointed in September but it was a month before it was discovered that she was not fulfilling Article 165 of the Poor Law Act. This specified that a person unable to read written directions should not be employed as a nurse. It was not enough to be able to read the printed word, as in the Bible or Prayer Book, a nurse had to be able to read what the doctor had written upon medications. So Nurse Goldsmith was dismissed. One would have thought the Board and the Master would have been more careful in their next appointment but perhaps the fact that she started work on the 24$^{th}$ December had something to do with it. It was late February before Louisa Matthews was called into a Board Meeting to sign her name to a form required by the Poor Law Board. Imagine the consternation of the members present when Miss Matthews informed them that she must decline to do what they wanted, having some years before made a vow never to write again! It was presumably a verbal resignation she gave to the Board when asked.

Her successor Mrs Nicholls did not stay long either. Her resignation was demanded when she refused to sleep in the Fever Ward. Her argument, that it was unfair to expect her to be confined to the ward both day and night, was not accepted by the Board. Few of the nurses stayed for long; either they disliked their duties or they were not suited to the post. References were not always what they seemed but the one from the East Suffolk Hospital concerning Mrs Rumage was a fine example of truthfulness. "She discharged her duties well, kept her ward particularly neat and clean but her temper was not good. Several charges of harsh treatment were laid by her patients but they were not proved." Mrs Rumage stayed but the Master was told by the Guardians to keep an eye on her.

It is not clear if it was this lady who had been on duty in June 1873 when Caroline Smith gave birth to a child that was either stillborn or died very shortly afterwards. The inquest that was held gives a little insight into the management of the midwifery side of nursing. When Caroline gave birth in the 'lying–in ward' the nurse was not in attendance. It transpired that the only way a woman in labour could summon assistance was by rapping on the floor with a stick that was provided for the purpose. The coroner recommended that a bell be used in future. The last we hear of Mrs Rumage was that she had been reported for inebriety and neglect of duty. (She not only had a Dickensian name, she lived up to the picture he drew!)

During the 1870s smallpox was again rife. The infirmaries of the Workhouses in West Suffolk were probably already overcrowded when they were expected to cope with an emergency that led to three 'out of district' patients being admitted to the Samford House infirmary. It was at two o'clock on the afternoon of Friday the 11th August 1871 that a gigantic explosion rocked the countryside for miles around the town of Stowmarket. For the second time in ten years, a major disaster had occurred at the factory that lined either side of the track at the town's railway station. Here the Prentice family employed at least 130 workers in the manufacture of gun-cotton, an explosive material used for blasting that was made by steeping cotton in nitric and sulphuric acid. The **Ipswich Journal** accounts of the aftermath of the accident, in which eighteen were killed, including two of the Prentice family, were horribly graphic; the reporter stated "a girl named Hales was burned to a cinder." Many of the survivors were severely burned; others suffered from the effects of inhalation of toxic fumes while of some of the workers there remained no trace whatsoever. Many of the wounded were taken to the infirmary at the Union House at Onehouse, others to Stowupland. Two cases were transferred to the East Suffolk Hospital in Ipswich but somehow, John Brown of Woolpit, Harriet Stirling and Simon Green were among the casualties who were brought to Tattingstone for treatment. While it is tempting to give the more dramatic details of this awful incident at Stowmarket, it is worthwhile noting that a number of those killed or badly injured were what we would now term children. Susan Wilding who died was only twelve. She lived several miles away at Creeting, from where she walked each morning to begin work at six. For her twelve-hour shift she earned sixpence a day giving her 3/- to take home to her mother at the end of the week. Perhaps this example helps to put life in the House into perspective.

When the smallpox reached Samford the fever ward was put on stand-by and the horse and cart used to convey paupers to the House from a distance was to be used as 'an ambulance' for serious cases. During the epidemic the Poor Law Inspectors came to see for themselves how the House was coping. They were not pleased with what they found. There were two wards, one for men, another for women – but there was uninterrupted communication not just between these wards but with the main body of the House, thus facilitating the spread of the disease. And, while the Inspector noted that a change of personal linen was given to patients, there were no separate arrangements for washing these clothes. Added to this, there did not appear to be a nurse specially appointed for these patients. The Master's wife had been entrusted with the duty but she had been ill herself and it appeared that nothing was done about the situation.

The Board swiftly sent a reply to the Poor Law Board stating:
1. A Nurse had been engaged.
2. There were proper arrangements for washing linen.
3. It was true that the wards connected but not the rest of the House.
4. All communication between Nurse and Officers and Inmates was prevented as far as possible.
5. When the wards were clear of infection the Guardians would give their attention to the Inspector's recommendations.

As if they did not have enough to worry about, the Board then found themselves having to deal with another medical problem. A released prisoner had been quickly dispatched from the County Gaol when it was discovered that he was suffering from pulmonary tuberculosis. He was taken to the Workhouse in Ipswich but the Master there, uncharitably maybe but also safeguarding his inmates, refused to accept him. So he was put into a cab and accompanied by a warder he was brought out to Tattingstone where he was taken in. However, the Board did not intend to be the 'dumping ground' so they sent a deputation the following Tuesday to complain to the Justices and to find out by what authority the governor of the Gaol had done this.

Contrary to what one may think, sudden deaths among the paupers were not accepted without question. On several occasions one or other of the Parish Medical Officers was called upon to explain why he had not attended at a certain case where death had ensued. This happened to the hapless Fleming. He was treating an out-patient who was seriously ill when for some reason he stopped visiting. The young man, Alfred Marsh had taken a turn for the worse and his sister walked seven miles to Fleming's house to get medicine. Fleming had refused to see the girl as it was a Sunday. When Alfred had died a few hours later, his parents had complained to the Board about the shabby treatment he had received. Perhaps remembering the outcry caused by the newspaper over the death of another young man, Whiting, the Board demanded full details. Mr Wrinch, the Guardian for Shotley said they should invite the parents, Mr and Mrs Marsh and their daughter to come and give their side of the story in full and the Revd. Hervey was adamant that the matter should not be hushed up. After the hearing in which both sides gave their version, but which was not recorded in any detail, Fleming was told he must be much more careful in future.

Dr Manning who took care of the poor of Bentley was similarly charged in a letter with lack of care in performing his duty. In his reply he stated that he had acted for both the good of the patient and for the general public. He had been called to deal with "a lunatic who had escaped from the custody of his attendants and was wandering the greater part of the night in gardens, lanes and roads of Bentley. The man, Thomas Smith, had threatened to murder one woman; he was dangerous to himself and the public at large and a terror to the neighbourhood." Dr Manning had found it necessary to place Smith under restraint and have him taken to the House for immediate admission. This was a course that he had always pursued in other cases of smallpox and he would continue to do so until he received the Poor Law Board's instructions to do otherwise. In due course a comment was received from the authorities at the Poor Law Board to whom the case had been reported. Their response was eminently sensible. If the man really was a lunatic then he should have been taken immediately to the Asylum. But they understood that as he had smallpox this was not an option. However, the question had to be asked, was the man really a lunatic? Was it not more likely that he was merely suffering from delirium brought on by the smallpox? And, furthermore, the so-called 'terror' among the neighbourhood was probably induced by a fear of the smallpox rather than the man himself.

A cause for concern for all the Medical Officers came in 1872 when the order went out that no medical relief was to be given to midwifery cases except where there was extreme necessity. The fees from attending a birth had considerably increased the doctors' basic salary so they were united in their outcry to the Board. They had even more cause to complain when later the same year there was a complete appraisal of all medical salaries and they found they had lost fees they had previously taken for granted.

In 1877, Dr Fleming had another run-in with the Board. He was asked to explain if his assistant who, it appeared, often did duty for Dr Fleming at the House, was properly qualified. The Master also complained that Dr Fleming's visits were often irregular and 'untimely'. It appears that he did not always come when the Master sent for him.

It was Fleming's turn to complain later in the year. His grievance was over those patients who had been returned to the House from the asylum at Melton as 'relieved' of their symptoms. They were now supposed to be fit subjects for the discipline of the House but, Fleming remonstrated that he did not think they should be "shunted to the House where there were no proper airing courts"' for them. It was quite clear that he felt the patients were not fully recovered and he said he would not take the responsibility for their care unless there were proper attendants to look after them when they went out. It is not clear what the outcome of this was but in 1880 Fleming was again summoned before the Board to give his reason for not attending a case of smallpox in the House when requested to do so. He had sent a message to the Master saying he would come on his next usual day, which was Thursday. He had however, sent his assistant to visit the patient, Mary Wallis on the Wednesday.

There seems to have been personal animosity between the Master, Harman Harris and Fleming but the doctor also appeared to delight in making trouble for the Board as he did in March 1881 when he drew their attention to the excessively high death rate among the aged poor. He pointed out that most of these deaths had been caused by diarrhoea brought on either by poor diet or insanitary conditions. He knew that he was on safe ground here because there had been loud protests earlier in the year about the bread that was distributed to the poor that was found to be contaminated. Similarly, there had been another report about the sanitary arrangements in the House and Fleming believed the water supply had been infected. The wells were tested and the analysed water pronounced good so, argued Fleming, it must be the food that was at fault. While he was pursuing this line of attack, he decided to tell the Board that he did not consider that there was sufficient heat-producing food being given to the young people between the ages of 9 and 16.

Another inspection of the drainage system revealed that in the Old Men's lavatory, the sink pipe was untrapped and ran straight into a drain in the yard. It was recommended that this pipe should be taken through the wall and delivered into a trapped gulley outside. In the kitchen, there was a sink that emptied directly into a cesspit that again was practically untrapped; that the course of the drain had been traced out and it was found that it emptied into a small cesspool in the garden ditch. There was also a closet near by into which a surface drain emptied. It would seem that Fleming might have strong evidence to back up his claims. However, the Local Government Board inspector, Dr Mount found that the House was scrupulously clean; there was nothing in the structural or administrative arrangements that could fairly be held responsible for the excessive number of deaths. It had to be assumed that these were the result of the very severe winter weather. The inspector did note however, "The Workhouse Medical Record Book was imperfectly kept with several columns being left blank. The Medical Officer is to keep the book more carefully."

The next argument to surface was over the diet provided for those diagnosed as lunatics. The Committee on Lunacy found that the food being given these inmates was not up to the standard agreed as being most beneficial for them. When the Master was questioned he said Dr Fleming had not sanctioned the special diet, so again Fleming was called to appear before the Board to explain. And this he did saying that the 'lunacy diet' had been tried and when there was no change in the mental health of those concerned, there seemed to be no justification for its continuance.

While Fleming was fighting his battles, Dr Norman, another of the District Medical Officers, was in trouble for prescribing cod liver oil without the proper authorisation. All the doctors had to cope that winter not only with smallpox but outbreaks of scarlet fever and dysentery while the animal population was stricken with foot and mouth Disease.

And then there was Dr Tertius D'Oyly Pain who sounds as if he had stepped right out of a Victorian novel. In fact he shares the same forename as the fictional Dr Lydgate in George Eliot's Middlemarch. He practised at Stratford St Mary and was the District MO for the surrounding parishes. His name first crops up in 1879 when he is mentioned as being unwell. But it was a year later that the Board received a letter from his wife to the effect that he was "suffering from disease of the brain" and was thus incapable of managing his own affairs. He had, she wrote, left the area and was now in London. It is likely that he had been admitted to one of the many private or public asylums in the city.

The treatment and understanding of mental health problems in the nineteenth century is an area that needs more research. We have already seen that the medical authorities were experimenting with special diets as a way of curing lunacy and much that was then labelled as such has since been found to be the result of physical defects. An elderly woman living in Holbrook was certified and sent off to the Melton asylum after she complained to anyone that would listen to her that her neighbours were hounding her. In particular, she believed they were poisoning her ducks. Today we would say she was suffering from dementia but we would be just as wrong as the medical profession were at the time. When matters were fully investigated, it was found that she had indeed suffered at the hands of malicious neighbours who were responsible for the death of her ducks. Dr Fleming got into trouble with the Board again when he refused to commit another patient as a lunatic. He maintained that the woman who had behaved violently was only showing a hysterical reaction to being forcibly restrained by her family. Mr Rodwell, the Guardian for Holbrook found another doctor who would certify her. As we know from novels of the period as well as documented factual cases, young women were often certified as insane when they failed to do what their fathers or husbands wished.

At the end of 1882 there was another outbreak of smallpox. Fleming, worked off his feet told the Board that a great deal needed doing to improve facilities. For a start, there was the so-called ambulance. This was so unfit for the conveyance of the sick that no one wished to be carried in it. It would have been no more than a rough closed cart drawn by a horse. (Older readers may remember that as children, when the old white ambulance went through the streets with its bell ringing, they turned up their coat collars and held their breath until the vehicle had passed. We learnt through the lore of the playground that this practice would save us from the fever! A pointless ritual that was a hangover from the previous century.) As for the fever wards themselves, everything about them was rough and old fashioned. They needed thorough renovation; new furniture and bedding. Improvements were called for also in the accommodation provided for the nurse. The Board promised they would look in to things once the infection had ceased.

But there were other epidemics to give concern. In January 1883 typhoidal diarrhoea swept through the asylum at Melton causing them to close their doors to all new patients. This meant that anyone being certified at that time had to be sent to the House. Eventually the Norwich asylum accepted patients from Suffolk until the crisis was over. This of course meant longer distances to be travelled and more time lost for those attending cases as well as additional expense. And while various diseases struck the human population, foot and mouth disease was still spreading throughout the county and bringing with it all it attendant problems.

At the Board Meeting in June, the Master was instructed to purchase six dozen bottles of wine for the use of the sick. Which wine was not specified but possibly it was port. The Medical Officer could recommend wine for a sick patient both within and without the House. However, the Relieving Officer was the one who had the power to deliver the bottle but he in turn had to fetch it from the Master at the House. One suspects that some bottles may not have been properly accounted for. A suspicion that is borne out later when we learn that Dr Fleming was to receive a letter from the Board requesting him to fill in all orders given by him for wine in the wine column of the Weekly Medical Returns.

At the end of the year Mr Lockwood, the Local Government Inspector reinforced many of Fleming's criticisms of the fever wards. In fact he went further; recommending that smallpox cases should be accommodated in a separate building. Again, drainage problems were noted, mainly that the closet drain ran along the yard immediately below the wards and under a passage. The whole system was fraught with danger. The Medical Officer was always to be informed when the cesspool was cleaned out, that being the most likely time for germs to occur. (I will save the exciting story of the new sewage farm to another chapter.) The Inspector also recommended that the House reviewed its Dietary Tables that had been in force since 1849. The Medical Officer was to be consulted as to what was best but certainly milk must be included in the diet for children.

In July 1889, the Board had to reprimand Dr Lawson, one of the District Medical Officers for charging too much for quinine. Laughable as it now seems, we have to remind ourselves that the Guardians were spending ratepayers' money and had to be accountable. The Clerk reported in a rather convoluted fashion to the Board that he had enquired of a good chemist the price of quinine. He then detailed the number of grains in an ounce of quinine costing 3s.6d. and the number of bottles supplied by Dr Lawson. All of which proved that Dr Lawson's charge of £5 was excessive. That was trivial compared to the shock they had that same month from the news of the death of Dr Fleming, who had been the Medical officer for the House for almost thirty years. In the same way that he had 'inherited' the post from his father-in-law, Dr Martin, so the Board now asked Fleming's son and partner to take over for the time being. Fleming junior was officially appointed to the post in August.

The question of a separate, purpose built infectious hospital on the Union House site surfaced again in October 1892 when Mr Humphreys produced two plans for an 'Ironwork Building'. One was estimated to cost £300.0.0. the other which had some unspecified refinements came out at £320.5.0. Neither of these plans included Mr Wrinch's estimate of £348.8.6. for the brick or concrete foundations the ironwork building would require. The Board approved of the costlier plan and decided that the £400 required for setting up the project would have to be raised by a loan. This was to be taken for three years at 3½ %. The land needed for the project was a meadow currently leased by a Mr Dale who had expressed his willingness to give it up. However, we now have an example of how little real power the Board had over major decisions. The Local Government Board, from whom the Guardians were hoping to raise their loan, let them know in June 1893 that they were not prepared to sanction the cash for an Iron Hospital. Such structures, they said, were not suitable. (This decision must have been altered later for I have early memories of the iron structures that formed Ipswich's Isolation Hospital and there were many similar buildings through out the country.) The Guardians were then in the difficult position of having to extricate themselves from their contract with Mr Humphreys.

Eventually a hospital of brick construction was built on a field to the west of the meadow behind the stables. The Minutes record that it was "similar to Mr Bisshopp's plan no.2 but with modifications". These were that there should be at least four beds in each ward and that the total cost including the architect's commission, drainage, water supply, fixtures and fittings should not exceed £1000. The whole project also depended on the Local Government Board consenting to provide a loan to be spread over thirty years. The hospital, which in time became screened by trees, was ready for use in the event of an infectious outbreak by 1898. While the Board waited to appoint a Caretaker, the current Master, Mr Jarrold was ordered to keep the beds and bedding aired; be prepared to send the ambulance (the old covered cart) when necessary and at the request of the Medical Officer. However, he was to be especially careful that no goods of any kind were sent from the Workhouse to the hospital or indeed that there was any communication between them when there was a case in the hospital.

1890 had brought the introduction of the Lunacy Act under which specialist inspectors now had powers to report on the care of those who were not serious enough to be held in actual asylums. With the growing financial burden imposed by the large numbers of those with mental problems being confined within Workhouses, it became necessary to classify them into three groups. A 'lunatic' was one with acute mania, usually labouring under delusions; the 'chronic' was one who was found after treatment to be harmless, not requiring the strict supervision of the asylum. This often included the senile, while the third group was labelled 'idiots' and was those who were regarded as imbeciles from a very early age. When the Inspector visited in 1898 he reported that "the imbeciles are well treated and have sufficient diet, getting four meat dinners weekly. The dormitories and bedding are in proper order. I thought the dress, especially of the men might be tidier. All of both sexes are bathed weekly." The 1891 census notes that of the seventy-eight inmates sixteen were classified as imbecile, many of them elderly. Among them is William Double. William was born in the House in 1831 when his parents came in during a period of unemployment. We do not know what impairment William suffered but it was sufficient that when his parents discharged themselves, he remained. He spent his entire life in the House. That such a fate was not common is borne out by the special note to that effect made by the Master when he recorded William's death in 1918.

As we approach the twentieth century, bureaucracy is increasing. In place of the Samford Hundred, we now have Samford Rural District Council and the number of posts connected to the administration of the Poor Law has increased to include for each district a Relieving Officer, registrar of Births and Deaths, Vaccination Officer and Collector of the Rates. But on the humane level, the local doctors were still crossing swords with the Guardians in the sort of case that would be quoted to show the iniquities of the system. Dr Turner was reported by the Relieving Officer for issuing a ticket for the purchase of two pounds of meat in order to make beef tea. The recipient was Jane Locke, a mother who, the doctor believed, was in need of nourishment following a premature delivery. According to the Relieving Officer the woman did not qualify for Out-relief as her husband and three of her eight children were in employment earning in total 31/- a week. When Dr Turner replied to the Guardians' letter, he explained that the family appeared poor to him and the woman needed the beef tea. If the Guardians were going to be difficult about it, then he would pay for the meat himself. The Guardians wrote that that would be perfectly in order! In the event, Mrs Locke paid for it herself.

Changes too were being made in other departments. Institutes were set up for the proper training of nurses for Workhouse Infirmaries, certainly not before time. The Guardians specified what was expected of their nursing staff.

1. All nurses must have practical experience.
2. The Matron was Superintendent of Nursing and attended personally all maternity cases.
3. The Head Nurse – elected on the understanding that she possess sufficient skills to meet all normal conditions with competent assistance
4. Assistant Nurse/s
5. Two Wardsmen and two Wardswomen assigned to the Sick wards
6. Night Nursing to be carried out by assistant nurses and ward attendants with access in emergency to head Nurse and Matron.
7. Application can be made to the Ipswich Nurses Home for help in an emergency.

The Guardians noted that fresh air, good nursing and warm water, were essential to the recovery of patients. Unfortunately, hot water was only available in the men's ward but the Board took the view that it would be desirable for the women to have it too, so that they could have hot food and drink as well as having the facility to make poultices and fill hot water bottles.

The Revd. John Hocking summed up the principle that was to underlie all nursing within the House. "The poor, the sick and the old...cure those you can quickly. Those who cannot be cured...it must be our common wish that their last days should be sweetened and alleviated by the gentle care which trained nursing alone can give."

And more attention was being paid to the comfort of those who had to spend much time in the infirmary. In 1899, the Medical Officer recommended that a waterbed be purchased. Although this was to cost £5.15.0. the Guardians agreed it and within a year or so, a second one was added.

Although attitudes to nursing care seemed to have softened, the same approach did not apply to members of the staff. In 1906, Flatman the porter announced that his wife was ill and asked that the Board should either send her to the sanatorium or give her three months leave of absence. Mrs Flatman was in charge of the Laundry so her absence would have entailed employing a temporary substitute. Before giving their decision the Board asked the Medical officer to examine her. He reported that the woman did indeed have the wasting disease known as pulmonary consumption but, in his opinion, she was still able to work. There is little doubt that the steamy atmosphere in which she worked must have contributed to her illness. Perhaps the reluctance to grant her time off was because earlier in the year she had taken time off to have a baby. On that occasion the Board had given her permission to have the baby in the House but only on condition that she herself paid for a substitute to do her work and that once the child reached the age of two months it was to be boarded out with foster parents.

Had the Flatmans belonged to the Hundred of Samford Mutual Assurance Benefit Society they might have been covered for a stay in the sanatorium. This Society had been formed in 1839. Within a year or two it had three hundred and fifty members each paying a small weekly sum that contributed towards their not needing outdoor relief in the case of sickness, old age, the apprenticeship of their children or the widowhood of their spouse. The treasurer at the that time was Mr Catchpole, the Master, no doubt doing his best to encourage membership in order to keep them out of the House. By the 1870s it had become almost essential for the workingman to make such provision. An order stated "That in all cases in which able-bodied men with families who are under thirty years and who have not gone into a Benefit Club apply for relief for themselves, their wives or families in consequence of sickness, no out-door relief shall be granted before a portion at least of the family have been received into the House." Income from a Benefit Club or Friendly Society was to be treated on the same footing as any other means of income.

A problem that faced many of the local Benefit Clubs was that they were too small to cater for the heavy demands upon them so during the next fifty years or so other Societies took their place. The Ancient Order of Foresters was particularly strong in this area from the eighteen nineties. Each group was known as a Court and to the Chelmondiston one (which presumably met in the public house known as the Foresters) belonged Charles Page. Charles was admitted to the infirmary of the House for treatment. He, or the Board on his behalf, applied to the Foresters for reimbursement for his maintenance. A straight forward case, one might think. But not so. The Foresters' Medical Officer refused to certify Page as being eligible for relief on the grounds that his was a mental problem rather than a physical one; he was diagnosed later by the Inspector for Lunacy as suffering from melancholia.

This was one occasion at least when the power of the Guardians came into play. They demanded a thorough scrutiny of the rules of the Order and finding that they stated clearly that provision was made for both mental and physical infirmity, they persuaded the Foresters to pay out. Court Elliott, the Tattingstone branch of the Foresters founded in 1897 actually held its meetings in a room at the House from that year right through to 1929 when they transferred to the Village Hut.

Standards of nursing care continued to rise, although there were still problems in keeping nurses for any length of time. In 1915, Mrs Carter reported Nurse Harding to the Board for her cruel behaviour toward the inmates. Apparently the nurse was abusive to the sick and infirm patients and when the Matron remonstrated with her, she was abusive to her too. Nurse Harding had refused to help the elderly women in and out of the bath and to assist with drying them. She had accused the old women of all sorts of misdemeanours, describing them to the Matron as "beastly old witches". Not unnaturally, Nurse Harding was given instant dismissal. In 1922 the Matron reported the nurses to the Board for failing to report and attend to the bedsores of an elderly patient.

Perhaps more interesting and illuminating was the case of John Lancaster. He was one of the inmates who had come from Woodbridge Union and was therefore chargeable to them, so if we wish to be cynical, we may suggest that that was the reason the Board took the decision they did. The Medical Officer, Dr Andrew, reported in November 1922, that Lancaster had a skin disease and needed to be attended to at the Leicester Square Skin Hospital. While they waited for an appointment, the doctor recommended the patient should have deep bath treatment that involved immersion right up to his neck. The Board ordered the Master to obtain a suitable second-hand bath for this purpose. There was little delay in either getting the bath or a hospital appointment. A suitable bath was bought for 38/- which only required re-enamelling but before this happened, Lancaster was off to London on 11$^{th}$ December for treatment that was to cost 7/- a day which fortunately the Board would not have to pay.

*Augt 29 1801*
*Board Room*
*Tattingstone*

I am directed by the Poor Law Board to acknowledge the receipt of your letters the 2 & 22 instant in the former of which you bring under their notice the the case of a Woman of the name of Whiting, aged about 60 years who has been offered relief in the Workhouse which she refuses to accept; and you enquire what course the Guardians of the Samford Union should adopt in the case, and whether they would be justified in adhering to their determination to afford her relief to her only in the Workhouse. I am directed to state, generally, that the Guardians have no power to compel any destitute person who applies for relief to come into the Workhouse if he

# VI

"What am I to do with the child? I can see nothing for her but the workhouse".
Mrs Brame thought the workhouse next in disgrace to prison itself. "Is there nothing but the WORKHOUSE?"

At the final meeting of the Directors before the House opened its doors to the new residents, the Revd. Stephen White presented the Corporation with a book entitled **An Earnest Appeal for Mercy to the Children of the Poor.** We can but hope that the Board and all those who would be in charge of the day to day running of the House took the opportunity to read the book and put into practice the suggestions it contained. There is no doubt that the care of children was going to prove taxing for many of those who came in were going to be, for one reason or another, without parents.

Maria Charlesworth writing in the middle of the nineteenth century echoed in the character of Mrs Brame the views of most of those who just managed to keep themselves above the poverty line. In the novel **Ministering Children** from which the above is taken, the motherless Patience, is abandoned by her feckless father. He goes, leaving Patience and owing five weeks' rent on the room they occupied in a lodging house. The landlady faced with his sudden flit seeks the advice of another of her lodgers, the elderly Mrs Brame, a former children's nurse as to what can be done for the child. Since neither woman can afford to keep her the Workhouse seems the logical answer. But since Mrs Brame, who has no real knowledge of the Workhouse, is reluctant to support the idea, the landlady suggests that Patience should be sent out to work as a general servant. This at least provided a roof over her head but the child was severely overworked and harshly treated. When she was taken ill with brain fever, her employer promptly dispatched her to the infirmary – at the Workhouse!

*"The parish authorities magnanimously and humanely resolved that Oliver should be 'farmed', or in other words, that he should be despatched to a branch-workhouse some three miles off, where twenty or thirty other juvenile offenders against the poor-laws, rolled about the floor all day, without the inconvenience of too much food or too much clothing, under the parental superintendence of an elderly female."* **Oliver Twist** by **Charles Dickens**. At the age of nine, Oliver Twist was sent back to the main Workhouse where, as we all know, he had the misfortune to become the spokesman for the hungry children.

It is reputed that Dickens used the Bosmere and Claydon Workhouse at Barham as his model for **Oliver Twist**. By coincidence, that and others in east Suffolk including the Parish Houses in Ipswich would have been known to Charlesworth too. Born at Little Blakenham in 1819, this clergyman's daughter spent her formative years in Ipswich. Her father, who, among other things, was the vicar of Elmsett, encouraged all his family to take an active and practical part in the care of the poor and neglected. Both Dickens and Charlesworth used the written word to bring the social deprivation of their time to the notice of a largely middle class audience. Where Dickens aimed to shock his readers with his larger than life characters, some of whom verge on caricature, Charlesworth adopted a more thoughtful, perhaps even genteel style. While never missing an opportunity to get her Christian message across, she is nonetheless sternly critical of the social problems she saw around her. What is more, she was prepared to make practical suggestions on how problems could be alleviated if not solved. As her reputation grew as a writer, so she gained the ear of many in authority including the reformer, Lord Shaftesbury.

So, what was to be done with the child? If we today have any problems comprehending what life must have been like in the eighteenth and nineteenth centuries, then the question of 'childhood' must pose the most difficulty. It was the mid-Victorian middle classes who invented the idea of childhood that we have built on. They idealised the close-knit family group in which parents ruled and controlled the development of the lives of their offspring, often keeping them solidly tied to the home well into adulthood.

The very rich had rarely done this; often they farmed out their infants to wet nurses, then consigned them to nursery and schoolroom before the sons went off to university, the Army or the Church. Their adolescent daughters went on extended visits to friends and relations in the expectation of finding a suitable husband while their own home provided hospitality to others in a similar position.

Among the working class there was little time for what we call childhood. The idyllic picture of carefree times with boys and girls 'coming out to play' is probably an illusion. Even before the Industrial Revolution had children working in factories and mines, children were expected to work at an age that nowadays we would think quite appalling. It may well be that the nursery rhyme got it right, perhaps it was only at night, after the day's chores had been done, that youngsters could have leisure time to relax and play. Parents were far too involved in working to have time to play games with their children and toys were practically non-existent. A rag or peg doll perhaps, a few stones for playing five-stones or 'alleys' in the ruts made by carts. But at least the country child had plenty of space in which to run about – or did he? As the enclosure of land took place in the eighteenth century, so the poor lost the right of use to common land. No longer able to exercise their rights to pick up firewood or let their pigs forage, the adults suffered but the children also lost their traditional playground. A child now caught on newly enclosed land or running in the woods could find himself accused not just of trespass but also of intended poaching, the penalty for which was hanging or transportation.

The country child was 'put to work' as early as five, helping with the simpler stages of preparation of wool for spinning. There was plenty too that a small boy could do on the land from bird scaring to helping clear stones from the fields after ploughing. Weeding the crops and helping stack the hay and corn were among the seasonal jobs available to help earn a few extra pence for the family. The girls naturally learned domestic work from their mothers, helping with the care of younger brothers and sisters and in an age when death in childbirth was frequent, girls as young as ten could find themselves taking on the role of housekeeper and mother substitute.

So, let us not be too sentimental when we consider the fate of the children who entered the House. Some came in as part of a whole family and knew, or at least hoped, that their time within the House would be short. Their father might be ill and so unable to work, or he was temporarily unemployed and when times improved, he would find work and they would once more have their own home. Others, like Anne Candler's children, were taken into the House because they had been deserted by their father. Mothers too, sometimes abandoned their children. Many were born in the House; some would stay until they were old enough to work while others might never leave. Amongst these were those who were handicapped in some way. In the eighteenth century there was very little provision for poor children who were blind, deaf or physically or mentally impaired. If they could not be cared for at home, then they were taken into the House where at least their physical needs were met. By the middle of the nineteenth century, as we shall see later, efforts were made to give the physically impaired the opportunity to learn a trade as a means of support. Those who were mentally afflicted but were not a danger either to themselves or others remained in the House while the more seriously deranged adults were removed to the Workhouse at Melton, near Woodbridge, which became the county asylum.

As we have already learned from the clothing that was initially ordered for the House, a distinction was made between 'children' and boys and girls. Those under seven were classed as children, those up to fourteen as boys or girls. From the age of seven, the sexes were separated and took up residence in either the male or female wings where each had their own schoolroom and exercise areas. Babies who came in with their mother or were born in the House, stayed with the mother until they were weaned, which could be as late as some time in their second year. While their mothers worked during the day the under sevens were supervised by elderly women, too old for any other kind of work. There was probably very little to stimulate the very young but then would there have been much more had they been living outside? At least they were fed, clothed and kept warm. By the mid eighteen hundreds, those babies who were orphaned or deserted might be fostered out around the parishes or as happened both here and in **Oliver Twist**, they might be sent to a Children's Home.

Once they had turned seven the boys and girls started learning to read and write. It should be remembered that this gave them an advantage over the children outside the House. Schooling was part of the regime of the House from the beginning in 1766 but it was to be nearly another seventy years before a school for poor children was established in Tattingstone, for example. Lessons were held on three days of the week and on the other three the children were instructed in knitting. Apart from the one in the House, most parishes had their own knitting schools where the children were instructed and supervised in making the stockings that were worn by young and old alike. If the parish was blessed with a good vicar who had serious minded young daughters, then it was possible that they might spend time reading to the young knitters and passing on to them knowledge of the Bible and perhaps other subjects too. In 1848, a form of nursery education was introduced. This was open to all children over the age of two who came into the House with their parents and all illegitimate children after the age of one if they were considered suitable.

The main aim of the Directors and Guardians was to ensure that each boy or girl who was in the House by the time they reached thirteen or fourteen should be found suitable employment. In this they were doing what a parent would have done. Richard Stopher, an auctioneer in Saxmundham describes how he apprenticed each of his sons in the first years of the nineteenth century. *"My son Robert I apprenticed to John Kemp, Harness maker. Thomas to Craig Raffe, Carpenter and James to Lionel Swann, Plumber and Glazier. Henry went on liking to Mrs Betts, Grocer at Stradbroke but stayed only his month. After that he went to Thomas in London to learn the Carpenter's trade."* Poor Henry wasn't cut out any more for carpentry than he was for grocery, so his father apprenticed him next to a local sea-farer. He had trouble there too, and after various adventures ended up working on board an American ship. His brother James decided he didn't want to remain in the Plumbing business but waited until his poor father had paid over the whole of his apprenticeship premium to Mr Swann before he ran away, thus leaving father out of pocket.

Ten pounds seems to have been the usual apprenticeship fee paid by the Guardians for a young boy to learn a trade. It was hoped this expenditure would be worthwhile in the long term by ensuring that the trained youth would support himself and any family he might have in the future and so not become a drain on the resources of the Poor Rate. All those leaving the House to go into employment were also given a set of clothing. When the House first opened it was decreed that children should return as far as possible to their native parish for work and pressure was put upon local employers to take them. However, as time went on, it was found necessary to seek employers further afield.

I have found no evidence that the Samford Guardians sent any boys off to the Army in 1793. At that time the British Army seems to have reached rock bottom; the artillery was the worst it had ever been and both men and officers generally were poorly trained. Many officers were promoted on the strength of the numbers of recruits they enlisted while others, totally unsuited, bought their commisions. In addition to men, at least three thousand boys were recruited for three specialist boy regiments that were to be deployed in the West Indies and other tropical locations. The idea of clearing out boys from the Workhouses was pleasing to the Guardians and many of the boys themselves were excited at the prospect. The aforementioned Richard Stopher, was for some years an Overseer of the Poor for Saxmundham. He describes taking *" John Shipp, a poor boy out of our Poor House to Colchester Barracks to put him into the 22$^{nd}$ Regt, of Foot. Col. Mercer received him and paid me one guinea for carrying him.... I also went with his brother Thomas Shipp to Ipswich and had him enrolled to serve for the Parish of Saxmundham at the time parishes had to find men for the navy."* Thomas, alas, went down with a ship sometime later.

John, however, went on to lead an interesting life. He wrote a book **The Path of Glory – Being the Memoirs of the Extraordinary Military Career of John Shipp** and it was the Parish Poor House he had to thank for his literacy, quite apart from anything else. He describes in more detail, the event mentioned by Stopher. *"One morning in or about January/February 1797, I was hard at work in a field by master's house, when who should I see but one of the Parish Officers making towards me with a large paper in his hand. Hastily running over my crimes I decided that I had done nothing to warrant the interference of such an exalted personage, so I stood up boldly and faced him. But he was all smiles and began, 'Shipp, I have frequently heard of and observed, your great wish to go for a soldier.' He then read me what was on the paper and asked if I was willing to go, for if I was the parish would rig me out decently, and he himself would take me to Colchester where the 22 Regt of Foot was then forming.(On return from the West Indies where it had gone in 1793 to recruit.) By four o'clock of the same day, to the honour and praise of the Parish be it spoken, I was rigged out in my new leather tights, new coat, new hat, new shoes, new everything... The next day, by 7 o'clock in the morning, I was on my way to Colchester and when I was seated on the front seat of the coach, I would not have exchanged situations with the grand pasha* *of Egypt or the King upon the throne of that land of which I was a native....We arrived at an Inn in Colchester where we dined....I was put into custody of the wife of the Drum Major, an old drunk Irish woman, but as good a creature as ever drank whisky. In the custody of this lady, the friend who came with me left me, first giving me a hasty shake of the hand and wishing me every happiness....I was soon deprived of my curly brown locks."*

Shipp, the poor boy from Saxmundham Workhouse rose through the ranks to Lieutenant. He travelled widely with his regiment, spending some time in India. Apart from his memoirs he wrote several books: two were fictional tales of army life, another, a serious treatise on Flogging. When he resigned his commission he became for a time an inspector in the newly formed Metropolitan Police. Ironically, his final post was that of Governor of the Workhouse in Liverpool.

During the 1790s when men were either recruited for military service or called up to serve in the local Militia, many children were forced into the House with their mothers who had been left without any means of support. In 1800 both boys and girls, like John Shipp would have found themselves 'deprived of their curls.' At a time when hair was generally worn long, a decree was issued at the Samford House that all boys and girls were to have their hair cut short. Although no reason is given, one assumes that it was for hygienic purposes, possibly caused by a severe outbreak of nits. It did however, have the disadvantage of singling out the shorn as being residents of the House. A hundred years later, when the children from the Union House were sent to Tattingstone School, the headmaster regularly blamed them as the source of all infestations, though in fact, they were probably more regularly inspected than the average village child.

However, there is no doubt that if nits could spread among the children, then so too could infectious diseases. A family admitted in 1802 brought measles in with them that quickly reached epidemic proportions. This put an added strain on the medical and nursing care both within the House itself and outside where the disease raged through the various parishes.

It was essential that boys and girls offered for work should be in the best of health and the Guardians were required to make a declaration to prospective employers that this was the case. Some times, the Guardians had to offer additional inducements to an employer as they did in 1800 for a boy who was lame. Anyone willing to take him as an apprentice was offered a premium of £15. Obviously, he would need a sedentary occupation; basket making and shoemaking were two of the possibilities on offer.

Once the Guardians were no longer tied to finding work for their young people within the Samford district, then the opportunities for varied careers became much wider. Obviously, Ipswich was the first place to be considered. This fast growing, lively town had much to offer. There were all the trades that were allied to being a port; ship building and repairs, rope and sail making, provisioning and of course, crew member of a merchant or fishing vessel. The town had industry too as well as craftsmen, all in need of both skilled and unskilled labour. Ipswich employers looked favourably on labour from the Samford House; the inmates were known to come from a country environment and therefore were more likely to be healthier than those born and bred in the overcrowded and polluted streets of the town.

So employers sent in their requests to the Guardians and in due course the legal papers binding a young person to an employer were signed and sealed. It is strange, but children who were in Workhouses were documented more carefully than those who were not. An inmate of the Workhouse could not just disappear without trace. Even if one did try to 'slip the net' that fact will have been recorded somewhere. The dockside parish of St Clement's, Ipswich was to become the eventual workplace for many boys and girls from the Samford House. When an agreement had been reached between employers and Guardians, the terms of apprenticeship were recorded by the Overseers of the Parish. From these records we know for example that on the 10$^{th}$ day of September 1821 "Sarah Smith maintained in the Poor House of Samford and belonging to Stutton is to be bound apprentice to Alexander Mackintosh of St Clement's, Confectioner."

Over the next three years a number of other young people found their way into St Clement's. The list below gives us an indication of the varied occupations into which they went.

Robert Yellop of Sproughton to Samuel Osborn, Basket-maker
William Bryant of Capel to Robert Martin, Chimney-sweep
Lydia Oxborrow of Sproughton to William Lee, Timber-hewer
Hannah Smith of Sproughton to William Hamblin, Straw-hat-maker
Jesse James of Shelley to John Perry, Baker
David Jerrard of Hintlesham to David Ringmead, Baker
William Ratcliffe of Wenham to William Bird, Mariner
John Phillips of Hintlesham to Alexander Christie, Mariner
Mary Baldry of Hintlesham to Thomas Trent, Bricklayer
John Garnham of Sproughton to Henry Otman, Tailor
Richard Roper of Sproughton to John Pinner, Fisherman
Mary Ann Jennings of Stutton to Robert Gaul, Whitesmith and Housekeeper
Joseph Seager of Woolverstone to John Brown, Mariner
Martha Tracey of Brantham to William Baker, Butcher and Housekeeper.

Lydia, Mary, Mary Ann and Martha went as maidservants. The first two as general servants to a family but Mary Ann and Martha were both bound as apprentices to men who supplemented their main incomes by running what we would now term 'a public house', so the girls would act as barmaids and possibly cooks if the 'house' provided refreshments.

In 1823 changes were made as to the age at which children could be apprenticed, reducing it to thirteen for boys and fourteen for girls although many outside the House were going into employment much younger than this. It was also at this time that all outside allowances for illegitimate children were stopped once they reached seven. If the mother could not support the child, then the only alternative was for the child to enter the House. In a further bid to cut the costs on out-relief, payments also ceased to needy families when a child reached eleven. These too had to become inmates of the House. In the case of a family where the father had been found guilty of a crime which carried the sentence of transportation, the wife was given out-relief for herself and children under the age of ten but those over that age had to come into the House.

The age limit on allowances changed again in the next few years. In 1836, the newly widowed Mrs Clark of Stratford St Mary had been left with six children, the youngest just two months old. The Guardians allowed her 3/3d. week, 1/- for herself and 9d for each of the younger children (that would have been three of them.) However, when they reached ten, the 9d was dropped and the child should either find work or come into the House.

*"The Act does not oblige you to be confined in any particular Parish because the Child follows the Settlement of the Mother till 16 years of age. The putative Father cannot be called upon till the Child is born – if relief is required it must be for the Child, (the Mother bearing the expenses of the confinement) the application must then be made to the Parish and the relief offered will be the Workhouse, should the Mother refuse that, there is no further claim upon the Father as the Parish are the only Plaintiffs."* (Printed notice on the inside cover of the 1841 Minute Book.)

One of the areas that changed with the introduction of the New Poor Law in 1834 was the attitude to women who had illegitimate children. Where, in previous years, putative fathers had accepted that they must pay for their offspring, it now became incumbent upon the woman to produce definite evidence that would prove who was the father of her child. This was by no means easy to do as Fanny Trollope demonstrated in her novel **Jessie Phillips.** Jessie, a poor but highly respected young woman in her community, fell in love with a rich man's son and believing he would marry her, she gave in to his demands and ended up pregnant and in the Workhouse. This was a familiar theme of many novels and plays of the mid nineteenth century. How could a young woman prove who her lover had been, especially if, as in the case of Jessie, the young man had always taken great care to make sure that their meetings were in secret and that when they were in the same company, he had studiously shown no interest in her whatsoever?

In 1838, thirty or so years after Anne Candler had finally managed to quit the House of Industry, her granddaughter Clarissa Lambert was admitted to it with a child prior to the birth of a second one. A note in the Minute Book states that Clarissa's mother may take out the first child to live with her if she were willing to provide for it. A further note states that Clarissa, when examined on the subject, had been unable to provide sufficient evidence for the Guardians to pursue for a maintenance order. (It was sad to discover that Clarissa spent the rest of her life in and out of the House. For a time she acted as housekeeper to her widower father but she ended her days in the House, labelled in the 1851 census as an 'imbecile.')

"Elizabeth Humphreys was ordered to be received into the House having no place of residence (and being pregnant) her father having turned her out and refused to provide for her." The names changed but down the years even into the late 1930s the House provided a shelter for the outcast woman and her child. Again, as time went on certain rules regarding unmarried mothers seemed excessively restrictive. At one time a mother who had found employment outside might leave her baby in the House until such time as she could have it with her. However, she was expected to contribute towards the child's upkeep from her earnings. It may be that this system was abused and that once they had left child and House behind them, some mothers simply disappeared. To overcome this a new rule insisted that when a single mother left, she took her child with her. This could be self-defeating as was shown by the case of Susan Bond. She applied for her child to be admitted as she was in danger of losing her job. The Guardians turned down her application even though she produced a letter from her employer stating what a good and valued servant she was. The Board stated that they no longer gave out-relief for 'Base' children and that if she could not support the child then both of them must come into the House. What is particularly interesting about this case is that Susan's employer had been Thomas Churchyard, the Suffolk artist who lived at Melton. His letter spoke warmly of Susan and the fact that he and his wife were willing to have her return to them shows, I think, that they did not regard her as a 'fallen woman' to be cast aside. Why, I wondered did they not allow Susan to bring the baby back with her or try to find a foster home for it nearby. Once one starts asking questions like that, one is off into realms of historical/romantic fiction!

By the late 1830s the current Governor of the House, Mr Catchpole, was trying to find methods of occupying the large number of children he had in his care. We read that he was given permission to buy in large quantities of worsted for the girls to knit up for outside sale while the little boys were to be employed in knitting stockings for the use of the inmates. This Governor had also "introduced several branches of employment for industry among the larger classes of the boys." Unfortunately, we are not told what these new initiatives were, neither do the detailed plans that he was asked to lay before the Board appear in the Minute Books. But more and more pressing was the need to find employers for the 'larger classes of boys.' There was always a steady stream of requests for lads to go to sea. Mr Hughes of Barking dropped a note to say that he was in need of two boys and that when he was next in Harwich he would call at the House to select a couple of suitable candidates. But April 1841 brought a letter that offered far-reaching prospects. The Chairman of the Board, John Gosnall told his fellow members that Mr George Hozier of 3 Sussex Place, Regent's Park, London was seeking to recruit four to six boys to work for him in Jamaica. Mr Hozier was at that time fitting up an Orwell steamer to add to his fleet and he indicated that he had heard very good reports of the standard of boys from the Samford Union. The positions he had to offer included millers, bakers, engineers, planters, warehousemen, porters or seamen aboard one of his cargo vessels that plied between the islands of the Caribbean.

After much discussion, Catchpole, the Governor, was ordered up to London to meet Mr Hozier and weigh up the prospects.

He duly reported back to the Board his belief that the potential was there for the boys to make good. Six boys aged between thirteen and sixteen were selected and the indentures that would bind them until they were twenty-one were drawn up. These promised that they would be given good food, lodgings with separate beds and medical attention when needed. The opportunity to earn up to £10 per annum was there if they worked well. On the 24 June, James and Samuel Cook of Capel St Mary, William Mudd of Woolverstone, Edward Goodridge of Wenham Magna, John Crisby of Washbrook and George Steward from Sproughton set out for London accompanied by the Clerk. Each boy had spent more than a year in the House and was either an orphan or had been deserted by his parents. Most, if not all of them, had probably never been outside the small area that made up the Samford Hundred. To travel to London by coach would have been a tremendous adventure, so what must have been their feelings about their ultimate destination, Kingston, Jamaica? There they would join the firm of Atkinson Hozier and Co. run by Hozier and his partner Charles MacGregor.

Each boy would have taken with him, besides the new outfits purchased for them by the Guardians, a personal gift of a Bible and Prayer-book. For most of them, this may have been the first thing that had ever truly belonged to them and as such was highly prized. Quite apart from the spiritual comfort the two volumes brought, they provided a source of education and challenging reading material. By the mid nineteenth century, the evangelical wing of the Church of England was taking its duty of educating the young very seriously and was responsible for initiating schools for the poor in both town and country. The present school in Tattingstone dates from 1841. Within the House as we know, both the school master and mistress as well as the chaplain had responsibility for ensuring that the children were instructed in the precepts of the Anglican faith. So well did they now perform this duty that fifteen girls from the House were presented to the Bishop of Norwich for confirmation on 14 May 1841. The service was held at the parish church in East Bergholt. So impressed was his Lordship on the conduct and appearance of the candidates that he wrote to the Board to compliment them. Not only that but to each of the girls, Mathilda James (15), Mary Norton (15), Joan Woollard (19), Sarah Banham (18), Sarah Cuthbert (14), Sarah Howard (15), Eliza Robinson (16), Elizabeth Hobart (14), Ann Worledge (14), Mary Mee (15), Rebecca (15), Sarah (14) and Louisa (13) Death, Eliza Hick (14) and Unisee Steward (14) he sent a personally inscribed book as a memento of the day. One cannot help feeling that this must have been a tribute to the Matron, Mrs Catchpole that she had made sure that the girls were all neatly and cleanly turned out. Among those listed we have Unisee (Eunice?) Steward whose brother George was soon to go to Jamaica and Elizabeth Hobart whose father had been transported to Australia in 1838 leaving her mother with six children, the eldest of whom was Elizabeth, to seek shelter in the House.

Originally from Stratford St Mary, the family had been living in Hadleigh at the time of Hobart's sentence and had had to seek help from the Workhouse at Semer. However, after three weeks there, under the Act of Settlement, they were returned to Stratford and thence to the Samford House. The Samford Guardians found themselves liable for costs to Semer of £2.15s.1½d. for their maintenance and another 4s.6d to the Overseers at Stratford for expenses while they were there. That would have included their transport costs. It is worth noting here that often it was the families of transported prisoners that suffered most. Many of those who were sent out to Tasmania and mainland Australia were able, once they had served their sentence, to start a new and sometimes prosperous life with a second wife and family.

With the introduction of the 1834 Poor Law came more and more centralised supervision. This was to pervade all areas and in 1851 we have evidence that those who undertook teaching within the House were now to be both properly qualified and adequately paid. At that time the school master was twenty-one year old William Mayer but he resigned, not because he was not properly qualified but because he wished "to devout himself to missionary labour among the Jews." Although most of us are aware of the activities of nineteenth century Christian missionaries in countries like India and Africa, or wherever Britain had a strong commercial interest, the work in this country of The Society for the Promotion of Christianity among the Jews is less widely known. There was a very keen local branch in Suffolk where annual meetings were held in the Town Hall in Ipswich. The Revd. John Charlesworth, father of the novelist was the first secretary of the Ipswich society in the 1830s. Another ardent supporter of the cause was the Revd. Charles Elliott, Rector of Tattingstone and it may be that he held meetings locally which inspired William Mayer to decide to become a missionary for the cause. Alternatively, having noted from the 1851 census that Mayer, (the name could be an Anglized version of Mier) was born in Bethnal Green, it may be that he was himself a Jew who had been converted. Suffolk had had a sizeable Jewish community but the success of the conversion programme had seriously depleted those who still actively attended the synagogue in Rope Lane.

Mayer was succeeded by Daniel Ray on three months trial. He did not last that long. The Inspector of Schools who came to observe him not only refused to recommend him for certification, he pronounced him as incompetent. So once again advertisements had to be placed in the **Ipswich Journal** and the **Suffolk Chronicle**. Charles Cowen became the next holder of the post.

Some fictional works of the period might lead one to think that once an inmate had left the House, particularly a young person, then the Guardians ceased to have any interest in him or her. This was not so. Take the case of Harriet Scrivener. Originally from Copdock, Harriet had been sent into service with a Mrs Fallows of Ipswich. After the Fallows' household moved to reside in Cambridge, 'friends', possibly the girl's relations, wrote to the Guardians saying that Harriet had complained of unkindness and ill-treatment from her mistress. The Board took the complaint seriously and ordered the then Governor, Alloway, to go to Cambridge to investigate the matter. At the next meeting of the Board, Mr Alloway reported that he had seen Mr Fallows but that Mrs Fallows was away from home in consequence of her ill health. Mr Fallows had offered no objection to Alloway conducting a private interview with Harriet who, he declared, was very "servant-like in her person, clean and decent." Harriet had said that she had nothing to complain of and the house was very comfortable but – she would like to be nearer relations. Mr Alloway thought that on the whole he saw no grounds for complaint and recommended no action be taken. He also said that he had not mentioned the letter the Board had received to either Mr Fallows or Harriet. Quite how he explained that he just happened to be passing the door in Cambridge and dropped in, we are left to imagine.

The new schoolmaster, Charles Cowen seems to have undergone a series of problems. We learn that after Mr Alloway had resigned as Governor to take up the post of Keeper of Ipswich Gaol, Cowen laid a complaint to the Board about him and other members of staff. Infuriatingly we are not told what was the nature of the complaint. Cowen was, perhaps, a liberal in his approach to the children. In August of 1852 he asked permission of the Board to take the children to Harwich for a day's recreation. We are not told on what grounds the Board refused his request; maybe they felt it might smack of a lenient attitude to the paupers generally. On the 26th August came the report of Cowen being taken ill while on leave from the House. A peremptory letter was despatched to him on the lines of get back at once or else...! A week later it was noted that he was still off and seriously ill. Nothing more was said on the subject but a Minute of 4th November states that a John Smith has been appointed schoolmaster. In the interim, we must suppose that the boys were instructed by – or supervised at least, by a responsible male inmate.

For the girls, life went on as usual. One girl, referred to only by her surname was looking forward to leaving. Her older brother had found good work for himself in Liverpool and wrote asking to have her join him. The Board agreed but expressed some concern as to the method and expense of getting her there. As often happened, the Master was charged with the task; he was to accompany her to London and then put her on to the Liverpool train. As for the rest of the girls, there was something very new in store for them. The block that contained their privies had caused numerous problems since the House was first built – not least that it backed on to the boys and that holes were often made in the party wall! After seeking various methods to alleviate the problems, including a new building at the end of the female wing, the Board decided to introduce a water closet alongside those with soil pans. The tender for this work was £5.10.0.

At the end of 1852 comes a note that makes one realise that however harsh the regime might seem, there was compassion and humanity. Among the newly entered inmates was Jonathan Balaam who had a small son. The child had what we would now call a food allergy; he was unable to eat meat. Rather than jeopardise his health, the Board ordered that he should have bread and cheese whenever meat was served. Remembering how often this featured on the menu anyway, the poor child would have had a very monotonous diet but at least it shows that some thought was given to his plight.

There was, however, no consideration given to Henry Crampin who was the schoolmaster in 1860. The Master, Harman Harris, reported that Crampin had accompanied him to Ipswich (why we don't know) and while there the teacher had "indulged in his old vice of drinking to excess". Alas, when he had returned to the House he was intoxicated. The miscreant was called before the Board and severely reprimanded but, "in consideration of his years" he was neither dismissed from his post nor reported to the dreaded Poor Law Board (which now had overall supervision of the Union Workhouses.) There is no indication as to how old Crampin was but he hardly seems a suitable person to supervise the young. The Board, perhaps anxious not to have to find another schoolmaster, in addition to the reprimand, imposed a ban on his leaving the premises. That at least would keep him from the drink.

Neither was all well with the schoolmistress. In October 1860, His Majesty's Inspectors of Schools reported that he would be unable to renew the certificate for the female teacher unless the next report was more favourable, especially with regard to spelling and arithmetic. Like her colleague, poor Phoebe Card was called before the Board to be admonished. It is perhaps hardly surprising that she resigned the following year. Her place was taken by Jane Balls. By this time another development had taken place, the teachers' salaries no longer came from the Poor Rate budget but were paid instead from central government; the office of HM Postmaster General allocating the requisite payments to the Board.

The pages relating to the Union House in the census returns for 1861 have been badly torn so it is difficult to say how many children were in long term care at the time. That numbers were dropping may be why in December 1867, the Board considered a request from the Ipswich Workhouse to take in some of the 150 under sixteens that they had. While admitting some of the Ipswich overspill would bring them in some much needed revenue, the Board decided that they would defer their decision until they saw what the weather was like in January. Severe conditions could bring an influx of their own people with children. Eventually it was decided to offer places to thirty healthy, orphaned or deserted little girls at 4/- per week each for a trial period of six months. For one reason or another this venture never came to anything.

By 1871 it had become law for all children to attend school and follow the syllabus laid down by the State. The Board received various posters on the subject and within a year or so, children from the House were attending the village school in Tattingstone, conveniently placed, just across the road from the Union House. Although now freed from the expense of providing board and lodging for their own school teachers, the Union had to find the necessary school fees for each of the pupils they sent to the school. Although a statutory requirement, schooling was not free but the small weekly payment could be hard to find for some families. So, from this time on, the Out-Relief payments sanctioned by the Board are likely to include the specified amount for the local school. Section 10 of the Elementary Act of 1871 stated; "that in every case in which the Guardians should decide to pay the School fee or any part thereof and declare the money so paid to be given by way of loan to the parent of the child such money shall be considered as given by loan and recoverable in accordance with the provisions of the Poor Law Acts applicable to recovery of other relief given on loan." The Pittock family of Capel St Mary is an example of how this worked. Mr Pittock was a farm labourer earning 12s.6d. a week. Of his seven children none was yet working, so he made an application for the school fee of sixpence (6d) a week for each of four of them. The Guardians agreed to pay half, that is 1/- a week as a loan to be repaid at Harvest time, traditionally the time when farm labourers could expect to make really good money. In order to enforce the new Education Act, a new member of staff appears on the Accounts Book, namely the School Attendance Officer.

The Local Government Inspector who visited the House on August 1877 noted among other things that "there are five boys and four girls in the House who went to the neighbouring public elementary school but out of school hours they were in the charge of paupers who were not capable of efficient management of children." This was a bureaucratic understatement. It turned out that one of the girls was employed in the kitchen, the other three were left in the care of a mentally disturbed woman while the supervision of the boys was left to a very elderly man. The Board's response to this was to consider sending its orphan school age children to St.John's Home in Ipswich where they had a school on the premises. This would cost the Board 6/- a week for each child. This still left the children who came in temporarily. They continued at the local school and needed after school supervision. Another group that needed special care were those designated 'Idiotic and Epileptic' cases. The Board had lengthy discussions on whether or not a separate ward should be provided for these children. It was decided to adapt the furthest room over the Able-bodied Men's Ward into a temporary ward. Their care was to be given over to the Nurse who would be assisted by a suitable pauper. The Nurse managed to get an extra 10/- a quarter for this additional responsibility. Incidentally, the nurse Hannah Baskett appears in the 1871 census as being 78 years old. Strangely, ten years earlier in 1861 she was 73. Perhaps it is not surprising that by late 1874, we read that she has been relieved of her duties and was herself confined to the Sick Ward.

Among those who appeared on the 1871 census was a family of three boys from Sproughton with the unusual surname of Loom. George was thirteen and his brothers Oliver and Caleb were 11 and 9. Caleb comes to our attention in 1876 when just before his fourteenth birthday arrangements were made for him to be apprenticed to Charles Mee, a tailor living in Bramford. For the first year of his five year term, the Board was to provide him with clothing and pay Mr Mee 3/- a week for his board and tuition. In his second year, Caleb was to receive wages of 1/- a week; each year he would receive an increase of 6d, so that in his fifth year he would be earning 2/6. Caleb went off to Bramford, presumably on a trial basis while the Vicar of the parish was canvassed for his opinion of Mee as a suitable employer. The reference that came back to the Board was not favourable so Caleb was recalled to wait for a further placement.

As the century progressed it became clear to those in authority that there was a great need to provide some form of training for those children who might otherwise find themselves drifting into vagrancy. In Ipswich a charitable organisation had established an Industrial School for Girls and now the Local School Board was looking for suitable premises for its own scheme. In some areas of the country, the falling population within Workhouses had led to the Boards of Guardians seeking alternative uses for their buildings and Industrial Schools seemed to provide the answer.

The following proposals were laid before the Board:
1. That the Guardians let the Women's Wing and the playground attached to it and 2 ½ acres of land and all the bedsteads and bed-linen and furniture therein to the School Board for fourteen years terminable after seven years.
2. All repairs and alterations were to be at the School Board's expense who shall not be required to restore the same upon quitting.
3. The School Board to be allowed to make such alterations or additions, as they require so long as they do not interfere with the main building.
4. There shall be no communication between the two buildings and the School Board shall make a separate entrance.

5. The School Board to pay the Guardians £50 per annum rent.
6. The Guardians shall be willing to let more land to the School Board should it be needed.

Like so many of the schemes that the Guardians considered over the long history of the House, this one failed to become a reality. Certainly, the Board could have done with the income. By late 1888 the cost of maintaining a child in St John's Home had risen to £2.7.2. The Board had to consider the children's return to the House if they could not persuade the Ipswich Guardians to lower their costs. They must have come to an amicable agreement as the children were still there in 1890 when the Board met at St John's Home to consider the children's future. Under discussion were Fred Whiting (14), Alfred Powell (13), Lucy Skeet (12), Alice Whiting (10) and Alice Upson (11). All but the last were orphans. Fred had an aunt living in Hintlesham who would provide him with a home if he found work. Alfred's brother in East Bergholt was willing to take him in if work could be found. However, the superintendent of St John's was anxious that Alfred should remain at the Home longer as he was both small for his age and near-sighted. Lucy had an aunt in Freston with whom she was given permission to spend a week. Alice Whiting had an aunt in Hintlesham who might take her but on the whole, the Board believed that all three girls would be better off going to Canada under Miss Rye's scheme.

The settlement of pauper children in Canada had been going on for some years. Belief that it was better for them to be taken out of some of the worst Workhouses or off the streets of big cities and given a chance to develop in the wide open spaces of north America was the motivation of many philanthropists of the day. Healthy young boys were in demand in the various aspects of farming and girls were needed as household servants, nursemaids and ultimately, wives for the settlers. Maria Rye was one of those enterprising Victorian social reformers who determined to improve employment prospects for young women. After opening and successfully running employment agencies in London, from 1868 she devoted herself to the cause of recruiting girls for work in Canada. She set up a home for waifs and strays in Peckham where she trained girls in domestic work and then sent them out to 'Our Western Home' in Niagara from whence the girls were sent out to work. She received support from many of the leading reformers of the day but doubt was eventually cast on her financial operations.

The Samford Union had used her before. In 1873, the Board had been contacted by a Mrs Ogilvie who was, it would appear, acting as a local 'recruiting officer' for Miss Rye. For the sum of £12 a piece to cover their travel costs to Canada, she would take two orphan girls off their hands. The girls in question were eight year old Alice Baldry and Ann Howard who was nine. If they remained in the House until they were old enough to go into service, then they would cost a great deal more than £24. At first, perhaps reluctant to let the girls go so far, they politely refused Mrs Ogilivie's request, saying that they intended to send the girls to an orphanage in Bristol. No explanation was given for that decision but something made them look again at the idea of Canada and Alice and Ann were sent off to the London training home. Others were to follow them over the years. And it may have been a letter in 1890 from Miss Rye that sparked off the idea of using her services again. She had written enclosing a letter from a Maud Edleston who had been sent out to Canada in 1873 and now wanted to know something of her past history, in particular, her parentage.

Miss Rye saw the girls in April, approved of them and agreed to take them either straight away to sail in May or to join the party that would be leaving in August. Lucy Skeet had spent the week with her aunt in Freston who had complained to the Local Government Board that Lucy was too frail, being small for her age, to be sent so far away. The Guardians answer to this was that it was that very smallness that would prevent Lucy getting a job in service in this country. The assumption was that the good fresh air of Canada would help her develop. More convincing was the argument that her stepfather was a pauper inmate and that the rest of her relations were unlikely to provide her with a desirable influence. There seemed to be no drawback to Alice Whiting going but Alice Upson's mother

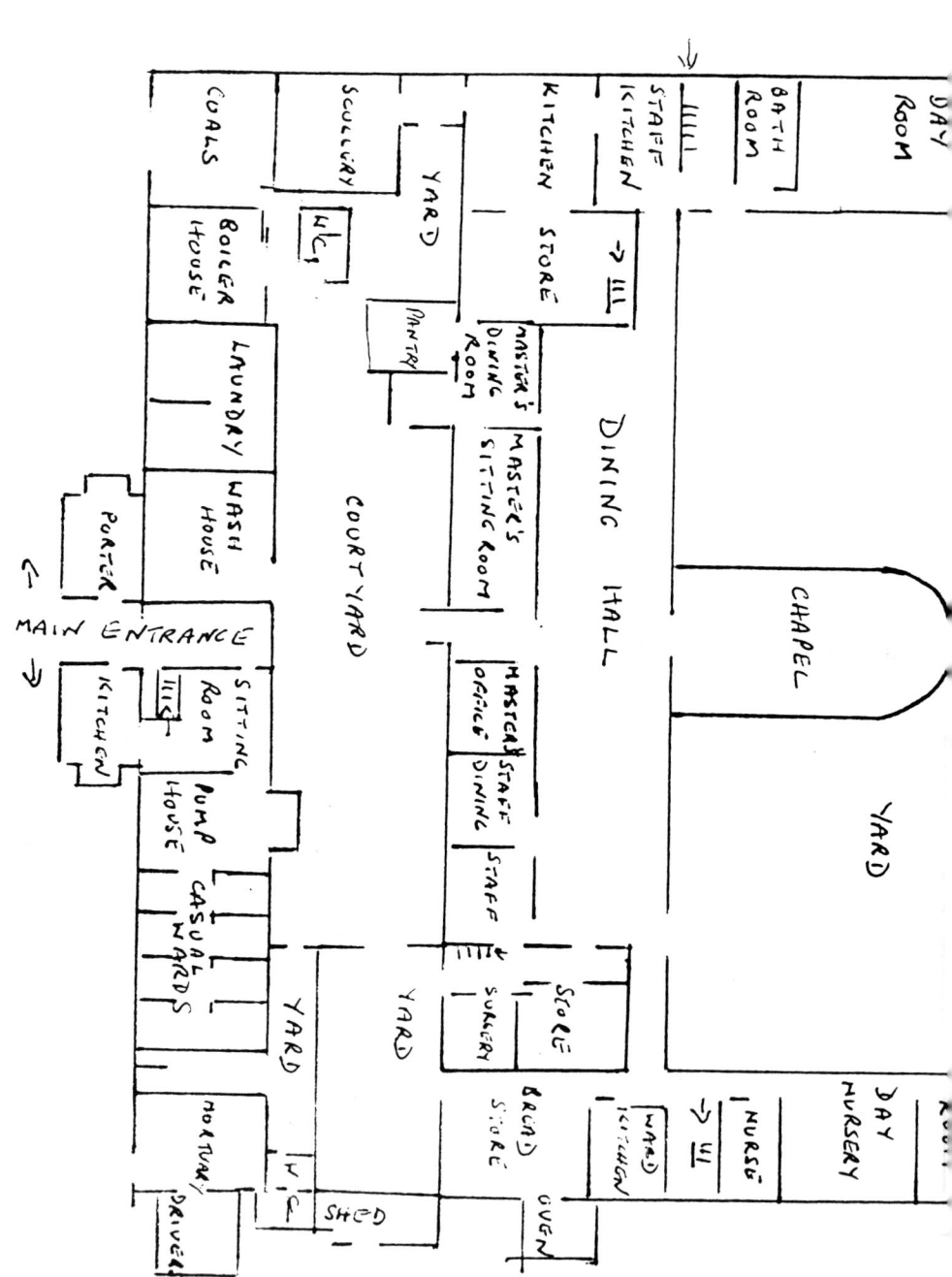

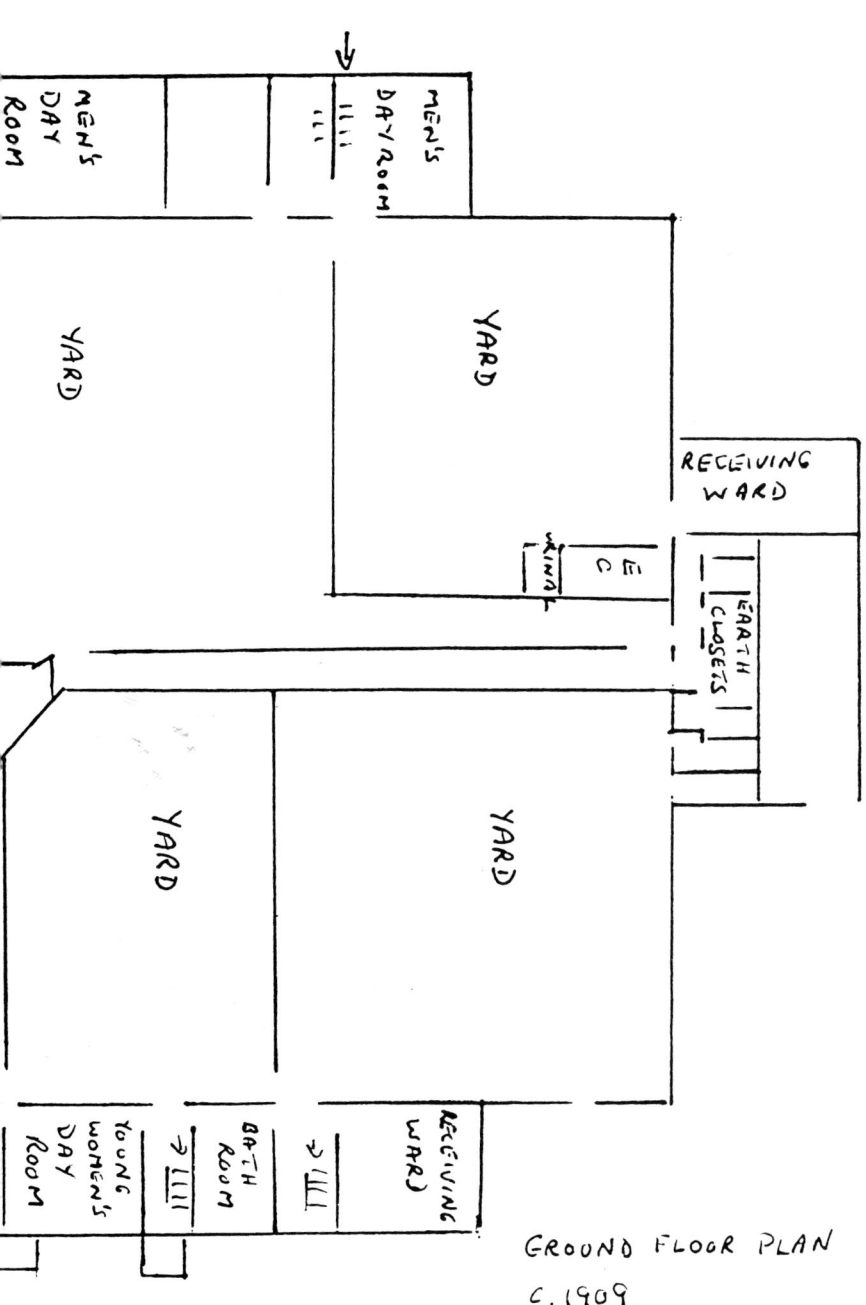

had a great deal to say on the subject. Her child might not bear a father's name but Mathilda Upson who was resident in the House with the rest of her children was adamant that her daughter was not going to Canada. Poor Mathilda, ever warm hearted, had managed to have a relationship with a fellow inmate, William Pettingale – not easy given the strict segregation in the House – the result of their liaison, young William Thomas was born early in 1890. Although Both Mathilda and Pettingale were severely reprimanded and lost all their privileges for a time, Mathilda does not seem to have been upset for too long. In 1893, she is again before the Board. One of her fellow inmates had revealed to the Master that Mathilda was in the habit of creeping out of the Women's Ward at midnight and making her way to the Porter's room. She was expecting his child within the month. Isaac Bush, the porter, forestalled any reprimand by resigning before the Board Meeting. However, when he was called before them he denied all knowledge of Mathilda's condition and said he was resigning to seek a better post.

For Lucy and Alice Whiting there was the excitement of going before the magistrates to sign the consent forms showing their willingness to migrate. Then they had thorough medical checks and were bought new clothes ready for the journey that started on the 13 August when the Matron took them up to London. Alice Upson on the other hand had to wait until October before she too went to London but for her it was into service with a Mrs Jackson. She was just eleven years old. What are we to make of the fact that now girls were starting work in service at an earlier age than they had a hundred years before?

In May of the following year a report was received from the Canadian Government Inspectors about Lucy and Alice. Lucy who was living with a Mrs Tidy in east Toronto was said to be well nourished and with a 'fair' intellect. Alice was with a family called Adams at St Catherine's. Her intellect was described as bright and she was attending both school and Sunday School.

Others followed them including Alice Howard and Louisa Gathercole. Six years after them, Fred Gathercole wrote to the Master asking permission to take his brother Henry out to Canada. I like to think that Louisa had kept in touch with her brothers and liked the country sufficiently to invite them to join her there. Henry, like all the other orphans was at St John's Home. The Master was ordered to visit the Superintendent and find out what fifteen-year old Henry was fit for and also to ascertain if Henry wanted to go. He did, as did his friend William Strange. Several others were deemed suitable to migrate under the auspices of the Waifs and Strays; the three Garwood children, Fred, William and Annie and Amelia Thrower. However, all was not plain sailing. In the following few weeks, Henry suddenly decided he wished to enlist in the band of the 4$^{th}$ Battalion of the Highland Light Infantry. Then, the Waifs and Strays Society was unable to comply with all the requirements of the Local Government Board, so everything was held up. As William Strange at 16 was well past school age he was promptly apprenticed to a farmer in Tattingstone. The other William was found to suffer from epilepsy so would need special care so that left Fred and Annie to go to Canada when the obstacles were finally sorted out.

Annie's ship was to leave on 20$^{th}$ July, Fred's on 24$^{th}$ August. Like their predecessors they went before the Justice of the Peace to give consent to their removal and they had a thorough medical check. Included in the Accounts Book are the costs for their clothes and travel arrangements. Older readers familiar with Ipswich may recognize some shop names.

| | | |
|---|---|---|
| Brand & Son | Outfit for Annie | 4.11. 9. |
| Martin & Newby | Boots & shoes | 12.10. |
| W.J.Walker | Prayer book | 2.10. |
| A.J.Shepherd | Railway to London & Proportion of Officer's Fare & refreshments | 10. 4. |
| City Clothing Co. | Outfit for Fred | 4. 2. 8. |
| | Prayer book | 2.10. |
| | Fares etc. | 1. 4.10. |
| | Total | £11. 7. 3. |

In addition the Board paid £22.0.0. for each child's passage money and maintenance. A further cheque for £6.17.8. had to be forwarded towards the cost of the annual inspection of them in Canada up to the age of 16. The first of these reports came in April 1900. Fred's stated that he was living with John May, Lower Melbourne, Richmond County where he was employed doing farm chores. He was said to be in good health. He was truthful and obedient, attended the local C of E church but at 14 was not attending school. He was paid £2.0.0. a month and had his board provided. The inspector added that he had been placed in a very good home and the boy said he had nothing to complain of. Equally, Mr May was quite satisfied with him. Just how far from him was Harrisburgh, Beverley Township, Brant County which is where Annie was with another farmer, a Mrs Robert Gray. She was employed in this "good home" doing general housework. Described as a healthy, robust girl, we are given the intimate detail that at 12 years of age, Annie weighed 104 lbs. She did not attend school but did attend the Methodist Church. She was said by her employer to be truthful and obedient. Mrs Gray found her rather tardy with her work, but nonetheless she was a very willing girl. She did not learn quickly but on the whole she was satisfactory. Annie liked both the place and the work she had to do and was treated well. She did not receive wages, only her board and clothes with which she was well supplied. It is doubtful that the inspector realised just how revealing her report was.

A further report was received in 1902. This time Fred was described as "a boy of very refined appearance". He was now earning a proper wage but remained with the May family who were said to be very fond of him. Thus, a very pleasing outcome for all concerned. Unfortunately the same could not be said for the now fourteen-year old Annie. The news came that Mrs Gray had sent her back to the Waifs and Strays Home in Niagara-on-the-Lake on 28 December 1901. The report from Canada continued: "The Matron had no suspicion anything was wrong otherwise than the girl being a little out of health. Upon being questioned she acknowledged, however, her unfortunate condition. Mrs Manning, the Visitor (for the Society) went to see the Grays twice and she also consulted the County Crown Attorney, who in the absence of corroborative proof, advised it would be hard to obtain redress. In the month of May, Miss Bayley placed her in the Salvation Army Rescue Home...I subsequently saw Annie at the Home. She has every comfort and the Matron expresses a deep interest in her general welfare and informs me that she will provide her with a place as a domestic servant when she leaves the Institution." Poor Annie. We had already been told she was a big girl for her age and not particularly bright, so she was an easy prey for whoever it was on the farm who had taken advantage of her. I suspect that many other girls sent out under the Society's scheme, found themselves in a similar position. In her case the Society made a further unsuccessful attempt to determine the paternity of her baby. Back at the Samford House, the Board directed that the Society should keep them informed and some months later they heard that Annie has been found a new job. But the story did not end there. Early in 1903 the Minute Book has a small note that as far as Annie Garwood was concerned "the only way to save her" was to send her back to England. One can only assume that she was either pregnant again or had fallen into "bad ways". There is no reference to the arrangements made for her return or indeed to her arriving back at the House; nothing that is, until 1907 when there is a passing reference to Annie and her illegitimate child. Of all the cases I read during my research, this one caused no little heart-ache. I imagined what it must have been like for the little girl to travel all that distance with the promise of a new and possibly exciting future ahead of her, her disillusionment at so young an age and having to return to the House 'in disgrace'.

By the beginning of the twentieth century, few children spent any length of time within the House. From the admission register of Tattingstone School it would appear that most of the children, some of them as young as three, who were enrolled by "Samford Guardians" stayed not more than a few months before they "left the House". In one or two cases, the family would move away, only to return some months later. Most orphan or deserted children of school age continued to be sent to a Children's Home (St John's) in Ipswich, where their progress was monitored by the Visiting Committee, in particular Miss Deane, who had joined the Board of Guardians. She also made it part of her responsibility to find good positions in service for 'her girls'. It was Miss Deane who requested that if a child from St John's went to a post which for some reason or another failed, the child should return to the Home while awaiting a new situation rather than being sent back to the Workhouse. But in 1907 there was talk of removing the children from there and housing them in 'Cottage Homes' or boarding them out locally. The following year plans were drawn up to build a pair of cottages for this purpose on the Workhouse Field facing the Church, probably on the piece of land next door to the thatched cottages. The idea never went beyond the planning stage as it was discovered that nine out of the ten children for whom they would have catered were soon to be released. Instead, those orphans who would have gone to St John's were boarded out locally and attended village schools.

Later, the Children's Home in Grundisburgh became an option. In 1975, Edgar Smith, who was then living in St Catherine's, Ontario recalled the time he spent there just after the First World War (1919). "I was only three and a half. I travelled from Tattingstone Workhouse with my two older brothers in a horse and carriage...There must have been about twenty children ranging in age from three to fifteen though a couple of the girls may have been older as they were kept there to help the Matron...Some of the children were orphans and so nobody came to see them. Mothers who were in Tattingstone Workhouse came to visit us about twice a year. When my mother came to visit me I saw the reason why I was in the Home though I did not realise it at the time. She had a baby in her arms."

Miss Deane then became chairman of the Committee for Boarded-out Children. To assist her in the task of visiting the foster homes she had three other ladies, Miss Boghurst and Mesdames Allen and Norman. Each had their own 'list' and each took responsibility for the children on that list. One of the main concerns of the ladies was that the children were not placed in overcrowded homes, so we read that one child was prevented from going to a home because the foster mother was already catering for two lodgers. That the Committee really had the best interests of the children at heart is shown in the case of a Mrs Gaunt of Hintlesham. She had applied to 'board' and Joan and Alan King were assigned to her. However, when the house was inspected, it was discovered that it contained just four rooms. Mrs Gaunt had three children of her own, one of them an invalid and two male lodgers. Joan and Alan were found alternative accommodation. Overcrowding was not the only consideration to be borne in mind when assessing the suitability of a foster home. During a routine call upon Mrs Pearson of Washbrook, it was discovered that both she and her home were perfectly satisfactory but, a slip-up had been made – Mrs Pearson was a Wesleyan and the children she was fostering were both Church of England. This was strictly against regulations. In this case, a compromise was reached, Mrs Pearson saying she would make sure that the children attended both church and Sunday school. On the whole, it looks as if most of the foster parents were widows (or deserted wives) who supplemented their family income with the fostering allowances. There were some homes where a husband was in residence and it was to such a one that Benjamin Whinney was sent in 1915, it being thought by both the Visitor and the local schoolmaster that he would be better off in a home with a man in it! Benjamin might have been in need of a firm hand but poor William Whittle was being brutally treated in his foster home. The Visitor discovered that the child was badly beaten, required to do unsuitable work and often kept locked up in an empty room for three days at a time. Such had been the case when the Visitor had called unexpectedly. The foster carer, a Miss Goodwin, accused him of stealing money, which it transpired, was only a few pence he had been given. It is heartening that the child was given an opportunity to present his side of the story though one assumes that the wheals from the beating must have been sufficient evidence. We are not told where William ended up but the offer of Mrs Cracknell of East

Bergholt to take him was rejected on the grounds that she was too old – she was 66 – and that her home was one and a half miles from the school.

Wherever the children were the Board of Guardians was still legally responsible for them and had to pay for their maintenance. And in those days before the setting up of what we term the Social Services, the Guardians were deemed responsible for many different aspects of life. In the case of young Fred Whittle whose mother was mentally incapable, the Board voluntarily took over parental rights for him and boarded him out in Bentley. But in 1916 they were made legal guardians of Alice, Dora and Henry Whidby when their father who had been declared a man of 'vicious conduct and mode of living' was stripped of all his parental rights. The children were placed in foster homes; nine year old Alice went to Capel St. Mary, and Dora and Henry eight and six respectively were lodged together in East Bergholt. Six shillings a week was paid for each child with a clothing allowance of 15/- a quarter. The children were able to attend the local school and have some semblance of a normal childhood.

The Board's responsibility did not necessarily finish once the child had left school. Neither did having connections with the Union House automatically bar a young person from either further education or the opportunity to enter the professions. Mary Gough, daughter of the erstwhile Relieving Officer for the Capel District had been in the Guardians care since 1905. She was obviously a bright and promising scholar but had not yet found employment when Miss Deane reported on her in January 1914. Too old at fourteen to remain in the Children's Home or to be fostered, Miss Deane had Mary's name down for a vacancy in the YWCA hostel. Meanwhile her brother Harold had been offered an apprenticeship in carpentry and while he was on a month's trial, he was to board at the Working Boys' Home. The following month we learn that Mary has been accepted as a pupil teacher at Capel School at a salary of 2/- per week until August. Thereafter her salary would rise to £10 per annum. The Board agreed to allow her 3/- a week until August and after that whatever sum might be necessary on top of her salary to support her.

With the Board's blessing and encouragement, it looked as if Mary was embarked upon a career that would more than provide for her in the future. Sadly that was not to be. In July of 1916, Miss Deane, who had continued to keep an eye on the girl, reported that Mary's health had broken down and she had been forced to give up teaching. The last we hear of her is that now she is sixteen she has to rely on Sickness Benefit plus further relief provided by the Relieving Officer.

Not only did the Board make their own arrangements for 'boarding-out' children from the Union, they also found themselves with yet another responsibility, that of examining the homes of prospective foster mothers in the area for other organisations. It came as a surprise to discover that a number of London based Societies for the care of unwanted babies, such as the Salvation Army and the Waifs and Strays as well as private agencies, recruited foster parents in the countryside. Records of all placements had to be kept and periodic checks made on the welfare of the children. If things went wrong, then the Union could, quite literally, be left holding the baby. This happened in November 1916 when a Mrs Bennett from Stutton complained to the Guardians that the father of little Frank Palin had not sent any money for him. Ben Palin of 22 Applemarket Street, Northwick was a munitions worker, so he should have been well able to pay for his child's keep. Since Mrs Bennett could not afford to keep the child, the only option open to them was to take the child into the House while they pursued the father for the arrears. Towards the end of January we read that little Frank has been taken by the Union nurse to his father. Mr Palin had sent £3.0.0. to cover the travelling expenses which, in fact came to £3.4.0. In addition he was committed to pay back maintenance at the rate of 5/- a week. (Incidentally, there are three Northwicks; the one in Gloucester is north of Bristol and Avonmouth, the Somerset one is close to Burnham-on-sea and the third is just north of the city of Worcester. Whichever it was, involved a long journey for the woman and child.)

That prices were rising during this time of war is shown by another case a month later. A widow who had been left with three young children applied to the Board for Out-relief. The Board in their wisdom decreed that two of the children should be sent to the Home for Waifs and Strays. This would be at a charge of 3/- per child. The Home had other ideas; they wanted 8/- for one child and 10/- for the other. Eventually a compromise was reached at 6/- for each. And in 1918 the clothing allowance for boarded out children had risen to 20/- a quarter.

By 1920 the Board was paying 12/6 weekly for each child boarded with the Waifs and Strays and St Andrew's Home while for those under sevens who were boarded out in private families the payment was 7/6 plus £1.0.0 for clothing. Some children cost the Board a great deal in one lump sum as happened in the case of Robin Edgar Briggs from Chelmondiston. The Board was asked to pay half his fees at the National Industrial Home for Crippled Boys so that he might learn tailoring. The Guardians agreed to the sum of £39.0.0 per annum plus incidental expenses. Although the Board did its best in finding suitable placements for its physically handicapped children, there came a time when the mentally impaired child was too old for an establishment that catered only for those under sixteen. For these there was no place except the House.

One girl whose name appeared regularly in the Accounts was Florence Parrish from East Bergholt. She is first mentioned in 1927 when the Guardians contributed towards sending her to a 'Special School', provided her with a surgical boot and also paid for her to have hospital treatment at a cost of 6/- a day. Her mother was asked to contribute 5/- towards Florence's maintenance. The following year, Florence has been settled in a Hostel for Crippled and Invalid Women Workers at Denmark Hill in London, for which the Board paid 25/- a week. Later that year in May, Florence needed alterations to her leg irons, so in came a bill for 7/6d., followed by one for 9/- for three pairs of stockings for her and 10/- for the fare for her holiday. In July she was sent for three weeks holiday at Westcliff and the Board was asked for 18/8d. for the fare. In 1929, she needed a new coat and dress and further alterations to her leg iron. Then she had an accident and had to be conveyed to Croydon Hospital by ambulance, the bill being paid by the Guardians and in October she was sent to St Luke's Hospital in Lowestoft to convalesce. It would have been interesting to follow Florence's subsequent history but that was not to be as the last entry for the Union House, as we had come to know it, was made on 27 March 1930.

# VII

"In future all male inmates (except the able-bodied) who may desire it and whose conduct is such that **the Master considers them deserving of the indulgence** be allowed tobacco to the quantity of one ounce per man per week." **Samford Minutes 1892.**

With such a disparate group of people gathered together under one roof it was essential for the smooth day-to-day running of the place that a code of conduct should be drawn up. When that code was breached in any way, then the wrongdoer had to be punished. We accept this practice in our daily lives so we must beware of thinking that the Workhouse was necessarily more punitive than other establishments dependent on strong discipline for the common good. It is, perhaps, the fault of fictional representations that we tend to think of all the inmates as weak and submissive, browbeaten to conform by the harsh treatment meted out by the Workhouse Master and his staff. That some Masters may have been sadistic, I have no doubt, but neither, by any stretch of the imagination, were the inmates all paragons of virtue. They were human beings; capable of losing their tempers and letting their fists do their reasoning for them in arguments, an action that applied equally to both men and women. They could harbour resentment and petty jealousies, they could be trouble-makers who stirred up those around them, in fact they could, without proper controls in force, easily turn into an angry mob resistant to any restraints the Master and his meagre staff might attempt.

One of the ways that the authorities attempted to keep temptation under control was by the splitting up of the various groups. Keeping men and women apart removed the opportunity for sexual tension as well as promiscuous behaviour – and the resultant increase in the infant population. Then within the groups there was further division of the unmarried from the married, the elderly and infirm from the able-bodied. Similarly, the children were divided by age as well as sex.

In the beginning the behaviour that would merit punishment was that which would upset the common good. Profane cursing and swearing, acceptable to a few but not to the majority was not to be tolerated. Neither was indecent or disorderly conduct. This could take many forms and indeed one of the grievances of mothers of teenage girls was that their daughters were in danger of being morally corrupted by having to share quarters with prostitutes and camp-followers. Neglect of or refusal to do the work that was set for the inmate, providing it was suitable to the person's age, strength and ability, could also be grounds for punishment. And in the early years of the House, it was usually sufficient to curtail food for a period of not more than twelve hours. The more hot-headed miscreant might be put into solitary confinement for the day.

These curtailments seem to have worked for some time but eventually, it was found necessary to introduce the stocks. This was both deterrent for the malefactor and a warning to others and to that end the stocks were set up in the Dining Hall where everyone might see. We should bear in mind here that during the latter part of the eighteenth century and the early nineteenth, the number of indictable offences generally had grown to enormous proportions. Many of these 'crimes' now seem negligible, yet in 1839 the Master was left to administer punishment to William Day who while out working on the land went into a neighbouring field and stole some peas. The argument that he was hungry would not have brought any sympathy.

1849 saw the introduction of a Punishment Book. Inside the front cover appeared the injunction, "The Master shall keep a Book in which he shall duly enter – Firstly, All Cases of Refractory or Disorderly Paupers, whether Children or Adults, reported to the Guardians for their decision thereon. Secondly, All Cases of Paupers whether Children or Adults, who may be punished without the direction of the Guardians, with the Particulars of their respective Offences and Punishments."

From the cases reported therein it is possible to gain some insight into the attitudes of both inmates and management. In the early years the most common punishment was to have "beer stopt" for a week. However, Thomas Cundy aged sixty did not respond to this punishment. Twice during September 1849 he wilfully destroyed his coat, waistcoat and trousers. When, in December now in possession of a third set of clothing, he tried to destroy that plus his shirt, the Master lost his patience and put Cundy on to bread and water for twelve hours. Today, we would recognise that the man was suffering from a form of dementia. Another problem with the older men in the House was that they were often used by the younger, able-bodied ones to act as go-betweens in attempted liaisons with the female inmates. Poor John Nunn, aged "between 67 to 70" had his beer allowance stopped for fourteen days when he was found conveying love-letters. It is distressing to report that these letters were intended for women in the psychiatric ward, then referred to as the Bedlam.

Without doubt, some of the inmates were born troublemakers – or people with spirit - depending on one's point of view. One such was twenty five year old Ann Beales. The 1851 census reveals that Ann was a single woman and that her brother Samuel was also in the House. Samuel was thirty-two at that time and his occupation was given as a tailor. They had both been born in Capel St Mary. Since no occupation is noted for Ann it is likely that she had kept house for her brother. She first came to the attention of the Guardians when she refused to work. For this she was reprimanded. Next she attacked a fellow inmate and followed that with threatening behaviour to the

Porter's wife. Her punishment was to be confined to the 'Lock-up' for ten hours. Quite where the 'lock-up' was situated is uncertain. In 1900 there is a reference to miscreants being shut up in the bell cage in the tower for several hours.

Refusal to work was most common among the young men and women in the seventeen to twenty-nine age group. Persistent refusal led to an appearance before the local magistrate who was most likely to pass a sentence of fourteen days 'hard labour' in Ipswich gaol. It is while following the adventures of Ann Beale that we learn of the work that had replaced the spinning and weaving of the old days. In 1852, Ann is brought up before the Master on three charges. The first was theft. She had stolen some copper coins from her fellow inmate Rebecca Death and a handkerchief belonging to the Cook. But it is the second and third charges that are more interesting, the one being that she refused to pick oakum and the other that she persisted in her refusal to do this. 'Picking oakum' is one of those phrases that crops up in Victorian novels where poor luckless prisoners are condemned to spend their days in this pursuit about which we may not be entirely sure of what was involved. In fact it was a nineteenth century form of re-cycling. Rope making was a very important industry that depended largely on imports of hemp from India or sisal from America. Shortages created by wars or tariff problems meant that valuable new rope could no longer be used for caulking, a process of using rope fibres and melted tar to stop up the cracks in wooden ships to prevent leaking. Instead the fibres from small ends or bits of reclaimed rope such as that washed up on the coastal beaches were teased out. This was a wearisome business that resulted in very sore fingertips. Inmates of both prisons and workhouses were given balls or bundles weighing about 1½ lbs. It was expected that at the end of the working day there should be no more than six ounces of material left that could not be used but occasionally we read that a pauper was found guilty of "wasting oakum", that is not persisting in getting as much as possible out of the bundle. The punishment for that was to have only bread and water for dinner. In Ann's case, she got not only the bread and water but a period of solitary confinement also. On occasions a miscreant would have his or her leisure time curtailed and be condemned to another session picking oakum.

It must, at times, have been very hard for the Master to maintain control especially when someone had returned from leave of absence – probably a man out in pursuit of a job – both dejected and totally drunk. One case reports a man in such a state breaking six panes of glass and two door panels. Another is described as wilfully breaking twenty-three squares of glass, which is quite a fair number of windowpanes. Such behaviour could endanger the lives of other inmates but it was also likely to inflame passions and incite them to 'insubordination' as the Punishment Book has it. One man did this by deliberately setting fire to his shoes and urging others to join him.

There was disobedience too among the school children. This ranged from the petty like "injuring the joints to the privy seat after being cautioned not to do so," to the more serious "entering the school and inciting girls to disobedience." On one occasion, fifteen year old Julia Barker of Wenham was "saucy and disorderly" in class. Having been reprimanded for this she took her revenge and locked the poor schoolmistress (and they were usually young women in their early twenties) in her bedroom. Julia then locked herself away, refusing to come out; when she was finally retrieved she was extremely insolent and ended the day by throwing her bowl of pea soup at the schoolmistress.

The boys were no better. Those privy seats were obviously a great attraction and one young man who damaged the seat in the Young Men's Privy while endeavouring to get through to the Young Women's facilities and removing their privy seat, ended up serving six weeks hard labour. One may smile now but at the time such episodes just meant more expense for the Board. More serious were the fights that broke out. The Powling brothers were not yet in their teens when they bit the lip of William Grimwood and struck Charles Plumb with a board causing a serious cut to his eye. And just for good measure they broke a window too. Perhaps it was a younger Powling who was inattentive in class, rude and insolent and threw his slate at the schoolmistress saying he would not do any more work for her.

The picture of the gentle down trodden pauper is belied when one reads of the twenty-three year old man whose catalogue of misdeeds included stealing someone else's leather gaiters and striking another man. He was then found washing out chamber pots in the "clean" pail, the one containing drinking water. He followed this up by urinating into the tub used for hand washing. He swore at and assaulted the Porter's wife and then went on a spree picking up large stones, which he then threw down into the privies. He also closed all the ventilators in the privies. His final gesture was to threaten the member of staff who remonstrated with him that he would 'knock his two eyes into one'.

Sometimes, when reading the reports made to the Board by the Master, Harman Harris, one cannot help wondering if he unwittingly stirred up trouble. It would be fascinating to know what was the exact cause of the trouble that occurred in 1867. The Master reported that during a search of the male wards, he had found 'house-breaking tools' said to belong to Henry Southgate and James Clarke. It appeared that the Master had "perused" some letters belonging to Southgate that had aroused his suspicions and so he had informed the police. The first question we might ask is why the Master was reading Southgate's letters in the first place. Had someone reported the men or was the Master following his intuition that something was afoot. We then have to ask what were these 'tools' and how did the two men come into possession of them. It was then revealed that Clarke was one of those who were constantly in and out of the House whenever he was out of employment. He was called before the Board, though not at that point to be accused of anything beyond trying to come back to the House on days when admissions were not taking place.

As the story unfolded, so it was possible to see perhaps, why the Master and Southgate did not get on. Although Southgate had been admitted with his children to the House, presumably because he could claim he had once been settled in the Samford area, he had, before he lost his employment, been Clerk to Maryleborne Workhouse. In other words, not only was he an educated man, he knew the workings of the Poor Law system as well as, if not better than the Master. Thus it was hardly surprising that Harris might be guarded in his dealings with Southgate who was resentful at finding himself in his present position caused by the desertion of his wife, leaving him to look after his five children, the youngest of whom was a cripple. Southgate took the allegations of the Master to the Board; in his view he had been wronged. One of the Board, Mr Wrinch tried to accuse Southgate of stealing his handkerchief – valuable items in those days – while in turn, the Master accused Clarke of stealing sheets from the House. The Board no doubt listened patiently before directing their Clerk to see the superintendent of Ipswich Police to ask for a detective to come to the House to see if it were possible to identify the sheets.

Nothing further was heard about this particular case but the following year, Southgate is again brought to our attention. With his expertise and knowledge he had written a letter of complaint to the Local Poor Law Board on his own and George Culpitt and Abraham Porter's behalf. He related that on the 2$^{nd}$ April, a Friday, the three of them had been given 3lbs of oakum to pick which, however hard they tried, they could not complete. The Master had had them arrested and taken to Ipswich where they were remanded to the county Gaol until Tuesday when they were examined in the Magistrates Court. The case was dismissed; the magistrates being uncertain whether or not the prosecution was invalid. Had the accused actually refused to pick the oakum? Furthermore, they felt it was cruel and unnecessary for them to have suffered four days' imprisonment when the Master need not have sent them into custody until the Monday. The members of the Local Poor Law Board were divided in their opinion on this case. There was a strong feeling among them that all three men were troublemakers.

Harris must have breathed a sigh of relief the next month when Southgate asked leave to go out to seek work taking with him his eldest son. The Board however decreed that he had to take three of the children, leaving the two younger ones who were unable to travel. Either he was unsuccessful in his attempt or he did not go as he was still in the House in August, as was Culpitt. In September they are again in trouble and were sent to the oakum picking room and expected to pick four pounds a day.

Southgate got his own back for this by taking up the cause of another inmate. He wrote to the Lords of the Admiralty to tell them of the plight of John Hazelton of Belstead. Hazelton was in receipt of a naval pension as a result of an accident on board HMS Princess Royal. According to Southgate, the former sailor, whose mind had gone, was semi-paralysed and incontinent, was not receiving any proper care. He wrote: " I ask you my Lords whether the Master of this House is fit to be so, to allow of treatment like this." He further accused Harris by stating that this was not the first case of brutality committed by the Master. The letter went not only to their Lordships, somehow it found its way into the press.

We are not told exactly what measures were taken by the Board but a month after the event, the daily family meetings that were permitted had been limited for Southgate and Culpitt to five minutes – and never together – and the porter had to be present when the family reunions took place. In January 1870, Southgate wrote to the Board complaining about these restrictions and an additional complaint that the Master denied him foolscap paper on which to write. By the end of April Southgate and his eldest son set out to find work and that was the last that was heard of them within the pages of the record books.

Occasionally there are references to members of staff who needed to be punished for some infringement. In 1839, George Wright, a pauper who was employed as shoemaker for the House and thus enjoyed certain privileges, was found guilty of behaving "improperly towards the Porter, committing an assault upon him." The Board reprimanded him thoroughly and recommended that during the following three months the Governor dealt with him "as a pauper". If Wright did not like that arrangement then he could quit his employment and take his wife with him, thus losing both employment and board and lodging.

Often it was the Porter who was in trouble. The nature of their job meant that at times these men could be over officious. In James Barker's case, it was while he was acting as Porter that he was found guilty of "improper language to girls." Too much to drink was the more usual crime of which porters were guilty. During George Garwood's reign, he was caught out drinking in a village alehouse after hours. The event might have gone unnoticed had not the village constable called into the house to remonstrate only to be forcibly evicted by the landlady's son. Naturally an official charge was laid and all those present in the house were duly noted.

Another one who had a problem with drink was Dougherty. On one occasion, after spending some off-duty time in Ipswich, he was so drunk that instead of alighting from the train at Bentley, he got carried on to Manningtree and consequently arrived back at the House much later than he should have done. Worse, however, was his treatment of some of the inmates. He was brought to book for his ill treatment of William Double. Poor William was born in the House and since he was mentally retarded, he never left. Mr Adams who farmed the House's land witnessed Dougherty knocking William about the head and William Page, a farm lad testified that he saw the porter push William down and kick him five or six times. Dougherty received the statutory one month's notice but his replacement did not stay long either. He too was dismissed for drunkenness.

A fondness for the bottle was not confined to porters and schoolmasters. In 1895, complaints were received from the Master, the Matron, the Nurse, the Porter and the Relieving Officer that Dr Fleming often turned up drunk. The Board had no option but to ask for his resignation as surgeon and physician to the House and Medical Officer for the Holbrook District. Sensibly, he agreed though this must have meant a considerable reduction in his income. We are not told if he continued with his private practice.

We are left to draw our own conclusions as to why the porter in January 1918 was given instant dismissal. The record simply states that it was for bad conduct. However, there is no doubt about what happened in 1928, when the Labour Master who was responsible for the daily work carried out by the inmates was reported to the Guardians for "violent behaviour". It was said that he threw knives and kicked anyone in his way before he forced his way into the Master's office.

Crimes of a sexual nature were bound to happen. In 1924, an elderly man was caught exposing himself to little girls on their way to the village school, and in that same year there was another case of a man carrying on a liaison with a woman who was a certified lunatic. Not only had the sixty-four years old been passing letters to her, he somehow managed to get into the women's quarters to meet her. And frequent too, are the references to young men scaling the walls to get into the women's yard and that in spite of the walls being raised and spikes added.

It was not just the House staff who were likely to run into trouble. Like the medical officers, even the chaplains were not immune to the reprimands of the Board. If one believed that those who died in the Workhouse were simply interred without much fuss, here then is a surprise. In 1905 the Revd. Walford was reported by one of the Board, Miss Deane, for failing to turn up in time for a funeral at the House. The funeral of Mathias Berry had been fixed for three o'clock in the afternoon and his friends and relations had duly arrived for the service. However, the priest failed to put in an appearance until 4.30 by which time some of the mourners had had to leave. Walford, asked to explain his behaviour, laid the blame upon the Master. It was customary, he explained, for a time to be fixed with the undertakers just after the death but there was always the possibility that the family might wish to take the body home, in which case, the chaplain's services would not be required. Thus he always awaited a confirmatory postcard from the Master that the funeral was still on. The day before this particular funeral, he had been preaching in the country and would normally have spent the night there. However, half expecting to hear from the Master he had returned to Ipswich but when the morning post arrived, there was no postcard! Thus he had assumed that other arrangements had been made. We must assume that when the Master realised that the chaplain had not turned up at three o'clock, he had sent a messenger, possibly on a bicycle, to the chaplain's home in Ipswich.

It was two years before the Master was able to retaliate with his complaint that Walford now held a service at 8am on Sundays, an hour that was inconvenient for both inmates and staff, presumably because it coincided with breakfast. The master's second complaint was that as the chaplain had now removed to the parish of Dallinghoo – and therefore become more difficult to contact – it was hard for him to arrange sick visiting and funerals. The Board were sympathetic to the Master's plaints and suggested to Walford that he should resign his chaplaincy. This he refused to do, changing instead his service times to 9am on the first and third Sundays and holding Evening prayer with a sermon at 3pm on the second, fourth and fifth. Every Wednesday he would say the Litany and give an address at 10am with ward visits immediately afterwards. And since he was so accommodating and the Board had no other fault to find with him, there was nothing they could do but accept that they were stuck with him.

# VIII

"The Guardians shall appoint one or more Visiting Commissioners from their own body: and each of such Commissioners shall carefully examine the Workhouse once in every week..."

From the very beginnings of the House in 1766, some of the Directors and Guardians had been deputed to take on the additional role of Visitor acting for the Guardians on behalf of the inmates. It was the Visitor's task to go into the House itself, as opposed to the Committee room, and see for himself what conditions were like for the inmates. The inmates were also to be free to take their complaints to the Visitors who would in turn pass them back to the full Board for consideration.

The system, like so many others, was formalised during the latter half of the nineteenth century so that in the extant copy of the Visitors' Book that dates from September 1870 we have the printed instructions laid out that require the Visitors to examine the House at least once a week; inspecting the most recent reports of the Chaplain and Medical Officer, examining the stores and affording, as far as was practicable, an opportunity for the inmates to make known any complaints they might have and then investigating those complaints. On each occasion a visit was made, the Visiting Committee had to consider the fourteen questions that were printed on each page.

1. Is the Workhouse, with its wards, offices, yards and appurtenances, clean and well ventilated in every part and is the bedding in proper order? If not, state defect or omission.
2. Do the inmates appear clean in their persons and decent and orderly in their behaviour; and is clothing regularly changed?
3. Are the inmates of each sex employed and kept at work as directed by the Guardians, and is such work unobjectionable in its nature? If any improvement can be suggested in their employment, state the same.
4. Are the infirm of each sex properly attended to, according to their several condition?
5. Are the boys and girls in the school properly instructed as required by the regulations of the Commissioners and is their industrial training properly attended to?
6. Are the young children properly nursed and taken care of and do they appear in a clean and healthy state? Is there any child not vaccinated?
7. Is regular attention given by the Medical Officer? Are the inmates of the Sick Wards properly tended? Are the nurses efficient? Is there any infectious disease in the House?
8. Is there any dangerous lunatic or idiot in the House?
9. Is Divine Service regularly performed? Are prayers regularly read?
10. Is the established dietary duly observed and are prescribed hours of meals regularly adhered to?
11. Are the provisions and other supplies of the quality contracted for?
12. Is the classification properly observed according to Articles 98 and 99?
13. Is any complaint made by any pauper against any officer, or in respect of the provisions or accommodation? If so, state name of complainant and subject of the complaint.
14. Does the present number of inmates exceed that fixed by the Poor Law Commissioners?

On the whole each item required a simple tick except for the variations in the number of inmates. In September 1870 there were 119 inmates while in February and March of the following year (the winter months when agricultural work was in short supply) this figure had risen to 166 and included three cases of smallpox. However, the local Committee could not afford to be complacent as there was always a Poor Law Commissioner to check that the Visitors work was being done correctly. In 1871, the Inspector's report was on the whole favourable but he did make strong recommendations that the Guardians should as soon as possible supply separate lavatories for the married women and for the "mothers of illegitimate children". He also recommended that wooden floors should be laid down in the schoolroom.

So did any of the inmates ever dare to complain? Or were they so totally browbeaten and downtrodden that it would be more than their lives were worth to say anything that might bring them to the notice of the authorities? There are a number of occasions when the Visitors highlight faults in the catering supplies. The Minute Book for November 1859 notes that the Visiting Committee had received complaints from the inmates about both the flour and the beef provided. Interestingly, the beef in question had been supplied by one of the Acting Guardians. In May of 1871 beef was again the cause for complaint being described as "so inferior, the Master is directed to return it to the contractor." Similarly on a number of occasions the bread served in the House or that supplied to the parishes for those on out-relief is of substandard quality.

It was the Visiting Committee who took note of what repairs most needed attention. Thus in 1889 they recommended that the cooking range in use in the back kitchen should be condemned and a new one purchased at a cost of £30 without delay.

During the early years of the twentieth century, one Visitor in particular, a Mr Marjoram, seemed to be very much 'the inmates' friend.' It was he who pressed for them to be allowed more liberty to go outside the House during free time. This may have been the result of pressure applied by the new inmates who had arrived in 1908. The sudden influx of paupers from the London borough of Edmonton must have had an impact on the existing residents and staff. The move for the men from an urban environment to the country must have been rather as it was for the evacuees during the Second World War. The men were so full of complaints that they were described as "dissatisfied and even dangerous". Apart from resenting the lack of opportunity to go out, they often complained that the food was improperly cooked. Their biggest grumble was that the weekly tobacco ration, which was given out on a Sunday, was not served to them until the evening. This apparently was the fault of the Porter. The Master issued the tobacco to him first thing on Sunday morning expecting him to distribute it as soon as possible. The position of Porter seems to have given some of the holders of that office, an undue sense of power. In some cases, the man might have been but one step removed from becoming an inmate himself, yet rather than being sympathetic to the plight of the others, he tended to abuse his position.

The Edmonton inmates won the battle of the tobacco distribution time and the privilege of being allowed out once a fortnight. We hear again of their dissatisfaction in 1909 when their complaint is directed towards the brick floors of the wards and day rooms which, they said, they found cold to their feet. And just for good measure they also drew attention to the fact that the puddings were not cooked properly. One wonders just how much better life had been for them in the House at Edmonton – or was it because they were troublemakers that the Edmonton Guardians had got rid of them?

Sometimes complaints to the Visiting or House Committee as it was also known came from members of staff about other members. Such was the case in 1919 when Nurse Hogan and Miss Tyrell accused the Matron of using improper language and abusive conduct towards both officers and inmates. The nurse reported that when an inmate fractured a leg, the Matron did not send for the doctor and the patient received no medical attention until the doctor attended in the ordinary course of events the following day. They also drew attention to the small amount of food being given to officers. The Board decided that there was insufficient evidence to substantiate the claim of negligence on the matron's part but they did take steps over the question of rations. Apparently during the cook's absence on leave, her relief had not provided a sufficient quantity of meat. To supplement this lack, an order was made for each officer to receive an additional weekly allowance of one pound of sausages.

There are no background details given to the case of Emma Fallows but as a result of her complaint to one of the Visitors, three Guardians paid an unannounced visit one evening to investigate her complaint about bathing. It may be that this was the same case that is mentioned in chapter V, where the nurse had behaved so badly to the elderly women over their bathing arrangements.

It is possible too, that the Visitor to whom Emma had made her original complaint was Mr Marjoram. He incurred the wrath of the Master on several occasions, mainly because he would come to visit on his own. According to the rules, the Visitors should come in pairs. Not only that, Marjoram, for obvious reasons, chose to visit when the inmates were having their meal. He would, according to the Master, talk to the inmates while they were eating and, even worse, in the Master's eyes, he would then go with the men into their Day Room to talk some more. Mr Marjoram had ignored the Master's request for him to leave the premises, so twice Mr Carter felt it necessary to complain formally to the rest of the Board about the Visitor's infringement of the rules. It may be that Carter who had not been long in the post was unhappy with what he saw as spying on him.

Mr Marjoram, however, was concerned only with the well being of the inmates and in 1921 he again raised the question of their being allowed to go out of the House on a regular basis. He recommended that those elderly men, no longer able to work should be granted more than the current one afternoon a week and a whole day once a month. Inequality of the sexes manifests itself here in so far as the women were to be taken out 'under supervision'. The elderly women were allowed the freedom to roam in the grounds but it was thought inadvisable for young women to have this privilege unless they were under strict supervision. It was reported that there were insufficient staff to undertake this. An eye-witness account of this period recalls that the old ladies, in their blue and white striped dresses and shawls were to be seen taking a weekly walk in a crocodile around the village.

Another complaint about food came in 1922 when the officers informed the Visiting Committee that they were being served chilled meat instead of fresh. The Master, who had been having problems in getting a cook at the time, retorted tartly that they really could not tell the difference when it was cooked.

Visitors unconnected with the Guardians had also been allowed from the beginning. Anne Candler mentioned that her friend Miss Firmin came to see her. An early report into the state of Melton House of Industry (before it became an asylum) notes that visitors wandered in and out quite freely. However, as the effects of the New Poor Law were felt, visiting times for family and friends of inmates – and staff too, did become more restricted. There is one case where an elderly lady asked permission to leave the House to visit family living near by. Her request was refused on the grounds that the family were perfectly able to visit her.

Other visitors had been welcomed into the House since the end of the nineteenth century. They came to bring gifts of fruit and sweets, tobacco and books at times like Christmas, Easter and Harvest festival. In 1915, for example, the public were invited to join the House for a Harvest festival service. A Colonel Adinsell, was particularly keen that the inmates should have access to newspapers and magazines. He supplied many of them and encouraged other members of the Board to do likewise. Mrs Adinsell occasionally brought in a concert party to entertain the inmates who, by this time, were mainly elderly. The idea of providing entertainment for the paupers had been initiated by an earlier Master, Mr Jarrold. He had a great love of music and was one of the first in the locality to own a gramophone. This was such a novelty that it is recorded elsewhere that in September 1903 he spent the afternoon at the village school where the children were entertained with "selections on his gramophone." The Tattingstone Fete Committee also provided entertainment. In January 1923 the Master reported that the Women's Institutes of Suffolk had sent a gift of eggs, cakes and oranges, thus beginning a tradition of WI care for the inmates that the local Institute carried on for many years when the House became St Mary's Hospital.

# IX

'Hark, hark, the dogs do bark,
The beggars are coming to town...'

"...as soon as practicable the Local Government Board should seek to obtain powers from Parliament to prevent the continuance of the unrestricted Immigration of Destitute Aliens into this country.
England is already overburdened with her own increasing population and the Immigration of poor foreigners seeking work cannot but impoverish her working classes. The imminent danger of these Aliens bringing with them the infection of cholera plainly calls for immediate action in this most important matter...legislation that will protect labour and the health of the Queen's subjects." **Letter from the Samford Board of Guardians 13 October 1892.**

The idea of the 'deserving and undeserving poor' is not, as one might think, a Victorian concept. The definition of a vagrant or vagabond is 'a wanderer, idle rover, a scamp or rascal'; in other words, one who *chose* to have no fixed habitation or steady employment was deemed to be idle and useless. Legal action against vagrants was first taken in the fourteenth century when under an act of 1349 it was forbidden for such people to be given alms. A later Act of 1388 introduced the idea that to receive aid, the wanderer must return to his place of birth. By Tudor times, the problem of roving gangs stealing from and menacing the law-abiding population was one that needed urgent attention. It was at this time that a distinction was made between the able-bodied and the impotent vagrant. The latter might earn some sympathy but the former could find themselves liable to punishment by branding, having an ear cut off or being bound into slavery for two years. Later, transportation became an additional option. Branding ceased in 1713 but other legislation against vagrants was not repealed until the early nineteenth century.

When the country went to war, as it did almost continuously during the eighteenth and nineteenth century, the army frequently had to rely on vagrants and vagabonds to swell the ranks. With very poor pay and living conditions, they were often the only manpower available to recruiting officers. But when the fighting ceased and they were no longer needed then the disbanded rabble once again took to the highways. A letter to the **Ipswich Journal** in February 1818 highlights the problem locally. The writer wished, he said, to "call attention to an evil of great magnitude existing and growing in this neighbourhood namely the increase in beggars…a greater number than usual of these unfortunate persons. Many of them young, hearty men, mostly professing to be Irishmen…The measures adopted in London (that is the refusal of alms) sends them to the country…An increase in crime is coincident with the increase in beggars…It is well known that unprotected females dare not refuse alms to the sturdy vagrant." The writer went on to remind readers that those who were considered to be impostors rather than bona fide poor travellers could be brought up before the magistrates and fined 10/-.

One of the effects of the Poor Law Acts of the 1830s was that the number of 'vagrants' was increased by the many newly unemployed who took to the road in search of work in different parts of the country. In 1839 the Samford Board of Guardians recommended strongly that anyone found begging in any of the parishes that made up the Union should be treated as a vagrant, brought before the local magistrate and then sent to the House.

John Glyde, writing in **The Moral Social and Religious Condition of Ipswich** in 1850 discusses the reduction of the town's

Poor Rate which would, he said, be much greater if it were not for vagrancy: *" The first thing to be mentioned is the enormous increase which, for several years, occurred in the number of vagrants. A meal in the evening, lodging and breakfast was provided at the public expense, for any person who thought proper to call at a Union House to obtain them. The certainty of receiving food and shelter tempted many to resort to a life of mendicancy; and thus that fund which should have been sacred to the necessities of the poor, was shared by the thief, the mendicant and the prostitute, who weekly crowded the vagrant ward, to the annoyance of those who, as **wayfarers**, were compelled by destitution to seek temporary aid"*.

Glyde may have taken note that in the years immediately before his report many of the vagrants were among those who caused trouble within the Workhouses. Having had their night's lodging and food, a number of them would refuse to do the work expected of them in return. 1846 was a particularly bad year for this type of rebellion not only in the Samford House but also in the several Workhouses in Ipswich. The **Ipswich Journal** reported that in one sitting, the local magistrate the Revd. George Capper of Wherstead sentenced Charles Littlejohn, John Curtis, Thomas Johnson, Thomas Woods, Thomas Syer and James MacDonald, all of the Tattingstone House to a fortnight's hard labour in Ipswich Gaol. Not only had they refused to work, they had destroyed the clothing issued them too. All of them were vagrants rather than bona fide inmates of the House. Remembering that the House was staffed only by the Master, Labour Master, Matron and Porter, the obstinate refusal of these six men to perform their tasks must have been intimidating. It is small wonder that the Master had to seek the help of the local magistrate.

By 1868 not only was there a further increase in the numbers tramping the roads but many of those who could actually afford to stay in the cheap lodging houses that abounded in the towns had found a way to circumvent the system and get free accommodation. They would leave what money they had in the lodgings and then go off into the countryside where they applied to the local policeman for admission to the nearest House. The year after, the Board tried to stem the influx by resolving that this practice of the police granting an order for a night's lodging and a meal should be stopped. Instead, all such applicants should be issued with an order to enter the House proper rather than the Casual Ward. In practice this does not seem to have taken affect for later that year we learn that all tramps wishing for overnight accommodation had to apply to PC Benham who was based at Tattingstone.

The Casual Poor Act of 1882 led to the Board arranging to have a portion of the building adapted for the reception of vagrants. Six years later we learn that tramps were to be discharged at 11am the day after their admission. They were expected to do some work before they went but the thinking behind letting them go before noon was that this would give them the opportunity to reach their next destination rather than their remaining for a second night. By 1892 the question of accommodation was still troubling the Board. The Master suggested the now redundant Brewhouse might become vagrant wards but on examination this was found not to be feasible so it looked as if they would have to patch up the original building as best they could. However, the Visiting Committee while on a routine inspection of the tramps' wards decided that the buildings next to the mortuary could possibly converted for around £20. This was then carried out, the area being turned into a series of small cells.

There was another alarming increase in the numbers seeking the one night's lodging in 1898. By that time, the tramps were being turned away from the House by eight o'clock in the morning, possibly, though there is no proof one way or the other, without breakfast. The result of this was that they then hung around the village begging. Frightened householders complained and the police were asked to make their presence felt in an attempt to warn them off. It was reported the following year that there was again a rise in the numbers of vagrants. The Board suspected that the newly appointed porter had not been sufficiently briefed as to the correct method of searching the vagrants and setting them to work. There was also a suspicion that the House was seen as an easy touch.

The Local Government Board came up with some ideas on how the Unions might deal satisfactorily with vagrancy. It was realised that if the Union were too severe on the tramps, then they would prey on the public's sympathy. In addition, if they made life intolerable for the vagrants then they would cease to use the Union and go instead to "those dens of crime" the cheap lodging house. John Glyde described the five common lodging houses in Ipswich in the 1850s. *"Four out of the five have large sleeping rooms, filled with stump bedsteads made of wood, having on them flock or straw beds. Upon these the vagrants of both sexes and of all ages sleep. Each bed is furnished with a pair of sheets, a blanket and a rug, which are frequently in the most filthy conditions. Ventilation of the rooms is entirely out of the question...Each lodger is charged threepence per night and before retiring must pay or be turned into the street. In most of the rooms there are eight or nine bedsteads; frequently three persons sleep in a bed, and married and single in the same room. No one is required to wash before going to bed, except those who may have been walking on a wet day, without shoes or stockings, whose feet have in that case to undergo the process of ablution. These houses are the receptacles for beggars, thieves and prostitutes, as well as for some poor creatures whose miserable existence compels them to lodge at the lowest possible cost. The police regard them as places where the dangerous classes are to be found."*

In comparison the Workhouse must have seemed like a palace. And it was recommended that conditions should be improved further; first by making all casuals have a bath on admission and then retaining them for the day following admission. The Master was allowed to use his own discretion on how he should treat special cases. The work given to male tramps was to include pumping the engines, digging on the Workhouse land, cutting wood and general labouring about the place and raising stone (for road repairs) on Union land when necessary. Oakum picking was only to be given to those who were troublesome or refractory.

The Board tried to carry out these injunctions but their problems grew and like many other Unions who felt they were under stress they subscribed to a petition to the government in 1902. Among the points they made was the particularly telling one that the admission of tramps to Workhouses promoted the spread of disease. They could have quoted what had happened in 1884 during a smallpox epidemic. They had already got three cases from Bentley in the fever ward in the House and there was another, a man in a cottage near the White Horse in Tattingstone who was refusing to come to the House, so there was every likelihood that the disease would spread even more. It was on the afternoon of 31$^{st}$ May that James Laughton and a fellow tramp arrived at the House for admission having come from the Lexden Union (Colchester). Mr Jarrold the Master saw him at the gate and at once noticed spots on his face. Demanding that Laughton remove his hat, Jarrold saw the telltale spots on his head and promptly isolated him. Dr Elliston confirmed the Master's suspicions the following day. Laughton said that he had felt ill while in Lexden and had asked to see the doctor there but he had been told he could not stop; he agreed with Dr Elliston that he had been 'hustled' on his way. What was even more disturbing was that by the time the tramp reached Tattingstone the disease was well developed so Laughton had probably infected those in Lexden, Braintree and all the other Houses he had stayed in since he had been in Oxford fourteen days earlier. The Vagrants' ward was closed for the time being but the episode highlighted a great problem.

Now a statement from the Bury St Edmunds Union notified them of the smallpox there and warned that tramps coming into east Suffolk could be carrying it. The Board like many others felt that Casual Wards were no longer fulfilling their original purpose, which had been to provide a night's lodging for the genuine traveller as he went from place to place in search of work. They asked too, to be given legal power to detain all habitual vagrants for up to 28 days as a way of containing infection and trying to break the habit of vagrancy. And to make sure that that habit was not ingrained in the next generation, they suggested that the children of vagrants, under the age of fourteen should be removed from their parents and placed in Industrial Schools where they might learn good habits as well as a trade.

That the problem was one that covered both sexes as well as children is borne out by the fact that when, at the end of 1903 a new Porter was appointed with his wife, as was traditional, taking on the position of laundress, she was given the additional role of Female Tramp Attendant. The Boards of Guardians across the country again petitioned the government, this time suggesting that they should look carefully at the system in operation in Belgium of forming labour colonies for the vagrants. In the Samford House fifteen hundred and nineteen tramps passed through the Casual Wards during 1902. The cost to the House was enormous. The Board questioned why the 'ticket' system had broken down. This needed the co-operation of all the Unions in the neighbourhood and Samford had actually never issued tickets, the Master merely signing those passing on to other Houses. The books detailing the casuals' movements were examined and it was discovered that a large proportion of them used the House when travelling between Colchester and Hadleigh and vice versa and Hadleigh and Wickham Market. Something had to be done. One suggestion was that more Police supervision might act as a deterrent. The Board resolved that the Master be requested to keep all tramps for two nights instead of the usual one and, to make life within the casual ward even more unappealing, each man would be required to pick the largest weight of oakum that was legally sanctioned unless the Medical Officer certified them unable to work. Finally, those who refused to work were to be prosecuted.

It did not take them long to put the last into action. Two tramps who refused to work were sentenced to seven days hard labour in prison. Things were becoming tougher. In the next case, the man in question was sentenced to fourteen days.

In an attempt to stop the spread of disease, measures had to be taken to disinfect the clothing of the casual traveller. It was reported to the Board that the best way to do this was hang the clothing in a cupboard that could be sealed and then heating formalin tablets over a lamp to produce a disinfectant vapour. The Board ordered the immediate purchase of the essential lamps and directed that a suitable cupboard or wardrobe be found for the purpose. So once they had been admitted to the casual ward, the travellers were stripped of their clothes, given a bath and temporary clothing to wear until their own were returned after fumigation.

The Local Government Board was supposed to pay a contribution for each passing traveller and it can be appreciated how necessary this was when one weighs up just how much the casual vagrants cost the House annually. Taking that figure of one thousand, five hundred and nineteen casuals for 1902, consider the expenses incurred in feeding, the provision of clothing and the staff to look after them. Conditions might have been rough but even the clean straw put down for bedding had to be paid for. Thus it is understandable that any tramp in possession of any money would be expected to hand it over as a contribution towards his keep. Word soon spread among the tramps of the Houses where this policy was in operation and so they took to hiding what belongings they had in holes in the hedgerows along the road leading up to the House. In Tattingstone small boys would wait and watch, so it was said, from the vantage point astride the white horse that is the sign of the public house of that name, to see where the tramps' little caches were made. So what the House did not get could be lost anyway to small pilferers.

1913 brought another rise in the number of vagrants. The Local Government Inspector recommended in his report that there should be provision for bathing other than in the receiving ward "which was considered unsuitable". It is not clear what this comment implied. Perhaps it was that the facilities were thoroughly outdated and there was no scope to improve them. More puzzling is the recommendation that "in order to prevent hardship or accident" there should be some means of providing warmth to the Casual Ward. One can understand the humane consideration of the need to provide some form of heating. But the use of the term 'accident' suggests a fear that the tramps were likely to start their own fire in order to keep warm.

The Great War brought some respite to the problem of vagrancy when in 1917 it was proposed that all casual wards should be closed for the duration of the war. This move came just after it had been agreed that Suffolk County Council would refund the Guardians 6d a night for each vagrant they lodged. However, one assumes that the closure of the casual wards was a sensible precaution against providing shelter for military deserters or enemy spies.

One would assume that following the war there would have been an even bigger influx of those using the casual wards. This may have been the case but there are no further references to vagrants in the Minute Books.

# X

'Taint the vittles or the fustian
Or the leathers I so mind,
'Tis my Betsey and the padlocks
And the old ways left behind.

When at night I lie so lone-like,
Do I know where Betsey be?
Somewhere down a mile of passage
But her face I seldom see.

Save on Sundays 'cross the chapel
'Mongst the other women stowed.
When I sight her nodding t'wards me
Thinks I, I must shriek aloud.

Parson he aint half a bad 'un,
Gov'nor, he is always civil,
But my Betsey and the padlocks,
Make me sometimes half a devil.

Would the upper gentries like it?
Would the keep cost any more?
Shouldn't we have better heart
To work the pump and scrub the floor?

The above verses appeared in the **Ipswich Journal** in 1894 and echoed a complaint continually levelled against Workhouses that they not only split up families but they deprived elderly married couples of the comfort of each other's company in their failing years. The poet Thomas Hardy took up this theme in his poem **The Curate's Kindness.**

"I thought they'd be strangers aroun'me,
　　But she's to be there!
Let me jump out o'the waggon and go back and drown me
　　At Pummery or Ten-Hatches Weir.

I thought: "Well, I've come to the Union –
　　The Workhouse at last-
After honest hard work all the week and Communion
　　Of Zundays, these fifty year past.

"'Tis hard; but, " I thought, "never mind it:
　　There's gain in the end:
And when I get used to the place I shall find it
　　A home, and may find there a friend.

"Life there will be better than t'other,
　　For peace is assured.
**The men in one wing and their wives in another**
　　Is strictly the rule of the Board."

Just then one young Pa'son arriving
　　Steps up out of breath
To the side o' the wagon wherein we were driving
　　To Union; and calls out and saith:

"Old folks, that harsh order is altered,
　　Be not sick of heart!

> The Guardians they poohed and they pished and they paltered
> When urged not to keep you apart."
>
> " It is wrong," I maintained, "to divide them,
> Nearly forty years wed."
> "Very well, sir. We promise, then, they shall abide them
> In one wing together, they said."

The poem continues with the poor man's growing desperation that after all he will not have the peace he had hoped for!

Although the Guardians had introduced strict segregation in the Samford House, it certainly did not maintain this rule into the 1890s as the anonymous poem suggests. As we see in chapter XIV, in the original specifications of the House in 1764, provision was made for apartments for fifteen married couples. In 1819 the Board gave orders that separate 'lodging rooms' for married people should be provided in one of the garrets. However, since they obviously did not wish to enlarge the House population, it would appear that these married quarters were in fact for couples over the age of sixty. From an entry in 1860 it looks as if to qualify for this accommodation both partners were expected to be over sixty. However, the Board was capable when necessary of showing compassion and bending the rules. Thus we read that John Daldry and his wife were to be allowed to live in the "aged couples apartments" even though Mrs Daldry was under sixty. The fact that John who was approaching seventy was paralysed and unable to look after himself may have had something to do with the decision. And can we draw any conclusion about the standard of care available at that time that he lived on for another six years?

One of the dangers of having husbands and wives with their children in the House was that given half a chance, the man would go off to look for work leaving the family and possibly not return either to collect them or pay for their keep. Another entry from 1860 refers to Edward Goodman and his wife. Edward who is described as an aged inmate applied for permission to leave the House in order to take work. His request was granted but he wanted to leave his wife behind in the House, as she was not only elderly but also infirm and ailing. Edward must have been going to earn sufficient to maintain them both as he was ordered to pay three shillings a week to the House towards her keep. To give him a chance to get settled, he was instructed to pay his contribution to the Overseer in Chelmondiston fortnightly. He must, however, have fallen behind with his payments because several weeks later he was ordered to remove her. A threat like that was usually enough to bring in the arrears.

Sometimes, the wives refused to accompany their husbands and this posed a problem for the Guardians. In Anne Candler's story we read of how she refused to join William until he had lodgings for her at Sproughton. A similar situation arose in the 1840s when William Page applied to remove himself, his wife and four children from the House. Mrs Page dug her heels in and adamantly refused to go on the very sensible grounds that he had no place to which to take them and they possessed neither bedding nor furniture of any kind.

As time passed the question of separating married couples became almost irrelevant as by 1914 there were only two married couples in the House as opposed to sixteen old women and the same number of old men most of whom were widowed.

As we have seen elsewhere, the Directors and Guardians had much of their individual power eroded as they were forced to carry out the regulations laid down by the Local Government Board. Occasionally, a humanitarian gesture by the Board would be stamped upon by the LGB and thus provide the sort of anecdotal evidence that gave the Workhouses such a bad name. One such example came in 1897. The three oldest male inmates were all called John – Messrs Barfield, Woollard and Milburn. The Guardians had ordered that these men should be allowed an extra pound of sugar a week. The LGB objected strongly to this. Their concern was not with the health implications of too much sugar in the diet, rather that the rules of the prescribed Workhouse Dietary had been flouted. The Samford Board was curtly reminded that these could only be altered on the recommendation of the Medical Officer. We are not told how they overcame this problem.

It seemed to me as I read through the business dealings of the Board, that there were numerous occasions when within the constraints laid upon them, they showed a very humane face. This was most evident in their dealings with children. In 1896, a widow Dale who had six children was receiving out-relief benefit. The eldest of her children, eight-year old Alice had been sent, at the Board's expense to be cared for and educated at Hope House Orphanage in Ipswich. Unfortunately, whilst she was in receipt of benefits, Widow Dale had another child. Under the rules governing out-relief, the baby was taken as an assumption that she was co-habiting and so with a man presumably now able to maintain her, she and the children lost their right to Poor Relief benefit. The widow, who was in fact on her own, struggled to support the family by taking in laundry. By rights, little Alice should have been removed from the orphanage and sent back home but the Board decided that it would be better both for Alice's moral welfare as well as her future prospects if she remained where she was. They therefore agreed they would go on maintaining her at Hope House.

Sometimes, the Board's attempt to show compassion bounced back on them as happened in 1893. The background to the case was not given but it would appear that little Walter Lloyd who had been sent by the Guardians to St John's Home must have somehow indicated to the authorities there that he was a Roman Catholic. This was reported back to the Board who were asked if they would agree to his being transferred to an RC Home in Bedfordshire. Even though this would mean the Guardians having to pay an additional one shilling a week for Walter's maintenance, the Board agreed and Walter was duly sent off to the new Home. However, word then reached Walter's mother of what had happened and she was very cross. We do not know if she was a long term resident of the House or if she had for some reason, relinquished the child's care to the Guardians. What is interesting, however, is that she had the final word on what should happen to him. For now she stated he was not a Catholic, and it was her wish that Walter should be brought up as a member of the Church of England. So, the poor boy was taken out of the Bedfordshire Home and returned to St John's.

Occasionally inmates would apply for leave of absence for a few hours. All such requests had to come before the weekly Board meeting. In 1848 Mary Shearman made just such a request, though her reason was not quoted in the Minutes. The Board agreed to her being allowed out on condition that she took her three 'base-born' children with her. They must have anticipated that she was intending to make a 'run' for it, abandoning the children, because whatever reason she had had for wanting leave it was not strong enough for her to comply with the Board's proviso. On the other hand the Board readily gave Ann Hill some hours off to enable her to go in search of a gown that she had loaned to Sarah Cuthbert. Presumably, when Sarah had managed to obtain her discharge from the House, the clothes in which she had entered were no longer wearable. Ann who had her own dress in store lent this to her friend on the understanding that it would be returned as soon as Sarah had found a garment for herself. Time having elapsed and the dress not returned to her, Ann was justifiably worried that when it was her turn to leave, she too would have nothing to wear.

It would have been interesting to know if Sarah Cuthbert had applied to the Board for a dress. There is no record of her doing so but in 1851 Sarah Stiff, another unmarried mother, asked for some clothing so that she might go in search of work. Her request was turned down on the grounds that she was 'undeserving'. The implication here is that she did not work sufficiently hard and again, the Board might have been fearful of being left with her several children. So Sarah had to remain in the House where she was employed in the laundry. She was one of those few who were destined to remain indefinitely. It may be that she was of limited intelligence as in middle age she is described on the census forms as an 'imbecile.' Perhaps the Board realised that she would not survive long in the outside world. That they were not denying all clothing at that time is shown when just after Sarah's request, Ann Pinner, a married woman with three children asked for shoes so that she might leave. The Board decided that her request and any similar ones should be left to the discretion of the Master. This was a sensible move; allowing a supplicant to be fitted out and take his leave immediately rather than having to wait perhaps several days before a Board meeting

Before the LGB tightened its hold, the Guardians did not always insist that mothers take their illegitimate children with them when they left the House for employment. For example, in 1837, Mary Abbott managed to find a place in service in London. The Board encouraged her to take the position and allowed her to leave the child in the House. She would, of course, now be in a position to pay a weekly contribution to the Board for the child's maintenance so it was also in their interest to encourage the mothers to find employment.

On a number of occasions, the attitude of the Samford House shows up the lack of compassion in other Unions. It was one day in 1852 that William Webb, a youth, probably aged between sixteen and twenty-one, presented himself towards evening "in a state of great weakness and destitution". Why he had made his way to Tattingstone we are not told. It may be that he belonged to one of the parishes in the Union. What the Master was able to discover from him was that he had been discharged that same morning from the Union House at Semer near Hadleigh. The "great weakness and destitution" of the young man caught the sympathy of the Board when the case was reported to them and they directed the Master "to write and enquire the truth of such apparently harsh treatment." It is interesting that the Master was asked to write rather than the Clerk to the Board. Did they suspect that a more forthright explanation would come from a Master to Master approach than from the more formal enquiry from the Board?

Conforming more to our stereotypical picture of the Victorian era is the story of Hannah Sharman. Hannah was no stranger to life in the House. According to the 1851 census taken when she was thirteen she was living there with her unmarried mother and sisters. Presumably the Guardians had secured employment for the girls and what little we can find out about them is that by 1867, one of Hannah's sisters is married and living in Stutton, while Hannah herself was in employment in Colchester. On a Saturday afternoon two weeks before Christmas, Hannah either had to give up her work or was dismissed as she went into the early stages of labour. She called upon the Relieving Officer in Colchester seeking the order that would allow her to enter the Union in that town for the birth. The Relieving Officer, while fully conscious of her state had to turn down her request because, during his examination of her pecuniary affairs, she had revealed that she had five shillings in her possession – probably her wages and what savings she had been able to make. Playing strictly by the rules, the possession of this money meant she was not a pauper. The Relieving Officer advised her to go to her friends for assistance. Somehow she made her way to Stutton that night and the following evening when she was almost ready to give birth, her sister brought her to the House to be confined. Although Hannah had a claim on the Samford Union originally, her long period of employment in Colchester meant that she was entitled to help from there. Samford Guardians again expressed their disapproval at the callous treatment of this young woman by writing to the Colchester Union.

That compassion was not lacking in all government departments is illustrated in the history of Henry Palmer. Henry had served in the Coldstream Guards and in 1897 became eligible for a special Campaign Pension of nine pence a day. He had some time earlier entered the House, possibly because he was unable to care for himself. However, the granting of this pension put him into the position of being a man of means and therefore not strictly eligible to remain in the House. Perhaps to our surprise, the Board decided to ask Henry what he wanted; did he wish to go back into the outside world and make his own arrangements or did he wish to stay where he was. Henry did not hesitate. He wished to stay. The War Office also showed a humane face. In a letter to the Board the authorities requested that the money should not all disappear into Henry's maintenance costs. They were anxious that he should have "some appreciable personal benefit." In the end, the full weekly pension of 5s.3d was paid to the Guardians but out of it Henry was given 2/-. to "expend at his discretion."

Many years ago, I recall hearing a poem entitled 'Christmas Day in the Workhouse'. The major part is long forgotten except for the fact that the Master is told in no uncertain terms what he can do with his Christmas pudding. The poem was intended to reinforce the stigma and horror associated with life in Workhouses. In fact it shows to the modern reader that those who were inmates did in fact get the opportunity to celebrate Christmas with a festive meal which again might not have been the case for those outside struggling to make ends meet. From the very beginning, extra money was earmarked in early December for the Master and Matron to purchase the necessary dried fruit to make the plum puddings and beef always appeared on the menu on Christmas Day. There is a note that in 1848 the current schoolmistress had complained to the Master about the Christmas Dinner. The substance of the complaint is left to our imagination. Neither do we know if she was complaining on her behalf only or for the inmates generally. What is clear from the Minutes is that however hard times were, the inmates were never deprived of this one important meal of the year. By the end of the nineteenth century, the local gentry were sending in additional foods and presents for all the inmates to add to the festive cheer. And when Queen Victoria was crowned in 1837 and her son in 1902 there was also a "modification in diet and discipline" to celebrate the respective coronations.

However daunting it must have been for the inmates or those seeking to become residents to appear before the gentlemen – and ladies too by the time we reach the twentieth century – of the Board, they must all have been aware that the Board would, if required, fight on their behalf. In the days before the Citizen's Advice Bureau or Legal Aid, to whom did the poor turn for help and advice on serious matters? In Isabella Clarke's case, it was to the Guardians. She was an inmate along with her husband and children. Unfortunately, Mr

Clarke misbehaved very badly, and was sentenced to three weeks hard labour in prison for his indecent assault upon one of the other female inmates. Understandably, Mrs Clarke wished to have no more to do with her husband and so she applied to the Board to assist her in getting a legal separation from him.

We have already seen in other places that husbands who found work were expected to maintain their wives and families who remained in the House and that some out-relief was given as a loan that was expected to be repaid. But what of those who were too infirm to work and had come into the House because they were homeless or unable to care for themselves. A contribution towards their maintenance was expected from their adult children. Usually, the cost was apportioned among the children according to their own circumstances and means but one could not simply put one's aged parents into the House and forget about them. Stephen Stiff's father was an elderly inmate and Stephen was responsible for helping to maintain him. Unfortunately Stephen fell into arrears with his payments when he became weighed down with first the illness and then the death of his wife. The arrears stood at 23/- quite a considerable sum accounting for perhaps two months or more. The Guardians asked Stephen to attend one of their meetings in late 1904. Contrary to the picture of hard-hearted men who were entirely lacking in sensitivity, when they heard his story, they waived the arrears.

A more practical expression of the softening of attitudes came when part of the high brick walls surrounding the House was taken down in 1921 and chestnut fencing was placed along the boundary wall facing the Church. And a few years earlier there was even a relaxation in the attitude towards religious practices when Julia Brown and her five-year old daughter were given leave to attend services at the Methodist Chapel in the village.

Here is one final example of the way that the Guardians showed compassion to those within their care. In 1913, six-year old Arthur Shemming who was mentally impaired had been sent from the House to one of Dr Barnardo's homes. When he reached the age of sixteen, he had to leave the Children's Home but since there had been no improvement in his condition, he was not in a position either to work or care for himself. There was no hesitation as to what should be done about him. He was returned to the House and the Guardians who had remained responsible for him. Whatever may be said of the system generally, it did not turn its back on those who were homeless and helpless.

# XI

"Lads under 18 years of age, if well-limbed and likely to grow, may be taken, for infantry of the line or general service, as low in stature as 5'3"." **The Ipswich Journal 1804**

Singularly little is said in the Minute Books about the impact of the Napoleonic Wars, yet it is clear from other documents of the period that the country was fully aware of the possibility of invasion during the seventeen nineties and the first decade of the nineteenth century. In April 1798 the country was placed on alert. The **Ipswich Journal** reported; "in case of an actual invasion on any part of the coast of Suffolk, they (the Loyal Volunteers) will be ready to stand forward like true Britons for the defence of their country." The newspaper continued that temporary barracks were being established in almost every empty house and warehouse in the town ready for the accommodation of the troops that were expected to arrive. By early May the French had still not made a move but the local gentry and others were able to assemble on Martlesham Heath to watch the regiments play out the tactics they intended to use when the time came. However, mid June brought panic when an express arrived in Ipswich from Aldborough [spelling of the time] announcing that a fleet of ships had anchored off the town. Since it had not replied to the signals from the shore it was assumed this must be the enemy. Troops were immediately placed on standby. Mercifully it was a false alarm; an innocent fleet of native ships returning from Hudson Bay had, because of "the thickness of the weather" been unable to read any signals from the shore.

Each parish had an 'escape' plan. Official forms demanded details of such things as the number of inhabitants; how many carts, carriages and horses would be available in the event of an evacuation, and what stocks of flour and animal feed were held in reserve. Presumably the House had its own plans though there is no mention of them in the Minutes. In fact, except for one reference to an application for out-relief for the wife and family of a Militiaman who were in distress, one could gain the impression that the war passed the House by.

Stuck inside the front cover of the Minute Book for 1850-53 are the printed **Orders re: Regulations for the Militia** that were no doubt received in preparation for the war that broke out in the Crimea in 1854. These are interesting now for what they tell us about the times but they would have been even more interesting to the Guardians since they offered a possible source of employment for their able-bodied paupers.

1. Volunteers must be aged between 18 and 35.
2. Those over 35 taken with medical approval.
3. Ex Army men with good character accepted up to 45.
4. Over 45 only with special sanction.
5. Men must be 5'4".
6. 5'3" accepted if eligible.
7. Must be resident in the County in which they engage to serve.
8. Volunteers are to be examined by the Military Medical Officer; or by two private Medical practitioners; if that not possible, then by one.
9. The allowance paid for medical examination, 2/6 per volunteer.
10. Volunteers must take the prescribed oath of allegiance.

11. Volunteers to be paid 10/- bounty and 10/- at the end of the first training period. Thereafter 2/- per month up to six months. Payment made monthly or quarterly.
12. Commanding officers may, after their second training, take the amount of the next six months instalment on their departure home.
13. Sergeants – or drummers on permanent staff – receive 15/- bounty on enrolment but are committed for five years. They need not have been residents in the county. Drummers accepted at 16 and under 5'3".
14. Volunteers may change their place of residence.

Unfortunately the Minute Book covering years of the Crimean War is very fragile and therefore not open to inspection. So again we know little of the impact that the hostilities had on the House.

The same can be said of the wars fought in South Africa in 1880-81 and 1899-1902. Only two significant facts emerge from this period. One was the growing number of vagrants who passed through the casual wards, suggesting that many men were attempting to evade conscription by keeping on the move; the other was that boys of school age were being taken to work on the land. This points to the numbers of agricultural workers who enlisted in the army leaving a shortage of manpower on the farms. The aftermath of both wars was a shortage of food supplies, potatoes in particular.

When we come to the First World War we have a plethora of diverse information. The first specific reference, although blandly stated must have caused major upheaval. On the night of 13th December 1914, the House played host to one hundred and fifty-six men of the 1st Highland Field Regiment of Royal Engineers. The payment received by the Board from the Army for this one night's billeting was £5.19.3d. Without going into the military history of the period, I would hazard a guess that the regiment was en route for Harwich for embarkation to the continent. The following year, on the 8th March 1915, thirty-nine men and eight horses of the 2nd East

Anglian Field Regiment of Royal Engineers also stayed for one night. That the House was able to cope with such an influx indicates how low the number of inmates had fallen. A table for the fifth week of the Christmas Quarter of 1913 gives the total to be just fifty-seven. Of these, sixteen were old men and ten old women. Both male and female Infirmaries held thirteen apiece. There were three children under the age of three and two boys aged between three and eight with one lad in the 8-16 age group. Although the war had yet to start, it is interesting that there were no 'able-bodied' men in residence. Also in the early days of 1914 a 'bed count' revealed that there were two hundred and eighteen available including three cots. Later that year, the Local Government Board was asking for details of what hospital accommodation could be offered "during the present crisis."

In March of that year, Mr and Mrs James gave up their post and were replaced temporarily by Mr and Mrs Ireland who held the reins until the appointment in May of William Carter and his wife.

During the war years there was an emphasis on self-sufficiency and we learn that the tenant farmer who had agreed to work some of the House land had prepared the site ready for planting three quarters of a ton of seed potatoes. There is a reference to the sale of surplus apples and walnuts for £4.12.0. and the House piggery did a steady trade in sows to market. And a nice touch – at the inmates' Harvest Festival Service, the public were invited to join them. A collection of 12/8d. was taken and this was spent on giving the inmates a 'meat tea' on the following Wednesday.

In November, the first of a group of able-bodied men and women arrived from the Tendring Union. With its proximity to Harwich, it is possible that the War Office had requisitioned part of the Union House there for the accommodation of troops. Several weeks later more inmates came from Tendring but the whole group returned to their own House after six months. By the autumn of 1915 the need to take Air Raid Precautions led to a reorganisation of the wards. The old men and women who occupied the sick wards were brought down to the ground floor and the active women were moved up to the first floor.

Once a week the Dining Hall (the only large space available locally) became a drill hall for the Volunteer Training Corps. This was probably a sensible arrangement since in the event of enemy invasion, the House might well have to rely on the 'Home Guard' to assist with its evacuation. And a further sign of the breakdown in barriers between the House and those outside came with the use of the Dining Hall for public whist drives, organised by two local ladies, Mrs Millbank and Mrs Kerrison (from Tattingstone Place) to raise funds for the Red Cross.

An indication of how vast were the casualty lists in the opening years of the war is that in 1916 Carter, the Master, found himself at the age of thirty-eight eligible for military service. He asked the Guardians to apply for exemption on his behalf but when it was put to the vote, the Board overwhelmingly decided against such an application. I do not think we should take this to mean that the Board was anxious to be rid of him. It was more likely an expression of the patriotic feeling that was sweeping the country; that everyone able to do so should answer the call to arms. When Carter was told of the Board's decision, he reported that Mrs Carter was both willing and perfectly capable of running of the House in his absence. However, she did not feel she could undertake the management of the Accounts. The Guardians agreed that Mr Alexander, the Relieving Officer should take on that responsibility. The only other question to be settled was whether or not the Board should supplement Carter's military pay to make up for his loss of salary. They deferred their decision on that for the time being. But having made all their plans, two months later, a recruiting officer informed Carter that he was classified as being in a certified (reserved) occupation. However, as is often the case, bureaucracy changes its mind and so on the 19$^{th}$ April of 1917, the Military authorities applied to a local tribunal to review Carter's exemption on the grounds that it was not in the national interest that he should remain in civilian employment. Within the week, Mr Carter had received his call-up.

Mr Alexander, the Relieving Officer whose duties included visiting all the villages within the District was diagnosed at this time as having a heart problem. While he was still able to work, his doctor had expressly forbidden him to continue to do his rounds on a pedal cycle. He therefore asked the Board if he might have an allowance towards the purchase of a motorcycle. Having gained the machine, he then ran into another snag – petrol rationing. He had been allowed six gallons for three months but to do his work he needed six times that amount. One of his duties was to act as registrar for births and deaths but, he told the Board, on his present fuel allocation he would only be able to carry out registration duties once a month. He was told to send the necessary certificates by post and conserve his petrol for emergencies. However, someone in authority listened to his pleas and the following month he was granted a licence for six gallons a month.

    Not so easily sorted out were the problems Mrs Carter was having with her staff. In her own right as Matron, Mrs Carter had overall responsibility for the nursing staff and the general welfare of the sick and infirm. In addition, she would, in the event of her husband's absence, have taken control of the general day-to-day management of the whole House. Reading between the lines, she began to show that she was not up to the task, and in November she and Nurse Grayson were involved in an altercation that resulted in the Matron stopping the nurse's weekend leave. The nurse retaliated by accusing the Matron of neglect of duty and took her complaint to the House Committee. The Board as a whole supported the Matron but whether or not they were right to do is open to question. That something was wrong may be borne out by the fact that within a few days of Nurse Grayson's problems, Nurse Helsdon resigned. The report of the Local Government Board Inspector – a Miss Warmsley, one of the many women who because of wartime conditions were able to follow a career – was presented to the Board on 28$^{th}$ December. Miss Warmsley did not mince her words.

    "The matron was suddenly taken ill on the day of my visit and she was off duty.

    "The nursing order of one sick woman and two infants was not satisfactory. There was evidence of insufficient changing of all three cases. The adult had a severe urine rash and both infants were sore. One, aged four months had acute diarrhoea. Some medicine, the nature of which was not recorded, had been prescribed and two pints of undiluted milk with 1 oz. (of it) supposed to be taken daily, but no record kept. Weights of neither children (sic) were recorded and they had never been out of doors although the mother of one of them is a scrubber in the Sick wards. The cots looked unkempt without sheets, quilts or covers over the mattresses and pillows, the babies being placed on mackintosh and wrapped in blankets. The atmosphere was close and too many beds for so small a room, especially as the young babies lived there night and day.

"The hours of the night nurse (15) on the days when the day nurse is off duty are too long. There is a danger of her sleeping on duty. This might be very serious as the distance between the wards is very great and the duty room is not in close touch with either male or female wards. I also think that a 12 hour day for eleven out of every fourteen days is too long for comparatively young women to keep fresh for the patients and interested in their work. Some free time during the day apart from time for meals should be given to every nurse."

The Board, having digested this critical report, asked that both the Medical Officer and the Matron should give their comments. Unfortunately, these are not recorded. But the Board had another problem to consider as they entered 1917, namely what was to be the long-term future of the House. With the decline in numbers entering the Workhouses, many were being closed down and given over to alternative use. The Committee appointed to consider closure decided that after the costs of maintaining and boarding out the inmates in other Institutions had been taken into account any saving made would be insignificant. The only way that the Guardians could save a substantial amount was if they could let the House for some other purpose. The Clerk was therefore instructed to write to the Suffolk District Asylum, which was always complaining of shortage of space, to enquire if they were prepared to board out at Tattingstone some of their chronic but harmless patients. Alternatively, would the

Asylum consider taking over the premises? The reply was speedy. The Asylum Board was not interested.

Within the House itself, staff problems were still occurring. Nurse Grayson finally decided she had had enough and handed in her resignation. Her post was filled by an applicant from a Workhouse in Norfolk. Then Nurse Helsdon, who had resigned earlier but had been persuaded to stay, decided that the time had really come for her to go. Her replacement came from Bristol.

With the Master's call-up it was left to Mrs Carter to supervise the introduction of the 'Revised Dietary for Wartime'. Food rationing, as such, was not introduced in the First World War as it was in the Second. Naturally there were acute shortages of those foods which were imported and home produced products inevitably rose in price. Cheese, a staple of the Workhouse diet, was one of the items to suffer. The supplier who tendered for the cheese contract made it very clear to the Board that he was expecting market prices to rise so there was no way he could accept a lower figure. We have already noted the personal impact of the fuel shortage on the Relieving Officer but it had a more far-reaching effect on supplies generally. One vital commodity for the House was coal. In the past this had been brought from Manningtree by road but during the war, the suppliers were unable to travel long distances. Only one supplier, Beaumont's of Ipswich was willing to supply coal and gas-coke to the House. However, it was stipulated it would transport it by rail to Bentley station and the House would have to fetch it from there by cart.

To add to the problems, the current porter and laundress, Mr and Mrs Taylor resigned. H.G.Waspe, a young man who had previously worked at the Basingstoke Union was appointed as engineer and porter but within a week or so of his appointment the boiler engine broke down. It was essential that the engine should keep going so the Matron was authorised to employ labourers from among the inmates to do the pumping. Then Miss Aldous, the cook, broke her leg and was unable to work, so a temporary cook had to be found. What, I wonder, did she make with the "quantity of pickled herring" that was the subject of a circular from the Ministry of Food?

Waspe's stay too, was temporary; towards the end of January 1918, he was given instant dismissal for bad conduct. This, of course, meant that a stopgap had to be found while the process of advertising and interviews was gone through.

It was not all bad news though. The field that had been turned over to potatoes had produced a surplus so that five tons could be offered to the Army Canteen Board at £5.0.0. per ton and some old cast iron bedsteads were sold at 4s.6d a cwt. to Cocksedges, an engineering firm in Ipswich who were, I assume, making munitions. It is a pleasing thought that the Union's worn out beds should have played their part in the war effort. And to help the House's finances, a number of inmates were taken in from the Woodbridge Union.

One wonders what was the reaction of the staff and inmates when towards the end of February a military representative came to look over the premises. Numbers were still very low but did they really want what the military gentleman had come to investigate, namely the possibility of taking over the attic and ground floors as accommodation for German prisoners of war. Obviously the two floors would be heavily guarded, and it was proposed that, if this scheme came about, the male sick wards would remain as they were on the first floor. We are not told why the plan came to nothing.

March saw the appointment of new staff; a labour master and laundress and a Nurse attendant. However, in July there was a mass resignation of these three plus the porter/engineer. On the bright side, the Cook had returned to her duties and to ensure that she stayed the Board raised her salary. This time the wife of the engineer was taken on as nurse. Interestingly, she commanded a slightly higher salary than her husband. But it was later found she was unable to carry out nursing duties, so she was re-appointed, at a marginally smaller salary, to act as Matron's assistant. So another nurse had to be appointed.

Throughout this period costs were constantly rising and more and more the staff were asking for higher salaries. Even the gentleman acting as Clerk to the Board asked for an increase. His £80 went up to £100. The porter and his wife resigned after six months having earlier told the Board they did not think the wage sufficient. The Board had attempted to see a way round an increase in wages by dropping the beer ration for Officers and giving them money in lieu but this was not enough to persuade the Coneys to stay. When their successors came they had a ten-year old son who was allowed to live-in with his parents though a charge was made for his food.

During 1919 there was an attempt to return to a more normal state of affairs and one way this was achieved was the re-introduction of the pre-war Dietary. An example for the week's dinners for Class 2 & 2a men shows the emphasis on potatoes and the use of tinned meat, presumably corned beef. The meat allocation varied between 3 and 4½ ounces. There was bacon on Mondays, tinned meat on Tuesdays, pork was served on Wednesdays and a meat pudding on Saturdays. It is not clear if Thursdays and Fridays were meatless but there would almost certainly have been meat of some sort on Sunday.

In the spring of 1919, Mr Carter was demobilized and returned to his duties in the House, no doubt to Mrs Carter's relief. She must have been pleased to let him take responsibility again, especially as she had just had to cope with all the commotion caused by a woman who twice managed to escape from the House. Poor Violet chose the end of January to make 'a bolt for it'. On that occasion she jumped out of the Board Room window. She made for Ipswich where for a week she slept rough before being picked up by the police. Violet was then returned to the House by her sister. But within three weeks she made a second bid for freedom via a bathroom window. On her return she was certified as an imbecile in need of care and protection.

As for the Board they could again concentrate on the business of how to balance the books. In this they were helped somewhat by taking in fifty or so of the Woodbridge Union inmates. But even more important was their battle against the Government's proposals to abolish Boards of Guardians and transfer all their duties and powers to the County Council. It took time but that was one 'war' the Board was to lose.

This is the last Will and Testament of me Harman Harris of Tattingstone Suffolk Master of the Workhouse I direct that all my just debts and funeral and testamentary expenses be paid and satisfied by my Executor hereinafter named as soon as conveniently may be after my decease I give devise and bequeath all my Freehold Houses in the several Parishes of Wix Essex and Brantham and East Bergholt in Suffolk as hereinbelow mentioned, To my son Charles Arthur Harris of Bromley le Bow London All those two Houses & Gardens in Wix now in the occupation of Isaac James and Faint To my son Philip Harris all those my Freehold Houses in Wix in the occupation of Robert Southgate and John Mills and Gilbert To my dear Wife Mary all those my two Freehold Houses in Wix Essex in the occupations of Wm Gilbert Robt Whiting Jas Whiting and Stephen Howard, To my son Richard Albert Harris all my said Freehold Houses in Brantham Suffolk in the occupations of Hearsum Woollard & Jennings & others. To my dear Wife my Freehold Houses in East Bergholt in the occupation of Potto and Potter & Nichols & all and every my household furniture linen and wearing apparel books plate fixtures china horses carts and carriages and also all and every sum and sums of money which may be found in my house or be about my person or due to me at the time of my decease And also all my stocks funds and securities for money book debts money on bonds bills notes or other securities and all and every other my estate and effects whatsoever and wheresoever both real and personal

# XII

"The situation of the door was peculiar. The sill was three or four feet above the ground...ruts immediately beneath suggested that the door was used solely for the passage of articles and persons to and from the level of a vehicle...(He) rang the bell, and received directions to back his waggon against the high door ...The door then opened, and a plain elm coffin was slowly thrust forth, and laid by two men in fustian along the middle of the vehicle. One of the men then stepped up beside it, took from his pocket a lump of chalk, and wrote upon the cover the name...He covered the whole with a black cloth, threadbare but decent, the tail-board...was returned to its place, one of the men handed a certificate of registry to (him), and both entered the door, closing it behind them."

**Far from the Madding Crowd, Thomas Hardy**

Even today the term 'pauper's funeral' has emotive connotations. The media may inform us that an unclaimed body is to be dealt with under that term implying that it will be 'disposed' of with little or no ceremony. The phrase came into being at a time when, if either the deceased had no money or the family was unable to pay for the necessary funeral arrangements, then the costs were borne by the parish Poor Rate. It was the duty of the parish Overseers to see that the deceased was buried with all due rites and obsequies. The Overseers' Accounts for the parish of Sproughton during the first half of the seventeen hundreds, show that Anne Candler's grandfather-in-law who was in receipt of parish relief for many years, had two wives buried at the parish's expense and when he finally died in his eighties, the parish provided not only his shroud and coffin but paid for the grave to be dug and the bell to be tolled at his funeral.

It was possibly the growth of undertaking as a business during the Victorian age with its emphasis on deep mourning and elaborate funeral processions that made the poorer folk of the early twentieth century so fearful that they would not be buried 'properly'. For some of them, there was a constant anxiety that when their time came, they and their family might 'lose face' by having to go into a pauper's grave. Some suffered that fate unnecessarily. It was in 1923 that old Mrs Gould of Arwarton died leaving no relations beyond her aged husband. Such was his state of health that he was brought into the House immediately. The vicar, judging by the poor state in which the couple had lived, gave Mrs Gould a pauper's burial at Arwarton and billed the Guardians for the cost of the funeral. It was then the duty of the local Collector to have the cottage cleared, taking into the Board's custody any items that might be of value. In this case there were two insurance policies which in due time the Board would be able to claim towards the old man's maintenance and funeral expenses. Similarly, any decent (that is saleable) furniture was stored until the old man's demise. However, as the Collector cleared some drawers he was more than a little taken aback to discover a small cache of gold sovereigns and half sovereigns. The final total was £197.10.0. The old couple had amassed a small fortune yet lived in penury.

How the dead were to be dealt with was just another item that had to be considered when the House was first built. Just after the first inmates were admitted, the Board resolved that a "Proper Place for a Burying Ground be set out at the end of Back Lane Field". At the same time, the carpenter from Holbrook received the first commission for the provision of the coffins to be used by the House. From a study of the Minute Books of the Samford Union, it is possible to gauge the economic health of the country by the fluctuation in the cost of coffins that came in three sizes and were made of elm or ash. In 1822, for example, in a cost-cutting exercise, the Porter, who was presumably a carpenter by trade, was making the coffins for the House rather than a local tradesman. He managed to produce them for 8s.6d., 6/- and 3/-. By the following year the larger coffin was costing 10/- and at the end of 1825 the prices had risen to 13/-, 9s.6d. and 4s.6d. 1828 saw a decrease of one shilling to 12/-. This may have been brought about by the use only of elm or a fall in timber prices generally. When the Porter was not able to produce coffins, then the work went back out to local craftsmen. All those who tendered for contracts to supply the House with whatever commodity, were expected to have samples "placed on the table" by 11 am on a Board meeting day. Macabre as this may now seem, sample coffins were there alongside samples of malt, cheese, meat, soap, candles or coals.

That the paupers were not simply shovelled unceremoniously into the ground as one might think, is shown by the fact that when the Chapel was equipped, a surplice, a burial book and a burying cloth were among the items ordered. And in those first years, at any rate, the sexton also tolled Tattingstone church bell for each committal service.

Not everyone who died in the House was buried in the pauper's burying ground. Those with relatives who could pay the costs were taken home for interment in their own parish churchyard. Others, who died at home, had their burial expenses paid by the Poor Rate. When the wife of Simon Wilson of Freston died in 1768, the Board paid out £1.2.0. for her funeral expenses and another 4/- to bring her family into the House.

During the first thirty years of the House's existence, the clerk would inscribe into the Minute Book the name of each person who had died, sometimes with an age and a cause of death. It seems likely that interments did not take place in the House's burial ground for several years – perhaps until the hedge had grown up. Certainly, the burial register of Tattingstone church records a number of paupers who had died in the 'Poor House'. Some of these were people who had been taken to the sick ward suffering from an infectious disease. One such was Mary Beaumont, a victim of the smallpox in 1797, of whom it is recorded that she was the maidservant of Lady Martin of Higham. Presumably, Lady Martin paid Mary's funeral expenses and had her interred in the village churchyard. Certainly no one dared bring back the body of someone who had died of smallpox and thus run the risk of re-infection.

At the beginning of the nineteenth century the Weekly Returns kept by the Master simply recorded the number of deaths. 1848 saw the introduction of a specific burial register and from 1852 this recorded details of the deceased including where the burial had taken place; either back in the inmate's home parish or in the Union burial ground. In 1851, the House, which had again been producing coffins for its own use, actually ran out of timber. To add to the problem, the carpenter who had been carrying out this essential work had just been discharged so the Board had swiftly to find a local contractor who could take on the work.

An inspection of the burial ground in 1872 revealed, "it was full of graves and required enlarging." In fact two hundred and twenty-eight burials had taken place in it from 1852 until the end of December 1873. It was recommended that another acre should be added to the existing site on the north and east sides. The new part was opened in 1874 with somewhat of a flourish. At three o'clock on the afternoon of Thursday, 26 February, the bishop of Norwich himself came to visit the House and consecrate the additional three quarters of an acre that had been prepared for future use. How usual it was for the bishop to carry out such ceremonies is not clear but since he was accompanied by the Revd. H.J.Hasted of Sproughton who was also the Rural Dean of Samford, it may be that he was paying what is known in church circles as 'a Visitation' to Samford. In those days, Suffolk was still part of the diocese of Norwich. Unfortunately it turned out to be a very wet day so the rites that took place in the burial ground were cut to the minimum and the official party then proceeded to the House chapel where all the inmates and many members of the local community were gathered for Evensong. According to the account of the event that appeared in the **Ipswich Journal**, the chaplain, the Revd.A.Woodd read the prayers, and the

Revd. Hasted read the lessons. Two appropriate hymns were chosen, accompanied on the organ by Miss Harris (the Master's daughter). J.M.Neale's 'Brief life is here our portion,'

> 'Brief sorrow, short-lived care;
> The life that knows no ending
> The tearless life, is there.'

and H.Bonar's equally thoughtful,

> 'A few more years shall roll
> A few more seasons come
> And we shall be with those that rest
> Asleep within the tomb.'

The bishop then gave his sermon taken from Job, chapter XIV, verse 10, 'But man dieth, and wasteth away, Yea, man giveth up the ghost and where is he?'

The new interments were to be numbered and twenty two year old Charles Sharman was the first to be so recorded when he was buried in June 1874. The occupant of grave no.4 was an unknown woman who, so the register states, was drowned in the river near the Ostrich Inn (now the Oyster Reach).

Originally an acre of land was acquired for the new burial area and a portion of this had been left unconsecrated. It is said that this section, which was in the northeast corner, was for the use of non-conformists and others. First to be interred there, in July 1876, was sixty-four years old Marcus Giles It is not recorded if Giles was indeed a Dissenter or member of the Chapel. Another possibility for his being placed there was that he had taken his own life and having committed such an act he would have been denied the privilege of a 'Christian' burial. Such was the case for all suicides until the second half of the twentieth century. The second occupant of this area was twenty-five year old Joseph Bourke who was buried on 26 March 1877. When I first came upon Joseph's name in the burial register I thought I was on the track of an interesting 'story'. Against his name appear the words 'brought from the County Gaol'. My vivid imagination had him down as a murderer or felon at least, who had been hanged but alas, the truth is much more mundane. Bourke was the man suffering from pulmonary tuberculosis who is mentioned in chapter V. Whatever his crime; it cannot have been very serious, as he had only served a two-year sentence. He had served his time in the County Gaol in St Helen's Street in Ipswich and when, on the day of his release, the prison medical officer had reported to the Governor that the man was very sick, the decision was taken to send him to the Ipswich Borough Workhouse. Accompanied by a warder, he was duly taken there but the Master refused to admit him. The warder then drove with his charge to the home of Mr Francis, the Relieving Officer for the Holbrook District, where he demanded that Bourke be admitted to the Samford House. The Guardians accepted him but complained bitterly to the Magistrates about what they regarded as the high-handed behaviour of Captain Crickitt, the governor of the gaol. The reason for all this was yet another example of bureaucracy at work. Bourke had been in the County gaol and the county did not pay towards the Poor Rate of the Ipswich Borough Workhouse. Thus, that Workhouse was under no obligation to accept the sick from the gaol. Had Bourke been in the Ipswich gaol, then that would have been a different matter.

As Bourke was dead within the month the matter was resolved. However, that leaves the question as to why he was laid to rest in the northeast corner. A clue may lie in Bourke's nationality. He was an Irishman and therefore it is probable that like the occupant of grave number three in the unconsecrated area, ninety-two years old Joseph Day from East Bergholt, he was a Roman Catholic. There was, at that time, still a very strong feeling in the country against those of the Catholic faith and so, like those other denominations outside the Church of England, their members could not be allowed to lie beside Anglicans in death. This does seem somewhat extreme but there are countless examples of refusals to bury in the parish churchyard those not professing to be members of the Church of England as the **Akenham Burial Case** highlighted. The House burial register merely states where Day was interred and that his service was conducted by Father C.Muller. Whatever the official view might be about adherence to the principles of the Church of England, the

Master was willing that a priest should visit the few Catholic inmates there were. On one occasion there is a note in the Minute book detailing the expenses claimed by the priest for coming to give the last rites.

Sometimes the burial register gives very detailed information; we know, for instance that in 1877, Joseph Mann from Great Wenham was in grave no.31 next to the road and the last in the row. While in 1880 Harriet Norman in grave 52 was at the furthest end of a row and that Alfred Ennals started a new row with his grave, no.53. For some reason in 1885 a new series of numbering was started with Sarah Jackerman becoming number one. But then in 1899 there are dual grave numbers, William Cook being assigned numbers 106 and yet another number one!

One person who most certainly did not find his way into the paupers' burial ground was a Mr Thomas Hawkins. One of the Board of Guardians in 1877, he most unfortunately died during a Board meeting. There is no mention of this actual event in the Minutes of that particular meeting. Instead, there is a reference in the following meeting's Minutes that an acknowledgement of the Board's condolences had been received from his widow following his death "during the last meeting."

If the life and death of Joseph Bourke failed to provide a mystery story, there is very definitely one surrounding Albert Chamberlain Daldry. We met Albert's parents in chapter X when John Daldry and his wife were allocated married quarters. John was a shoemaker by trade and the family lived for some time in Washbrook. John may have been married twice, if not he certainly came to fatherhood rather late being forty-nine when his first child, Ellen was born. Albert, born in 1846, was the second of his three sons. It may be that when John and Jemima were admitted to the House following John's paralysis, Albert came with them because he was sick or infirm in some way. Whatever his story, he died in the House, just after his seventeenth birthday in 1863 and was buried in the Union graveyard. But here is the mystery. Why, amongst all those hundreds buried there, should Albert be commemorated with a headstone? The only one in the whole burial ground. It has been suggested that one of his brothers did well in life and that he paid for his brother's memorial.

Every so often over the years that followed, the question of improvements to the burial ground would be discussed, but there were always more pressing matters that needed attention. However, in 1921, one of the Board, the Revd. Miller annoyed the Master by complaining about the unkempt condition of the graveyard. The Master stated categorically that he could see nothing wrong with it. Nevertheless, having raised the question, the rest of the Board gave consideration as to what could be done to improve matters. It was suggested that a proper system of marking the graves should be adopted. The Master was therefore given the task of finding out the price for crosses that were either numbered consecutively or had a space for inserting a name.

At the next meeting the Board were presented with designs and estimates for crosses and numbered pegs. As usual, economy governed the decision and it was agreed that the pegs should be marked with numbers corresponding with those in the burial register. This was done but was later to cause some confusion. There are as we have already noted, three graves marked with the number one while others have two numbers. The last of these dual numberings was for Sarah Collins, buried in 1907 in a grave that is marked 223 and 70. Adding to the mystery of just what was going on is the fact that George Searle's grave is marked 221 and 69 but in between is Ruth Hounslow with the number 222 but no other. Could it be that some of the very early graves were being re-used?

The proposal that a large cross should be fixed in the centre of the graveyard was also defeated. That idea surfaced again in 1925 when there was a proposal that the entrance to the graveyard should be marked either by a cross or some other suitable symbol. The question was never resolved for, as it was pointed out in 1928, very few Unions were still using their own burial grounds.

The last recorded burial, that of Joshua Scoggins, (no. 308) was in 1930. For the next sixty odd years, the burial ground lay untouched, except by the hand of nature which slowly turned it into woodland. In spring it is filled with a 'host of golden daffodils' and in early summer the song of the nightingale fills the air. Thus the old paupers' burying ground has become, perhaps, one of the earliest examples of a modern 'green burial site.'

# XIII

"Applicants to be diligent and attentive...and of humane disposition."

The number of staff actually employed in the House was very small considering the size of the building and the number of people it contained. From the outset it was intended that as much of the day to day 'domestic' work as possible should be undertaken by the inmates themselves. The original Officers, as they became known, were the Governor or Master and his wife who acted as Matron, the Porter, Laundress, Nurse and Baker. To these were added the Schoolmaster and mistress, an assistant nurse and, in place of the baker, a Cook. One can only assume that in the beginning the cooking was done by female inmates supervised by the Matron. In addition were the salaried Medical Officers, Relieving Officers and the chaplain but these of course, did not live-in on the premises.

The most important member of staff was the Master. On him fell the responsibility of maintaining a smooth-running establishment that would satisfy the requirements of the Board. Initially, the man appointed was a master craftsman in some aspect of the wool trade and as such he would have been used both to managing his employees and conducting business transactions. That he needed to be both literate and numerate is taken for granted and the handwriting of some of the early Masters who took on the role of Minute clerk for

Board meetings testifies to this. What follows is merely a brief outline of each of the Masters and some of the other Officers. Although mention is made of the Matrons, in the early years we often know little more of her than her name.

**Edward Pearson** was born in Norwich in 1719. He was married to **Mary** (b.1726) and they had at least two sons, Robert who followed his father as Master, and Henry who died in 1778 at the age of eighteen probably from smallpox. It is possible that they were also the parents of the Revd. Edward Pearson, MA, DD, who was a fellow, and later master, of Sidney Sussex College, Cambridge. A scholar who wrote treatises on theological and ecclesiastical questions, he is known to have visited Ipswich and preached there on several occasions.

In 1766 when he became Governor, Edward was forty-seven. His salary was £40 a year and Mary received £15. They lived rent and board free in their own living quarters. The settled life must have suited them for eight years into their tenure of office when Mary was forty-eight, she produced twin girls who were baptised Mary and Charlotte in Tattingstone church.

There was no question of retirement from work in those days unless one was forced to do so through ill health. Consequently when Edward died in 1786, aged 67, he was still in post. His death meant that Mary would have automatically lost both her job and her home but when the position was advertised, their twenty three year old son **Robert** applied for it. Having been brought up within the House he would have been more familiar with its working than most external applicants for the post so he and his mother put in a joint application which was accepted. Robert received the same salary of £40 that his father had done twenty years before but he did have an additional £10 for acting as clerk to the Guardians. There is no indication as to why Robert resigned after ten years. It may be that he wished to pursue a career elsewhere, perhaps with a wife. While Mary, having reached seventy-one, may have felt it was time to give up. She spent the next four years in Ipswich but on her death in 1801, her body was brought back to Tattingstone to be interred beside her husband in St Mary's churchyard.

Of **Charles Twitchett** who became Governor in 1797 there is little information. Even his name causes problems, it being spelt with both one 't' and two and either an 'e' or an 'i'. He was already in his fifties and probably not in very good health. He too suffered the loss of two children in their early twenties, his son William and a daughter Mary, who bore the same name as her mother. His salary had by that time risen to £13.11.0. per quarter, but he was not to enjoy it for long as he died aged 59 in 1801.

His replacement was **Richard Steward** who with his wife **Mary** came from Wisbech. Steward had to look after the House during the period of the Napoleonic Wars, a time of economic depression. Although Steward was a master craftsman in the wool trade, it was during his reign that 'a labour master' was brought in to set up and supervise the manufacture of cloth on the premises. When he retired the Board presented him with a gratuity of £25 for his work in promoting the cloth trade. Although one gains the impression that he was a strict man with the inmates, he may have had a weakness for drink. He certainly blotted his copybook with the Board after he had resigned, when it came to their notice that he had "clandestinely slept in the House on two occasions." One wonders whom he had returned to visit.

When the post was advertised late in 1818, the notice that appeared in the **Ipswich Journal** asked that applicants should have - "Proper testimonials to their being of strict moral conduct (a reference perhaps to Steward's drinking?), be diligent and attentive to business, writing in a good hand, conversant in accounts, of humane disposition and members of the Church of England."

**William Catchpole** who came from Ipswich must have convinced the Guardians that he had all the necessary requirements when he was appointed in 1819. He was a wool draper by trade, that is he was a businessman knowledgeable in the buying and selling of cloth rather than a craftsman. With a 'labour-master' whose job it was to supervise the workers in the manufactory, Catchpole could devote himself to the essential business of selling the cloth produced in the House. He took up the post in March and at Christmas the Board presented him with £25 over and above his salary by way of thanks for reducing the expenses of the House. Is this another implied criticism of Steward's term of office? There is little mention of Mrs Catchpole but we do know that the Board had a bonus in Catchpole's daughter. She organised the knitting schools for the children within the House, a job she did so well that with her father they set up similar arrangements in many of the parishes. Not only did the Board reward Miss Catchpole for her efforts but she has even claimed a place in history by featuring in **Sidney** and **Beatrice Webb's** treatises on the Poor Law.

Catchpole seems to have been very well liked and trusted by his employers. In 1834, following an unspecified illness that lasted for eight months, the Board granted him a donation of £30.0.0 towards his expenses for a journey to Bath for treatment. Having made a good recovery, he continued to serve the Board well for a number of years. The Board delegated to him the power to make decisions that once would have been up to them, and he seems to have spent quite a bit of his time travelling on their behalf, negotiating apprenticeship agreements and investigating complaints. Most surprising however, was the discovery that when Catchpole gave up the post of Master, presumably through failing health, he still remained very involved by continuing to act as the Clerk to the Board for which he received the same salary as he had as Master. His continued presence may have been one of the reasons that his successor did not stay for long.

**John and Elizabeth Alloway** were examples of the keen upwardly mobile young people of their day; he was in his mid thirties, Elizabeth ten years younger. John came originally from Reading, his wife from Colchester. There is no indication of where they worked before, but they came at a difficult period for the House. In 1848, for example, the Master must have been under considerable pressure to cut expenses when the accounts for that year showed receipts of £1965.0.0 against expenditure of £2034.3.5. In that same year he reported to the Board that the schoolmistress had complained about the Christmas dinner – what the exact nature of her complaint was we are not told, but Alloway was informed in no uncertain terms that it was his place to maintain authority over the staff. That he may have found discipline difficult is somewhat ironic in view of the employment he took next. He resigned as Master when he was appointed keeper of Ipswich Gaol in 1852, a position he held until his death in 1871. One titbit of information about Alloway is that he was left five cottages on White Horse Hill in Tattingstone in the will of a John Newman. There is no indication why this legacy was made to him. However, he did not live long enough to inherit, so the property passed to his eldest son, Josiah, a clergyman who at the time of his father's death was living in New Zealand. A long and protracted correspondence with the other side of the world took place while he established his claim to the property, which he then quickly relinquished, his agent selling it for him at auction. Coincidentally, one of those cottages was bought by Alloway's successor as Master of the House.

According to the census records, **Harman Harris** was born at Wix in Essex in 1808. His wife, **Mary** who was a year younger than her husband, came from the adjoining village of Bradfield. When they took up their post they brought with them their youngest children, a boy of nine, called Phillip and the baby, Joseph. Three other sons, Harman junior, Charles and Richard must have already left home and been in work. Harman and Mary were in their early forties when they came to the House and within a couple of years they had increased their family by the addition of a daughter, Sarah. Sadly, their eldest son, Harman died at twenty in 1854 and Joseph died when he reached twenty-two. It is possible that many of these post-adolescent deaths were the result of tuberculosis. Quite what Harris's credentials were is not revealed but of the four candidates called for interview he won almost unanimous approval from the Board, gaining nineteen of their votes against his nearest rival's six. If the Board were seeking a strict disciplinarian, then they would appear to have found it in Harris. It was he who had problems during

1869 with the inmates who made complaints against him to the Poor Law Board. However, the fact that he remained Master almost thirty-three years, when death relieved him of his office, suggests that both he and the Board were satisfied with the way he ran things.

What is intriguing about Harris is his business acumen. Unless he had inherited family property, over the years he must have used savings from his salary to make some very shrewd investments. When he died, his will revealed him to be a man of considerable property, leaving to his wife and sons "all my freehold houses in Wix, Brantham and East Bergholt" (there were at least six in Wix, each divided into three or more tenements each) and "all my stocks funds and securities for money book debts money on bond bills notes or other securities". All this was quite apart from the household contents and money found in the house at the time of his death. That was the will drawn up in 1879; by the time he died he had added four cottages and a shop in Tattingstone to his property portfolio. Harris must have been a keen and probably very important member of his Masonic lodge. Following his death in 1885 and that of Mary in 1892, a rare commemorative stained glass window bearing Masonic symbols was placed in the church at Tattingstone.

**John Henry Jarrold** came next with his wife **Jane** and young John Henry junior. By the time they took on the role of Master and Matron, the House was fast becoming a home for the elderly and sick. One senses that it was during the Jarrolds' reign that there was an easing in the enforcement of discipline as well as more contact between the House and the village. Mr Jarrold was very musical and often entertained the inmates. We may assume that he was a member of the Tattingstone Choral Society and it was through his influence that the Society gained permission to hold a public concert in the Dining Hall of the House. We also discover that Mrs Jarrold did not confine herself solely to duties within the House. It was she who accompanied two of the girls who were to emigrate to Canada in 1890 up to London. It is possible that Jarrold himself may not have been in the best of health. Perhaps he had failing sight as at one point he asked the Board's permission to use the services of a young man to help him with his record-keeping. The Board gave its blessing to the plan as long as Jarrold paid the youth from his own pocket and also paid for his board and lodging within the House. In 1908 his ill health forced him to resign.

Whether it was because there was acute unemployment at that time or that the position of Workhouse Master had become more highly sought after, there were **eighty three** applicants for the vacant post which initially offered only a two-year contract. Five couples were invited for interview by the Board and their details give us some insight into the backgrounds of the applicants who came from all over the country. They were all quite young for such a position and all came with experience of working within the Poor Law service. Three were already in position as Masters and Matrons; they were Mr & Mrs Atkins aged 31 and 32 currently employed in Launceston, Cornwall; Mr & Mrs Damen 33 and 34 from Ringwood in Hampshire, and from Calne in Wiltshire, Mr & Mrs Fox aged 35 and 31. Mr & Mrs Hayward-Heathcock 35 & 37, were employed as Porter and Assistant Matron at the Leicester House and Mr & Mrs James 36 & 37 came from the Hertford Union where they were employed as Porter and Portress. One assumes that the Hertford establishment was much bigger than Samford and took in many more women thus necessitating the need for a female to act as admissions officer.

Each member of the Board voted for his preferred candidate. On the first ballot it was a close run between Fox (8) James (7) and Atkins (6). On the second ballot Fox and James tied with 8 each but the third vote gave James 13 to Fox's 10.

So **William and Sarah Louise James** were duly elected to the office at salaries of £60 and £40 respectively. They had two children and James was expected to pay 4/- a week for each child's food. The Jameses appear to have carried on the liberalising regime of their predecessors. Their daughters, Ethel and Lillian went to the village school and their mixing with the local children did much to break down barriers and some of the mystique that surrounded the House. Mr James was obviously a well-educated man. Not only did he possess beautiful handwriting but also his comments in the Master's Journal show a fluency of thought and sensitivity rather than a mere listing of weekly activities. He recorded with genuine feeling the many acts of kindness by donors of gifts to the inmates. In recent years, it had become commonplace for ladies and gentlemen, either associated with the Guardians or simply living in the locality, to give extra groceries and little luxuries to the inmates around Christmas time. However, Mr James recorded his appreciation to Col. Murray who regularly sent in newspapers, books and magazines for use in the House. One cannot help believing that this was the result of James's influence.

Again the reason for their departure in 1914 is not recorded. Given that they were still young, one would assume that they went for promotion, perhaps to a busier House with more inmates, for by that time numbers in the Samford House had fallen to fifty-seven; sixteen elderly men plus twelve sick or infirm, and ten elderly women and thirteen others of whom six were mothers with their children.

For the two months before the **Carters** took up residence, **Mr and Mrs Ireland** acted as temporary Master and Matron. There are still people living in the village who have memories of Mr Carter. He was not very tall, about 5'4" and he had dark hair and a moustache. Within a very short time of his arrival war was declared and numbers within the House rose with the introduction of inmates from the Essex Union House at Tendring. I have dealt in some detail with the Carters elsewhere (chapter XI) so suffice it to say here that following Mrs Carter's death in 1928, Carter must have been sufficiently well respected in that he remained in office as a widower. The Board was prepared to accept a separate application for the post of Matron and **Miss Agnes Dewhurst** was appointed. Mr Carter was still in office when the House passed into the jurisdiction of the County Council in 1930. A letter written in February of that year by the Woodbridge Guardian whose duty it was to inspect the Samford House to make sure that the Woodbridge inmates were well looked after, paid glowing tribute to Mr Carter:

"I found everything in splendid condition and highly satisfactory and all inmates seemed contented and quite happy. I was particularly impressed with the high esteem in which the Master seems to be held by old people and very pleased to observe the way in which the little children flocked round him which evidently proves that their little lives are made brighter by his kindness and fatherly ways towards them. I consider the Samford Union are to be congratulated upon having such a splendid man in charge."

Bearing in mind that members of the Board included many clergymen, one would have assumed that the **Chaplain** to the House would have would have commanded great respect from the Master and the staff. This was not always the case; there were occasions when the chaplain was taken to task for failing to perform his duty adequately – or perhaps, more to the point – that for which he was paid. In the same way that medical men were not always considered by their fellows as social equals, such too, was often the case with those clergymen who came from more humble backgrounds. Nineteenth century novelists like George Eliot and Anthony Trollope frequently depict clerics who without private means had only very small stipends on which to support a family and therefore welcomed the opportunity to increase their income by taking on additional work as the chaplain of a Workhouse, hospital or set of almshouses.

In 1880 the cost of the chaplaincy came under discussion following the retirement of the Revd. Woodd. Apart from the salary paid to the reverend gentleman he, like other wage earners of the period was now asking for a pension. The Board considered that instead of making an official appointment, as had been standard practice since the inauguration of the House, they should ask the Rector of Tattingstone to allow the Indoor Poor to attend one of the Sunday services at the Parish Church. In addition, in return for an agreed stipend (which would not have superannuation requirements attached to it) the Rector would also officiate during the week in the House. The question was put to the Bishop and he having consented, the **Revd. Hawkins** agreed to accept the post at a salary of £60.0.0. There was, however, one proviso. The Rector suddenly discovered there was not enough room in the church to accommodate the Poor. This would suggest that the weekly congregations at St Mary's church were so large there would have been insufficient seating for those who would join them from the House. The only accurate figures available for the seating capacity comes in the Religious Worship Census of 1851 when it was revealed that the church had two hundred seats free of pew charges and on the day the census was taken there were 76 adults and 26 children present for morning service and 152 adults and 26 children for the afternoon. Unless things had changed dramatically, and with the growth of the Methodist Chapel membership it seems unlikely, it would seem that room could have been found in the morning. Was this not more a question of the susceptibilities of the congregation being upset by the inclusion of the paupers? So, the poor continued to attend in their own chapel. And within a short space of time a new chaplain, the **Revd Beauchamp** was appointed. He left in 1899 and was replaced by the **Revd Walford,** vicar of St Mary Key, in Ipswich.

Because of his position, the chaplain was often able to see aspects of life in the House that were not always apparent to the Board members. The more caring of the chaplains were responsible for trying to make life more comfortable for inmates. For many of the elderly inmates in particular, attendance at Chapel was the highlight of the week, bringing both spiritual uplift and comfort as well as a welcome break in routine. But, for those who were hard of hearing, this was a pleasure that was being denied them. To help remedy this state of affairs the Revd. Walford applied to the Board for the provision of ear trumpets. The Board listened sympathetically to his requests but directed the Master to consult the Medical Officer as to the efficacy of such instruments and of course, the cost of them.

We are not told the result of this request but it was not long after that the chaplain was again making representations to the Board. It was in November that he asked permission to discontinue holding services in the chapel throughout the winter. The place was, he complained, far too cold for the elderly inmates to endure for an hour or more at a time. No doubt he too suffered from the chilly atmosphere and, quite rightly, he was aware that he could not give of his best if he was conscious only of his cold hands and feet. On this occasion the Master was directed to make sure that the room was properly warmed. One cannot help wondering if a personal feud between the Master and the chaplain accounted for the fires not being stoked up in good time. It was to be some years before central heating pipes were laid beneath the floor of the chapel.

Having attended to the ears of his 'parishioners' the chaplain then turned his attention to those with failing eyesight, asking if spectacles might be provided for those who needed them. The Board took immediate action here and invited Mr Scarborrow, an optician in Ipswich, to visit. He carried out the necessary eye tests and supplied spectacles at 1s.6d. per pair. Outside the House, many old people were unable to afford the eye tests that would give them a correct prescription to have made up into spectacles, relying instead on either a single magnifying glass or the purchase of cheap magnifying spectacles that would allow them to read some print. Perhaps the Board felt that the chaplain was getting too carried away with his requests because they turned the next one down. The Prayer Book of the period had undergone some amendment and the clergyman asked to be supplied with a copy of the new one. The Board directed the House Visitors to inspect the book concerned. This they did and their conclusion was that a new book was not needed. In their opinion all that was required was the purchase from the relevant quarters of the additional leaf that contained the amended service. This could then be inserted into the present (and quite adequate) Prayer Book.

While the chaplain ministered to the spiritual and occasionally the bodily needs of the inmates, the post of Relieving Officer brought the holder into very close personal contact with the sufferings of his fellow man. He it was who had to carry out the dictates of the Local Government Board as relayed to him via the Guardians. How hard-hearted he must have seemed when he refused to sanction out-door relief to a family or approve the ticket that would purchase food or drink for the sick. In his other role, he had to collect money from those who, once they were in work, were repaying their loans from the Union or the maintenance payments for a child, a mentally ill husband or wife or an elderly relation. Not a popular man among his fellows, one would assume; seen as he was as the detested agent of those in authority. How difficult then, when the Relieving Officer himself fell on hard times as happened to Mr Gough.

J.S. Gough had been Relieving Officer and Collector of Dues as well as registrar for births and deaths for the Capel District of the Union for a number of years, never giving his employers any cause for concern. So it came as a shock when at the Board meeting of the 13 August 1905, the Clerk reported that he had had notice that relief had not been paid in those parishes that made up the Capel District. He further reported that nothing had been seen or heard of Gough for the past two days. When he had also been told that some payments for the previous week had not been made, the Clerk had immediately visited Gough's home and removed all the books and papers that concerned Union business. And so that people should not suffer, he had arranged immediate benefit payments to those in need, enlisting the help of a Mr Robert Death in the administration of this.

On examining the books he found that everything was in order up until the $2^{nd}$ August after which there were no entries at all. As far as Gough's Collector's books were concerned these recorded all the money paid over to the Treasurer up to the $30^{th}$ June. The counterfoils of his receipt book showed that receipts had been given for all money subsequently received with the exception of an amount of cash that was found in his room. The Clerk then reported that Gough had now returned home. Medical Officer Stewart who was Gough's doctor, told the Board that the poor man had suffered a complete nervous breakdown brought on by overwork. He recommended that his patient have a thorough rest and change of air. The Board listened sympathetically and offered Mr Gough four weeks leave of absence – unpaid of course.

At the meeting held two weeks later on the $31^{st}$ August, the news was given that Gough had left his home on the $17^{th}$ and no one at all had any information as to his whereabouts. When his four weeks of leave was up in mid September, the Board asked for the latest details and at first sight things looked rather suspicious. There was still no news of him or the £22.19s.4½d. he owed to the Board. But on the other hand, he was due £24.4s.5d. in salary. Since the work of his office had to go on, the Board had no option but to suspend him.

More important though was what was to become of Mrs Gough and her four children. She had now been without any financial support for a month or more and although there is no direct information about her, it looks as if she too had been taken ill. It is a tribute to the humanity of the Board members that they showed such concern that instead of bringing the family into the House as would have happened to others, the children were immediately placed in foster care with a Mrs Goddard in Capel. She was paid the going rate of 4/- a week per child with a quarterly allowance of 10/- for each for clothing. It is significant that Mrs Goddard asked for certain items of clothing to be provided immediately; a request that was met from the Union House store. It may be that Mrs Gough had had to sell or pawn some of the children's clothes to help buy food or that she had been too grief-stricken and ill to wash the children's clothes. Imagine what a blow it must have been for this poor woman to find herself now having to rely on the support of Poor Relief.

At the end of September the Board took the only option available to them; they applied for a warrant for Gough's arrest on the standard charge of deserting his wife and family and leaving them chargeable to the Union. In the meantime, an advertisement went out in the **East Anglian Daily Times**, the **Poor Law Journal** and the **Local Government Chronicle** for a successor to Gough. The new holder of the post was to be aged between 30 and 40 and live in an approved place in the District. A salary of £80 per annum was offered with a 10% commission on all the amounts collected. As a security a pledge of £100 for the post of Relieving Officer and £50 for the Collector's was demanded from the successful candidate. Mr Alexander was appointed.

The sad end to Mr Gough's story was that he was found some weeks later, wandering near a railway in the West Country. He was arrested and brought back to Suffolk where it was quickly established he was in no fit state to stand trial. For a time he was cared for by his mother but finally he was sent to the asylum where he died in August 1907.

Over the House's long history there were a great number of Porters and Laundresses, far too many to deal with individually. What we can do is look at what the post of Porter actually entailed. Initially, he would be the first person encountered by the new inmate. It was his business to scrutinise anyone wishing to enter, and to receive officially those who had been told by the Board via the Relieving Officers that they were to come into the House. His other duties included keeping a watchful eye on the inmates during their exercise period, reporting troublemakers and those who in any way infringed the rules of the House. The Porter was also responsible for the supervision of the pump that provided the House's water supply and he came into close contact with the inmates who were detailed to work it. His duties included the maintenance of the heating in the building, the fires in the early days, the boilers as time went on. In fact, by the end of the nineteenth century, the title of Porter had changed to engineer and the holder of the post was expected to be qualified as such.

The good porter was very much the Master's right-hand man, often deputising for him on his day off or while away from the House on business. In 1874, the porter Dougherty carried this idea to extremes by refusing to hand over certain keys to the Matron when the Master was absent. It may be that the Master rather wished he had not brought an official complaint about this to the Board because Dougherty then revealed that the Master was often out very late, some times all night. Two weeks after this indiscreet revelation, the Master complained to the Board that he was concerned about the Porter's temper. It seems he feared the man might strike him. Mrs Dougherty too seemed to have an inflated opinion of her role and refused to help clean up after the annual white-washing. Her argument was why should she do this menial work when there were three able-bodied paupers in the House who were quite capable of doing it. The Doughertys had replaced the Tweeds who had resigned hurriedly in order to avoid inevitable dismissal when Mr Tweed was named as the father of an inmate's baby. He was ordered to pay 2/- weekly for its maintenance. However, he pointed out that as he was now temporarily out of work he could barely manage 1s.6d.

Many of those who presented themselves as applicants for the post of Master had had experience as porter in another Union. That the position was one that could be misused, we have ample evidence. We know there was the opportunity to have illegal relationships with female inmates, abuse children, and verbally and physically mistreat those within their care. Many of those who were unable to carry the responsibilities that went with the job seem to have turned to drink as a means of support.

The porter was usually appointed with his wife taking on the role of Laundress. She herself would not necessarily have done the actual work in this department but she had to have knowledge of it and be able to supervise the female inmates who did the washing and ironing. Her working day would have been spent in a damp steamy atmosphere, so it is small wonder that several of the porters' wives suffered ill health or died. Sometimes, the porter's wife had nursing experience and she carried out that role, often becoming assistant to the Matron or she might have acted, as Mrs James had, as portress, carrying out many of the porter's supervisory duties among the female inmates. If the wife had other qualifications the post of Laundress was advertised separately and occasionally, as with that of Cook, if no one suitable was found outside, the job was given to a female inmate who had shown she was capable of doing it. Both posts, at different times, went to unmarried mothers who had been forced into in the House to have their babies. Once they became paid members of staff, they had the opportunity to save and eventually leave the House to take other employment. On the other hand, members of staff could find themselves becoming inmates as happened to the nurse Hannah Baskett who after a lifetime of service to the Union ended her days in the infirmary with all the other elderly women. And as late as 1915, Walter Scott who was employed at the House as a stoker lost his job when he became ill. With no savings behind him, he became an inmate but was quickly put into the male infirmary where he spent the last few days of his life.

One role that receives occasional mention is that of Labour Master. We have mentioned by name the men who came in the early days to set up the cloth manufactory and we know that in 1823 for example, the current Labour Master had plenty of work to do in providing employment for sixty people in the House. We know too, that there were others who supervised the mid nineteenth century oakum picking. How far this was actual daily work as opposed to punishment is not entirely clear nor is it certain when it ceased to be part of the House routine. This leaves the question of how the inmates were employed in the latter years, as they must have been, since the position of Labour Master was still operational when the Union passed into the hands of the County Council in 1930. It would seem that farming occupied most of the able-bodied men who were admitted to the House. Since they were not encouraged to stay long, much of the work would have been suitable for the unskilled. They would be found tasks in the fields of the Workhouse farm and in the gardens of the House itself. In addition they would help look after the livestock, particularly the pigs. They were also, as is mentioned elsewhere, hired out to local farmers for busy times such as harvest.

One job at which the men took turns was manning the pump that drew up the water needed for the House's daily requirements. There are numerous mentions of 'working the pump'; sometimes it was a chore allotted to vagrants, sometimes it was used as a punishment. A Minute in 1851, describes the installation of a new engine pump in the fifty-five feet deep well that was situated in the entrance yard. One imagines them turning the heavy wrought iron handle attached to the rising main pipe that raised the water to the storage cistern some 17 to 18 feet above ground.

The Labour Master presumably drew up the daily or weekly lists of duties to be performed. This would include the women who were detailed-off to work in the kitchens, laundry and sewing room. Two trusted men and two women were also selected to work in the infirmary as ward orderlies. When work was scarce during the nineteen twenties, the local county council came up with schemes to employ many of the able-bodied inmates. These included the widening of the road from the Bentley crossroads down to Brantham and ultimately as far as the bridge at Cattawade where the River Stour Drainage Board also offered opportunities for work.

Like the position of Porter, that of Labour Master was open to abuse. Working as closely as they did with the inmates gave them plenty of opportunity to mistreat or overwork their charges. One was described by a villager as 'a little Hitler'. Could this have been the man who had the unfortunate surname of Death? He was sacked in 1924. The reason is not given but if it was for bullying then his successor was no better. A rather garbled report appears in the Minutes to the effect that one of the inmates had charged the Labour Master, a Mr Shemmings, with knocking him down. The Labour Master answered this accusation by stating that he had found another inmate named Holmes with a black eye, which he believed had been inflicted by the first man. When accused, the man had become abusive and threatening and to defend himself he had pushed him away. This has caused the man to fall. The matter was smoothed over but it is worth noting that Shemmings did not stay in his post for very long.

# XIV

## PARTICULARS
## OF THE
## SEVERAL ARTIFICERS WORKS,
Necessary to be done
In Building a **HOUSE OF INDUSTRY**

According to the Plan, Elevation, and Section, that are approved of.

***********

In the absence of any extant plans to give us an idea of the original layout of the building, we can instead make use of the detailed schedule drawn up by Andrew Chandler for the craftsmen engaged in the building. The directions for digging the footings have already been given in a previous chapter. What follows (you may wish to skip!) gives us references to the way in which the building was constructed as well as the various rooms and offices. Each tradesman was given his instructions, starting with –
**Bricklayers Work**
"All the Foundations (below the Ground) of the Outside Walls of the main Building to be two Bricks and a Half, with a Footing of one Brick, as shew'd by the Section; the Party-Walls in **Cellar** and Foundation two Bricks, with a Footing of Half a Brick; the Ouside Walls from the Setting off to the first Floor two Bricks, and from thence to the Eaves one Brick and a Half. The Party-Wall

next the **Hall** to be one Brick and a Half to the first Floor, and above that one brick; to have a Tuscan Cornice done in Brick-work all round the Building under the Eaves, as shewed in the Elevation, to have one Brick Arch over all the Windows, set in well-beaten Mortar; to be camber two Inches. The Foundations of the Walls of the **Brewhouse** and other Offices to be two Bricks, and above that to the Eaves one Brick and a Half; the Piers of the **Gates** to be three Bricks: The Foundations of Walls of the **Enclosures** to be two Bricks two Feet high; and from thence to the Top one Brick and a Half, eight Feet high: The Chimney-Jambs in low (ground floor) Rooms to be one Brick and a Half, with a Footing of half Brick; the Size directed by the Ground-Plan: The Shafts of the Funnels to be carried three Feet above the Ridge of the Roof; all the Walls to be wrought fair on both Sides, all the Building to be covered with good sound plain Tiles on Heart-of-Oak Laths properly nailed; all the above Works to be done with good Mortar properly prepared, and the Work well flushed. The Cellars and the Bottom of the privies to be paved with red Bricks, and all the low Rooms of the Building, and Rooms marked O.P. in the Ground-Plan, to be paved with white Paving-Bricks. The Brewing Office and the Yard before it, as far as the Entrance in of the back Gates being fifty-eight Feet in length and thirty feet wide, and Stable to be paved with Lumps Edge-ways; an Oven, as shewed in the Plan, eight Feet Diameter at mein; three Wells four Feet six Inches Diameter each; all the Hearths to be laid with Foot Paments; all the Sash-Frames to be set in a 4 Inch Revel.
**Carpenters Work.**

"The Door-Cases in Cellar and Offices to have Oak Cells, (sic) Jambs, and heads of Firr, 5 by 4 Inches and ½; the Doors of yellow whole Deal, rebated and ledged, Joints beaded, free from Sap; all the Outside Door-Cases to have Oak Sills, Jambs, etc. of Firr, Scantling 6 Inches by 5 Inches; Door-Cases to be framed with two Lights over the Doors; the Doors to be framed flush with four Pannels of Inch yellow Deal, beaded; the Framing to be two-inch yellow Deal; all the Floors to be framed with sound yellow Firr Girders or Beams, 12 Inches by 11 Inches, Joists 7 Inches by 3

Inches; Framing Joints 7 by 6 Inches; Part of the Girders to be plained, and a Grove cut in the Girder to receive the Plaistering of the Ceiling; to have Wall-Plates all round the whole Building under each Floor, 7 Inches by 5 Inches and ½; the Girders not to exceed ten Feet asunder, to have one Foot at an End in the Wall; Lintells over the Windows 5 Inches and ½ thick; and as wide as the Recess requires; bound Timber below the Cells of the Windows 10 Inches by 3 Inches; middle bound Timber 4 Inches and ½ by 2 Inches and ½; Tassels and Discharging-Pieces to each Chimney, 5 Inches and ½ thick by 4 Inches and ½; the principal Rafters of the Roof to be framed into the Girders of the Garret-Floor as shew'd, in the Section; principal Rafters 10 Inches by 9 Inches; small Rafters 5 Inches by 3 Inches; Collar-beams 6 Inches by 8 Inches; Purlins 8 Inches square; Ridge-piece 6 Inches by 2 inches; all the Trimmers to be framed two Feet clear of the Breast of the Chimnies; to fix Hip-Rolls to all the Hips; to have 19 Dormer-Windows in the Roof next the Courtyard, Cell of Oak, Jambs and Heads of Firr 4 Inches and ½ square; Cheeks boarded with yellow whole Deal, rebated Tops covered whole Deal, with proper Bearers to receive the Lead, to have 18 ditto (Dormer windows) in the back part of the Roof framed in two Lights in order to receive Casements; each Light to be 2 Feet 4 Inches high and 1 Foot 3 Inches wide in the Clear, Cheeks and Top to be covered as before, and the Girders over Cellars in little Rooms to be Oak 10 Inches square, Girders over ditto in Store-Rooms 12 Inches square, Joists as before; all the Timbers in general too be free from Sap, folded Joynts; to have five Stacks of Stairs in the main Building and two Stories in the Offices, as shew'd in the Drawing; Steps and Raisers to be whole Deal free from Sap; Newels 4 Inches square, Rails molded with proper Strings and Carriages, a Dado of whole Deal instead of Ballisters; Partitions to part the Stairs in Chamber Story, and Garrets to be Brick; Noggin, the Quarters 4 Inches and ½ by 4 Inches, skirted with ¾ Inch yellow Deal, inside of the Rooms to receive the rendering, all the Timbers not to exceed a Foot asunder, and Skirting in all the Garrets with ¾ Inch Deal the Width of a Board, and whole Deal Window-boards to all the Dormers in Garrets.

The Rooms marked in the Ground-plan E,F,GG and the Room marked D, in the Chamber-plan, to have whole Deal Window-boards and ¾ Jamb Lining, beaded and skirted with ¾ yellow Deal the Width of a Board, with framed whole Deal Chimney Fronts, with Cornice and Shelf over each Chimney; in Room mark'd G, a Closet with proper Whole-Deal Shelves each Side of the Chimney. The Committee-Room to be wainscoted five Feet high, Framing yellow whole Deal, slit Deal Pannels, Ovolo (convex moulding of quarter circle or quarter-ellipse section, receding downwards) [OED] knee'd round the Chimney-piece, with proper Freeze and Cornice over ditto: The Surgery to be fitted up with a Counter, and proper Shelves and Drawers, as shall be directed: To have a Double-Deal Dresser in the Kitchen, 16 Feet long and two Feet three inches wide, with proper Bearers etc. and Drawers under ditto the whole Length, and proper Pewter-Shelves over ditto; Oak Curb to Sink in ditto, four Inches square, and proper Whole-Deal Shelves in Pantry. One of the Garrets in the Wings to be divided with Whole-Deal, and slit Deal Partitions into fifteen Apartments for Married people; each Apartment to have a Light with a Casement. All the Doors to the Lodging-Rooms and Store-Rooms to be framed with four Pannels, out of inch-and-half Deal; Pannels flush on one Side and beaded. All the sash-frames to be Case-frames, Oak Cells and Pully-pieces, and inside Beads; outside Linings inch Deal, fram'd; inside Lining 3-qrs. Deal with Deal square inch-and-half sashes, single hung: Sash-frames to be 4 Feet 9 Inches high, and three Feet two Inches wide, in the Clear. Pediments over the Doors in the Court-yard according to the Drawings: The Privies to be floor'd with Oak Joists, five Inches by four Inches: The Floors, Seats etc to be done with yellow Whole-Deal, free from Sap: Ceiling-Joists and Rafters as before: Two pair of Gates; Stiles to be two-inch-and half Deal, ledges fram'd into them, and whole Deal beaded and nail'd to the ledges, so as to make them flush on the Front-side, cap'd with Oak, moulded. Oak Curbs to the Cellar-Windows four Inches square, with Whole-Deal Flaps and Cheeks to ditto. One Story of Oak Steps out of the Cellar into the Brewhouse-Yard, with Whole-Deal Flap, etc. to ditto.

**Plaisterers Work**
All the Ceilings and Roof to be plaister'd with good Lime and Hair, and good Sand in it, on Heart of Firr Laths, well nail'; and to be sloped and whiten'd: The Rooms marked in the Ground-Plan E,F,G,G, and the Rooms mark'd in the Chamber-Plan A and D, to be rendered, and the Back-side of the Partition and nine-inch Wall to be rendered; all the rest of the inside Walls to be sloped and whiten'd.

**Masons Work**
"To fix a Portland Chimney-Piece in the Committee-Room, with Slips, and Noseing, and Blocks, and a Slab two Feet wide. Four Portland Stones, four Inches thick, to cap the Piers at Front, and Back-Gates. Eight Stones to receive proper Hooks to hang the Gates on. To lay the Bottom of the Sink with Yorkshire Stone in Tarras [or Trass - volcanic earth formerly imported as cement-material. OED.]

**Smiths Work**
"Iron Bars to the Mantles of all the Chimnies, two Inches and a half wide, and half an Inch thick; the Kitchen-Bar double in Breadth: Hinges, Bolts, Locks, and Latches, to all the Doors as shall be required, not of less Value than Five Shillings for each Door at an Average, and Fifty Shillings for two pair of Gates; eight Hooks for the Gates; Iron Straps two Inches wide and 3/8 ths of an Inch thick, to cluch [clutch? The OED gives one meaning as a 'gripping-piece'] the Foot of each principal Rafter, and bolted with a 3 qrs. of an Inch Iron Bolt into the Girder or Beam, with proper Irons to fasten on the Hip-Rolls; and to have 50 Iron Casements, with proper Hooks and Fastning to ditto; To have 3 qrs. Iron Bars to all the Cellar-Windows.

**Painters Work**
"All the Outside-Work to be done three Times in Oil; all the Inside-Work to be done twice in Oil, and once in size.

**Plumbers Work**
"The Dormer-Windows in the Roof, and pediments in the Court-Yard, and Rolls, to be cover'd with lead, seven pounds to the Foot; to have four Pumps fixt in such Places as shall be directed:

Valley [internal angle formed by intersecting planes of roof – OED] to be laid with Lead, 8 pounds to the Foot, two Feet wide each.
**Glaziers Work**
"All the Windows to be glazed with Crown Glass. [made in circular sheets without lead or iron – OED]

"All the above Works to be done in a Workman-like Manner, for the sum of ....£4029 –9s –0d.....(signed) Andrew Chandler...
And if it is thought proper or necessary to alter any of the above Works here annex'd in the Designs, it shall no ways break, or make void, any of the above Proposals or Agreements, but shall be allowed in Proportion; and if the Work should be reduced, then the Value to be deducted in Proportion out of the total Sum.
N.B. There is to be no Pediment in the Front, althou' shewn in the Drawing.

***********

No building remains unaffected by the passage of time. Not only does it suffer the accepted wear and tear caused by wind and weather as well as that made by its human occupants, but it also has to adapt to whatever is required of it at any given time. Minor repairs and regular maintenance had taken place but by 1802 the House was in need of some quite major work. An advertisement placed in the **Ipswich Journal** in that year invited "Such persons as are inclined to do the carpenters and bricklayers work at the Poors House to deliver their proposals to the Weekly Committee." It was not specified what extension or repair work was going on at that time but by 1819 the House was in need of renovation, so a re-building programme was put into operation. We read of an order for 50,000 sound hardburnt, red bricks, good Memel (Scandinavian) fir and 1¼ inch yellow deal square framing for the work in hand. And at the same time, tenders were invited from bricklayers, carpenters and tilers. It is not made clear how much of the labouring work was undertaken by the inmates themselves but doubtless the Board would have been anxious that their own men should be employed where possible.

To meet the costs involved, it was necessary for the Board to raise further funds and this they did as usual by offering mortgages and selling off part of the anticipated Poor Rates.

The Board Room, as we have seen from the original schedule, was an oasis in the midst of austerity. The gentlemen of the Board could not be expected to sit in surroundings similar to those of the inmates and so their meeting room, which was used at least once a week by the Visiting Committee in addition to the Board's Meetings, was made to resemble as far as possible a comfortable office or sitting room of the period. Fifty years on, the Board Room like everything else needed updating. First, in 1811, they purchased some new chairs, that one hundred and twelve years later were to be mentioned again. It was in 1923 that it was reported that some of the Board Room chairs were broken and the suggestion put forward that they might be sold, an offer of twenty-five shillings apiece having been made for them. One cannot help wondering who the astute prospective buyer was. No decision was made at that time but a little later it was reported that Messrs Green and Hatfield, antique dealers, who had a shop on St. Margaret's Plain in Ipswich, had offered to purchase fifteen of the chairs for £60.0.0. Now realising that the chairs were obviously worth more than that the Board decided to accept instead a quote of £8.0.0 to repair them. Where they are now and how much they eventually sold for is not recorded.

New windows were put in at the west end of the room in 1813 and for winter comfort, a new stove was purchased. Possibly the Board members were anticipating the move they were to make in 1814 to hold all their meetings in the House rather than, as previously, at the White Elm, Copdock, the Swan at Washbrook or the White Horse in Capel St Mary. Comfortable though their room might be the Board had to wait until the end of the 1840s before they were provided with a water closet for their specific use. Part of the passage way near to the entrance of the Board Room was enclosed for this purpose, an operation that cost £3.10.0.

A reference appears in the Minute Book for 1819 concerning the development of separate lodgings for married couples in the garrets. This raises the question, were the original married apartments mentioned in the specifications not carried out at the time or were these additional apartments? Perhaps the latter since on the ground floor doors in the kitchen and storerooms were removed to extend the kitchen area. There must have been an exceptionally large number of inmates at that time as each of the existing dining tables was made narrower in order to get in three extra tables down the centre of the Dining Hall. The tables, of course, would have been simple boards placed on trestles and as such able to be dismantled easily when the room was required for another use such as the daily family meeting time. And it was its very size of the Hall that made it ideal for military drill practice during both the Napoleonic and First World Wars.

Initially, a room in the main body of the House had been set aside for religious worship but when more space was needed, it seemed sensible to use that room. The proposal was made that either a different space should be found for the chapel or better still they should build a proper one. So in 1824 Mr Whiting submitted plans for a new chapel in the centre of the yard "breaking out from the Hall". The design with its Georgian rounded end was a very welcome relief to the essentially angular lines of the main building. Mr Whiting's estimate of £330.0.0. was accepted by the Board and the chapel was completed and ready for use by March 1825.

The following year Mr Whiting was again doing business with the Board when he was asked for estimates to build a new infirmary for serious cases of illness. The need for this had become only too apparent in the previous year when there were not only outbreaks of smallpox throughout the district but also what is simply described as "much sickness" – very likely typhus. The Board resolved, "that the present Sick House be taken down and that infirmaries be formed in the roof of the Poor House". So again, the garret space in one wing was utilised and a proper staircase put in. Mr Whiting was allowed £190 for the demolition and removal of the old building and £215 for the interior alterations. In many ways this was a temporary solution and the question of the right provision for the sick was one that would recur over the years.

Each year in late spring, the interior walls of the House, like those of most cottages, were lime-washed. But while one could freshen up the inside, the building itself continued to suffer from natural wear and tear. For example, some of the brickwork of the east wing on the yard side fell down into the boys' recreation area in 1839. When this was examined, as is so often the case, it was discovered that this was only part of the problem; in this instance settlement in the roof structure indicated that immediate attention was required. That was dealt with but the 1850 plans to alter the Men's Wards were deferred, possibly because of cost, though essential alterations were made so that the privies used by the boys and girls were made "sufficiently separate". The question of lavatory arrangements, as we have seen elsewhere, was a constant one.

On the 28th February 1860, most of the country was hit by hurricane force winds. In Ipswich the storm that came from the southwest and then veered to west north west lasted from 11-30 in the morning till 3 in the afternoon. The local newspaper reports that tiles were ripped from the roofs of houses in the Norwich Road; lead was stripped from the roof of the hospital of the Cavalry Barracks and a chimney collapsed at the Grammar School in Henley Road. Still in that area, the gable end of a house was blown out at the Arboretum Nurseries and in Christchurch Park thirteen beech and poplar trees were uprooted. On several of the large estates surrounding the town, such as that of Lady Harland at Wherstead, the devastation of so many trees ruined some magnificent landscape designs. The House did not escape either. The inmates may have felt it was somewhat ironic that the main damage was to the Board Room where the chimney was blown down taking with it a good many roof tiles. For Mr Fulcher, the local builder, it was a case of an 'ill-wind', he being called in immediately to repair the damage and re-erect the chimney-stack.

When one looks at that vast roof area, it is hardly surprising that it should require periodic attention. The problem that occurred in

1867 like so many others was not specified, but a reference to the need for troughing and tanks to take excess water suggests that the roof was leaking.

Rearrangement of accommodation again became necessary in 1862 when the House was once more the subject of a letter in the local press. This time it concerned the practice of young males having to share beds. The complainant's objection was not on moral grounds but that his bedfellow was 'lousy'. The Board took note of the publicity and promptly ordered seventeen single beds to help alleviate the situation. However, there was insufficient space for this number of beds in the room so a general reshuffle took place. In 1896, the problem was reversed when the LGB Inspector insisted that the living room occupied by the old women was too large. He recommended division in order to afford separate accommodation for women coming in for the first time. At the same time, there was a shuffling of other accommodation. The Master asked permission to utilise the now redundant dispensary as his office, so that his present office could be made into a private sitting room for the Porter and the Cook who were married. Frustratingly, within a very short time of making this change, the Porter and his wife resigned.

Under the Casual Poor Act of 1882, it became necessary for a portion of the building to be set-aside specifically for vagrants. Again, the building had to be adapted to meet those needs. This time the area chosen was that adjacent to the old mortuary where a series of cell-like rooms was carved out.

As the nineteenth century entered its last quarter, standards of hygiene generally had been raised. At the House proper bathrooms and water closets were built, particularly for the sick wards. But by the 1890s the very necessary question of the disposal of sewage had to be properly addressed. Matters came to a head when Roger Kerrison, the lord of the Manor and owner of most of Tattingstone, wrote to the Board to complain about the offensive smell from the Workhouse drain. For the uninitiated Board members it was revealed that the House drainage consisted of a series of dead wells. From these, glazed and brick drains led the overflow into one common drain that ultimately discharged into the stream at the bottom of the hill.

The Committee set up to tackle the problem came to the hardly surprising conclusion that this was not the best practical way of rendering harmless the matter that flowed into the stream. They decided to look at a number of systems to see which would be the best for the House. One cheap and obvious way was to utilise what they already had, backed up with a simple network of filtration beds. More long lasting and up-to-date was the septic tank system that was in use at Exeter, the Dibden system used at Sutton in Surrey or that of Col. Ducat in Hendon.

It may seem hard for us to understand the enthusiasm with which the committee appointed to look into the different systems set out upon their mission. Messrs Hocking, Thwaite and Edgell visited Hendon on the 25 April and Sutton on the day following. The report they presented to the rest of the Board is worth repeating here, not only for the benefit of students of nineteenth century sanitation but also for those of us who tend to take such matters as sewage disposal for granted. The sewage farm in Hendon was of considerable area and "considerable stench". There they found **Col.Ducat's Bacterial Self-Acting Filters** at work under his own personal supervision. On each square yard, 250 gallons of raw sewage was treated daily; the crude sewage without precipitation or treatment ran on top of the filters and issued automatically from the base as effluent. This was perfectly inodorous and of sufficient purity to be safely turned into streams and rivulets. There was no residual sludge. The filters required the minimum of attention and since the filtering material never needed washing or changing, it was possible for one man to superintend the purification of up to one million gallons a day.

The committee, having got this far with their report then became technical as they extolled the virtues of Ducat's system with its perfect aeration of all layers of the filter. "A frame, twelve feet square and of eight feet height is built up of 3inch drain pipes laid close together in Portland cement and held together by brick corners. The pipes have an inward fall of 3" so no moisture runs out from them. At the bottom of the pipe-built walls, there is a row of oblong outlets, from which effluent escapes and runs by a little gutter on each of the four sides of the filter to a larger gutter that carried it away. Immediately above these outlets, a run of larger pipes connect with a hot water heating apparatus, necessary in winter as microbes will not work in temperatures under 37F. The space within these pipe-built walls is filled in with strata of broken 'hards' (probably coke residue) from the Gas Works, coarse and fine shingle and other suitable material. Between these strata a row of pipes are laid to carry air into and through the whole mass of filters. Although crude sewage was flowing plentifully into the top of the filter, your Committee were unable to discover the slightest unpleasant smell even at the open mouths of the pipes."

It was apparent from the rather sketchy report of the visit to the Surrey sewage farm where **Dibden's Sunken Filter Beds** operated that the Committee were in favour of Col.Ducat's system. It was estimated that the scheme would cost between £120 and £150 to set up. In addition, royalties of ½ d per 1000 gallons were payable to the inventor. It was estimated that for the House these would work out at two guineas.

There then followed various proposals about the situation of the new system. Fortunately the Guardians owned all the land between the site and the stream so there was ample arable and meadowland on which to purify effluent before it reached the stream. When tenders for the project came in they were much higher than the Committee had estimated ranging from £225.10.6 to £240.10.0. One of those who tended for the contract was a Mr Thwaite from Richmond Road in Ipswich. There is no way of knowing if he was related to Thwaite, the Committee member, but if he were, it did not secure him the contract! The building of the new drain to Ducat's filtration system was completed and in 1899 the Board congratulated itself and all concerned with its new "Hygienic Temple". And as a finale to this sanitary saga, in 1903 Mr Wright presented the Board with a plan showing the drainage system of the House. The Board were so impressed by this, they ordered the Clerk to have it varnished and it was duly hung in the Committee Room. However, late in 1904, it was reported that the filter was in bad order having silted up; so more expense was incurred when the top layer of rubble was removed and fresh shingle introduced.

During the next year, a building inspection revealed that the garrets in the women's wing were in a very poor state of repair; the roof and walls had bulged, necessitating the insertion of iron rods and ties. At this time too, it was discovered that much of the woodwork needed renewing and the whole exterior of the House needed repainting and the guttering or troughing repaired. Perhaps it was to help pay for these essential repairs that the Board now gave serious consideration to taking in the inmates from other Workhouses. As early as 1893 they had been asked to accept one hundred elderly men and women from the Chelsea House but had refused so large a number. 1905 brought overtures from both Hackney and Camberwell to take some of their able-bodied paupers and a few months later they were asked to consider taking fifty old men from Rochford. All these requests were, at the time, turned down or came to nothing because maintenance costs could not be agreed. However, the Board did give the whole matter their serious consideration and the Chairman, Alfred Harwood delivered a report on **The Desirability of Boarding Paupers from Other Unions.** The gist of this was that the House had accommodation for one hundred and fifty in addition to its own inmates but to take that number would involve considerable outlay. Therefore he suggested eighty as the optimum number. But before they could consider receiving more there were certain alterations, repairs and new installations that would be needed. To cope with the additional large quantity of laundry, a new drying chamber should be attached to the laundry. It was pointed out that the present laundry was now totally inadequate and extensions would be necessary any way. Two additional coppers were needed in the kitchen and extra washing accommodation needed on the men's side and additional privies for the women. Finally, slight repairs and alterations were needed in the attic rooms. All this could be accomplished for £300 that could be taken out as a loan, while a further £300 for the additional furniture and clothing could be taken from the House's current account.

Much higher was the bill that was presented by the House Committee in 1907 when definite arrangements had been made with Edmonton to take in a number of their inmates. The Committee showed that a new steam cooking apparatus together with boilers and a boiler house to provide a hot water supply to the bathrooms that the Local Government Board had laid down as a future requirement would cost £794.10.0. Also required were a steam engine and shafting for the Workhouse and the laundry; a hot water heating system for the Dining Hall, the sick wards and the Board Room and a new bathroom and lobby for the men's wards, all of which would add another three hundred and seventy pounds to the bill. But essential now to meet the needs of the present inmates was a new water tower and tanks that would cost £285.

Internal alterations were made again in the 1920s. The Woodbridge Guardians, who were at that time sending some of their inmates to the House, recommended that the wards for the sick and infirm should be moved to the ground floor. At around the same time, the House Committee suggested other changes. The Nurses' Day room, they thought, should have linoleum upon the floor. The rest of the Board threw up their hands in horror when an estimate for £20 was received and deferred their decision on this. However, they did approve the installation of six lavatories and two baths for the women's side of the building. A further recommendation that each inmate should be supplied with an individual towel and a numbered peg on which to keep it was amended to a 'sufficiency of roller towels.' Again this may horrify the present-day reader but even in the 1920s most working class families would have shared a communal towel. When so many houses still did not have bathrooms, daily ablutions took place at the kitchen sink and the ubiquitous roller towel hung on the back of the kitchen door. The nurses did get their lino the next year, obtained at a price of £11.1.4. But by then, the stove that heated that room was declared worn out and a replacement was needed. Again price dictated what should be installed. An estimate was given for one costing £9.4.9. but the Master considered that an open grate with an oven attached was more suitable and that could be had for a third of the price. The Board did not hesitate to recommend its purchase.

That was not the case when it came to replacing the iron ventilators in the sick ward. The proposal was that swing windows should be fitted there but the Board decided to leave that till later. They did, however, initiate the installation of washbasins in the Men's wards and had their lavatories converted from earth to water closets. In 1927 the brick floor of the kitchens was replaced with red tiles. Another sign of more modern times came with the provision of accommodation for the chauffeurs of the Board members. Just after the House was built in 1766, a carriage house had been provided for the use of the Board though no specific mention was made of where the grooms or drivers were to wait. Now, nearly two hundred years later, with the proliferation of the horseless carriage - and perhaps more concern for the well being of employees - the now redundant wood-chopping shed was furnished with a heating stove, some lighting and reasonably comfortable seating for the uniformed chauffeurs.

Modernity was slowly be making its way into the House but the District Inspector was aghast in 1928 to discover that there was no telephone within the House. Until that time, any telephone calls had to be made from the public kiosk in the village. At a time when the installation of a telephone relied on the availability of a line which might well have to be shared with another subscriber, it was not surprising that the rector of Tattingstone took advantage of this opportunity to share a party line. At the same time a telephone was installed at the office of the Clerk in Ipswich and another was provided for Mr Alexander, the Receiving Officer.

Sometimes small-scale alterations were necessary. One such occurred in 1928 following the death of Mrs Carter, the Master's wife and Matron. The posts of Master and Matron went together so on the lady's death, Carter's post was automatically terminated. The Board however, had such confidence in him that they recommended his re-appointment. There were twenty-three applicants for the post of Matron, many of them widows of Masters or those who had had nursing experience in Workhouses. The post was, of course, a living-in one so the question of accommodation for a single lady had to be taken into consideration. The Master's living quarters were quite spacious and it was fortunate that one bedroom was situated across the corridor from the rest of the rooms. The Board gave instruction that this should be turned into a bed-sitting room for the new matron, Miss Agnes Dewhurst.

From the end of the nineteenth century several Union Houses in Suffolk closed; some took on a new role as in the case of the Nacton House while others were demolished to make way for other development. In 1923, the Cosford Union at Semer advertised that as it would be closing it had certain items for sale that might be of interest to those establishments still in business. These included fifteen bedsteads at ten shillings each and nine other bedsteads at eight shillings. There were one hundred and fifty blankets and sheets and fifty quilts at six shillings, four and sixpence and six shillings respectively. Five dozen knives and forks at twelve shillings a dozen, four dozen pint mugs and three dozen chamber pots as well as forty shirts and one hundred pillowcases were on the list that the Board gave the Master to bid for. He was told that he might buy whatever else he considered desirable and we read later that he had indeed purchased two cot bedsteads, three night commodes and a carrying chair.

The acquisition of the cots is a sign of the direction in which the House was moving at that time. Although by the 1920s most of the inmates were elderly and infirm, in need of what we now call 'long term care', the House catered more and more for the unmarried mother and her child. And to this end, just after the purchase of the cots, the Master was authorised to purchase a second-hand perambulator for not more than fifteen shillings at the jumble sale in Tattingstone. Further, he was deputed to buy some additional cot blankets.

Two cases show the diversity of circumstances that led to a woman going into the House to have her baby. The first concerned Mary who was diagnosed by the local doctor as being 'mentally defective.' Her parents had been advised that Mary should be placed in a Home for girls with similar disabilities but they had refused to sanction this. Unfortunately the young woman then became pregnant so the only option now open to her parents was for Mary to be admitted to the House for indefinite detention. There are numerous cases throughout the long history of the House where a girl was forced to take refuge in the House because her parents, usually her father, had thrown her out of the family home. But the girls were not always totally alone. In the case of Alice, when she made application for admission to the House to have her baby, her mother came with her to speak to the Guardians. The Board probed deeply into the parents' financial circumstances but more importantly, they were most interested in what accommodation was available at home. They must have been satisfied with the answers they received for Alice was admitted. Furthermore when the baby was born, the Board took out an affidavit against the putative father who eventually accepted responsibility for its maintenance to the tune of two shillings and sixpence a week.

Again, we must not allow sentiment to cloud our vision. Although life within the House was hard for the unmarried mother, many girls in a similar position outside found it difficult to cope with the social and financial pressures put upon them. My recital of the story of the Samford House ends when in 1930 when Suffolk County Council took over the former Poor Law establishments but there is one point I should like to clear up. In July 1999, an article appeared in **The Guardian** about a woman who had had a baby in the House in 1934. The journalist wrote, *'Even today Tattingstone is a rural backwater. Then it was like the last place on earth. The sky weighs down on the earth as if trying to flatten it. Even on summer days the wind whips hurtfully across the flat landscape. It is a place to make you look inwards.'* Those of us who know and love the village find it difficult to recognise that description. We can, I suppose, allow the reporter her bit of poetic licence, but I cannot forgive her for not doing her research thoroughly. She continued, *'in the year Mary was born, seven other illegitimate births were recorded, which seems high for such a small, close-knit community. For something to which such a stigma was attached, it seems to have been surprisingly common.'* Quite apart from impugning the morals of the population of Tattingstone, the reporter had got it very wrong. Had she looked carefully at the birth register from which she got her figure of seven, she would have seen that Mary's mother alone came from the village. The rest of the women came from as far a field as Woodbridge and Felixstowe.

The early records do not give any exact account of either the way in which the accommodation was laid out or measurements of rooms. However, when the County Council took over the running of the House, a thorough inspection was made of the premises. The drawing that accompanied the resulting report in November 1931 was very basic but the report itself does offer some helpful detail.

ACCOMMODATION.
Office: 1 room 14'x 13' for Master.
Boardroom: 1 room 18'6"x 28'
Master's quarters: in central block; sitting room - 28 x 13, dining room -16 x13, bedrooms:   1) 29 x 20, 2) 16 x 18, 3) 18 x 19, bathroom -14 x 5.
Staff quarters:  dining and sitting room faces north and has the disadvantage of being entered from Inmates' Dining Hall. Has been converted from two rooms, used by five nurses, cook and labour master. Four staff bedrooms in central block on first floor, north facing, and three on second floor.
Porter's quarters: four good rooms.
Kitchens:  Convenient for Dining Hall.
Dining Hall: 100' long – worn brick floor – heated by steam pipes and radiators. Deprived of certain amount of light by erection of chapel at later date.

## ACCOMMODATION FOR INMATES

**Nurseries:** Day nursery – west wing ground floor on through way to Old Women's day room. No lavatory or WC attached to nursery. Night nursery on $2^{nd}$ floor next to Maternity ward. No WC. Only 7ft. high and only two windows, one north, one south.

**Women's quarters:** Day room on ground floor – sufficient WCs but require more light and ventilation.

**Infirm Women's dormitory** – central block, unsatisfactory – only means of cross ventilation via fireplace. One part of room next to the chapel deficient in light. The dormitory accommodation for women **the poorest of any in the county** – extremely narrow, only 14'.

**Dormitory 2:** grossly overcrowded – thirteen beds instead of 6.

**Dormitory 3:** 18 beds in place of 9. No lavatory or WC on $2^{nd}$ floor and no heating.

## EAST WING

**Men's quarters:** Day room – ground floor – three rooms – each requires the insertion of windows in eastern side which being the outside wall was left unpierced. Number of infirm Old Men accommodated on ground floor for sleeping. Overcrowded. Two small high windows on east. No lavatory or WC. Rest of men on second floor – no WCs.

**Sick Wards:** three for women – very clean. Lack of windows. Only one WC. Maternity ward – no water available. Totally unsuitable.

Over the next fifty years the building would again be adapted internally to meet the needs of the elderly patients who came to spend time in St Mary's, as it was renamed, when it became a NHS geriatric hospital in 1948. Gradually, the stigma of the 'Workhouse', which many of those old people could recall from their youth, has now passed into folklore. In 1990 the doors of the building were closed and for ten years it looked as if the old place would be left to crumble into oblivion, aided and abetted by the thieves who stripped the roof and the vandals who broke glass and tore doors off their hinges. But the dawning of the twenty-first century brought new hope to the derelict shell. Sensitive and imaginative redevelopment of the major part of the building into the unique housing complex known as Chedworth Place, has given Andrew Chandler's original construction a third phase in its long life.

# SOURCES

| ADA7/ | Samford Union | Suffolk Record Office |
|---|---|---|

| | |
|---|---|
| AB1/1 –28 | Minute Books of the Samford Union 1765-1930 |
| AB6 | Boarding Out |
| AC6/3 | St John's Home |
| AE/1 - | Weekly Returns |
| AG2 | Register of non-settled paupers 1906-1923 |
| AH1/1 | Probate of Will of Thomas Payne, 1669 |
| AH1/2 | Probate of Will of Ephraim Daldy |
| AH1/5 | Lease of land |
| AH1/6 | Mortgage |
| AH1/9 | Abstract of title to farm and land |
| AH1/12 | Lease of Pound Grove |
| AH 2 | Particulars of Artificers Works to be Done |
| AL/1 | Register of boarded out children 1905-1916 |
| AQ1 | Letter books 1905-7 |
| AQ2 | Letter books 1911-13 |
| | |
| CB1 | Births 1848-1946 |
| CB2 | Baptisms 1813-1943 |
| CB3/1-3 | Deaths 1848-1946 |
| CB4 | Burials 1899-1930 |
| CB5 | Register of married couples 1914-39 |
| CB8 | Register of mechanical restraint 1892-1916 |
| CB9/1-2 | Creed registers, 1893-1914, 1918-1945 |
| CB10 | Property register |
| CB11 | Punishment register 1848-1936 |
| CB12/1 | Admission and Discharge register 1915 –30 |
| CC1 | Visitors Book 1870 |
| CC2 | Master's Journals 1913 onwards |
| CD2 | Clothing receipt and expenditure book 1924-32 |
| | Register of Lunatics 1889-1918 |

HF1              Register of persons receiving infants for reward
1902-29

Letter regarding Mrs Whiting, the property of Mr & Mrs Keeble of Brantham Hall
Extracts from a letter re: Grundisburgh Home
(I offer my very grateful thanks to Mr & Mrs Keeble and the Edgar Smith and Hilda Tuck for the use of their material.)


Useful reading
Jessie Phillips by Frances Trollope
The Workhouse, Norman Longmate pub.Temple Smith 1974
The English Poor Law, 1780-1930, Michael Rose, pub. David & Charles 1971

## Subject Index

Act of Settlement
4
Air raids
171
Alcohol
9,28,33,42-3,138,191
Apprenticeship
34,102,105-6,109,117
Army
4,57-8,149,169-71
Bastardy
30,38,44, 107-9, 164
Building
15-16, (design: chap.XIV)
Bureacracy
47-8, 91-2, 184
Burial
23-4, 179-80
Chapel
28, 180,212
Chaplains
110, 139-41, 196
Child migration
109, 119-23
Children's Homes
116, 118, 124
Clothing
8, 20-1, 38, 193
Commissioners, Poor Law
48-9
Confirmation service
110
Dietary
26-8, 86, 89, 143-4, 165, 175, 177
Doctors (chap.V)
23,66-6,73,84-5.141
Education
31,101, 110-14
Fostering
94, 124-8
Friendly Societies
73,74,94
German prisoners
176
Gordon Riots
58
Gun Cotton Factory Explosion 81
Family meetings
137
Furniture
7,8,18,19,22
Infirmary
29, 212
Isolation hospital
23,33, 90
Knitting
101
Labour masters
46,47, 203
Laundry
23, 93,202, 204, 217
Leather working
28-9
Loans
14-5, 34, 37, 90, 211-18

Local Govt. Inspectors
49,50,86,89,143,152,155,173
214 219
Lunacy
87, 91, 94,100,177
Manufactory
31, 46,47
Measles
102
Militia
104,169-70
New Poor Law
Chap.III
Nursing
79, 80-1, 95, 174-5
Opthalmia
78
Porters' duties
201
Privies – sanitation
114,134,215, 218
Punishment
37,44,131-6,150, 154
Relieving Officers
69,74,1 92,26,172,184,199-200
Salaries
23, 115,189,194,196
School fees
115-6
Segregation
159-160
Shaving
28
Smallpox
22, 32,81-2,153,181

Tobacco
52, 144
Transportation
107, 111
Typhus
212
Vagrancy
Chap.IX

# INDEX OF NAMES

## A
Abbott Thomas
Adams
Adams George
Adinsell, Col
Alderton Fisher
Alderton Thomas
Aldis
Alexander
Allen Mrs
Alloway John
Arnold John
Askew Ann

## B
Bacon Henry
Baker Robert
Balaam Jonathan
Baldry Alice, Mary
Banham Sarah
Barker James
Barker John, Sir
Barker Julia
Baskett Hannah
Beales Ann, Samuel
Bennett, Mrs
Berners Henry, Revd.
Berners William, Esq.
Berry Mathias
Betts John
Bloomfield John
Boghurst Miss
Bond Susan

Bradstreet Robert
Briggs Robin
Broke Philip, Sir
Brooke Cooper William
Brooke, Dr
Brooks William
Brown Julia
Bryant William
Bush Isaac

## C
Candler Anne, William
Canning Richard, Revd.
Capper George, Revd.
Card Phoebe
Carter William
Catchpole
Chandler Andrew
*Charlesworth, Maria*
*Churchyard Thomas*
Clarke James
Clarke, Widow
Clubbe John, Dr
Coal William
*Cobbold Elizabeth*
Cocksedge Engineering
Collinson Charles
Collinson, Esq.
Condor
Constable Golding
Cook James, Samuel
Cooke John
Cowen Charles
Cox Martha
Cracknell, Mrs

Crampin Henry
Crisby John
Cuff, Mrs
Culpit George
Cundy Thomas
Curtis John
Cuthbert Sarah

**D**
Daldry Albert, John
Dalton, Mrs
Dardy Thomas
Day Joseph, Sarah
Deal Ann
Deane William
Deane, Miss
Death Louisa, Rebecca, Sarah
Dickerson David
Double William
Dougherty
*Ducat, Col*
Dunnett Joseph

**E**
Edgell
Edwards, Dr
Everett Isaac

**F**
Fallows Emma
Fenn Simon
*Firmin Mary*
Fisher James
Fleming Albert, Dr

Flory
Fulcher

**G**
Garnham John
Garrod William, Revd.
Garwood Annie, Fred, George, William
Gathercole Fred, Henry, Louisa
Gaunt, Mrs
Gilders Anne
Giles Marcus
*Glyde John*
Goldsmith Miss
Goodridge Edward
Goodwin, Miss
Gosnall John, Thomas
Grant Andrew, Revd.
Grayson, Miss
Grimwood William
Grosse, Dr

**H**
Hall John
Hare Barzillai
Harris Harman
Harwood
Hayward
Hazelton John
Helsdon, Miss
Hervey, Revd.
Hibbs, Revd.
Hobart Elizabeth
Hocking John, Revd.
Hogan, Miss

Howard Alice, Ann, Sarah
*Howe John, Lord Chedworth*
Hozier George
Humphreys Elizabeth
Hutchinson Isaac

**I**
Ireland
Iron, Finch William

**J**
James William, Sarah Louise,
Jesse, Mathilda
Jarmain Thomas
Jarrold John, Jane
Jennings Edward, Mary Ann
Jerrard David
Johnson Thomas
Josselyn John
Juby John

**K**
Keane, Dr
Kerrison Roger, Esq.
King Alan, Joan
Knight Lott

**L**
Lambert Clarissa
Lancaster John
Lawson, Dr
Lewis John
Lewis, Mrs
Littlejohn Charles
Lloyd Richard Savage, Sir

Locke Jane
Loom Caleb, George, Oliver

**M**
MacDonald James
Manley William
Manning, Dr
Marjoram
Marsh Alfred
Martin, Dr
Mason Joseph
Matthews Louisa
Mayer William
Mee Charles, Mary
Miller, Revd.
Moore William
Mount, Dr
Mudd William
Muller C. Revd.

**N**
Nicholls, Mrs
Noble Charles
Norman Mrs
Norton Mary
Nunn John, Revd. Martin

**O**
Oxborrow Lydia

**P**
Page William
Pain Tertius D'Oyly, Dr
Palin Ben, Frank
Parker William

Parrish Florence
Pearson Edward, Mary, Robert
Peck Joseph, Richard, William
Pettingale William
Phillips John
Pinner Ann, Joseph
Pittock
Plumb Charles
Porter Abraham
Powell Alfred
Powling

**R**
Ratcliffe William
Ray Daniel
Robert Harland, Sir
Robinson
Robinson Eliza
Rodbard, Dr
Rodwell
Roper Richard
Rumage Mrs
Rush Hayward
Rustat Tobias, Revd.
*Rye Maria*

**S**
Screiber C.A.
Scrivener Harriet
Seager Joseph
Sewell James, Esq.
Shaphard Robert
Sharman Charles
Shave John

Shipp John
Skeet Lucy
Slemming Arthur
Smith Caroline, Hannah, James, John, Sarah, Thomas
Southgate Henry
Sparling Benjamin
Spurgeon, Dr
Squirrell Isaac
Staunton Thomas, Esq.
Stebbing Titus, Revd.
Steward George, Unisee
Stopher Richard
Strange William
Stubbin John
Syer Thomas

**T**
Talmarsh William
Tarver Lark
Taylor
Thompson
Thrower Amelia
Thwaite
Tracey Martha
Turner, Dr
Twaits James
Tweed Joseph, Revd.
Twitchett Widow
Twitchett
Tyrell, Miss

**U**
Upson Alice, Mathilda

**V**
Vesey William

**W**
Walford, Revd.
Wallis Mary
Warmsley, Miss
Warren Thomas, Revd.
Waspe H.G.
Whidby Alice, Dora, Henry
Whimper Nathaniel
Whiney Abraham
Whinney Benjamin
White Stephen, Revd.
White Thomas, Esq.
Whiting
Whiting Alice, Fred, James, Susan
Whiting, Widow
Whittle William
Willes John
Wilson, Mrs
Woods Ann
Woodward Thomas
Woollard Joan
Worledge Ann
Wright George
Wrinch

**Y**
Yellop Robert